ECONOMICS OF SOCIALISM

ECONOMICS OF SOCIALISM

BY

HENRY D. DICKINSON

BOOKS FOR LIBRARIES PRESS

FREEPORT, NEW YORK

First Published 1939
Reprinted 1971

INTERNATIONAL STANDARD BOOK NUMBER:
0-8369-5834-9

LIBRARY OF CONGRESS CATALOG CARD NUMBER:
73-160966

PRINTED IN THE UNITED STATES OF AMERICA

PREFACE

THE purpose of this book is to investigate in the light of modern economic science the fundamental problems involved in the organization of human productive activity for the satisfaction of human needs in a society based upon the twin postulates of economic freedom (both for the worker and for the consumer) and economic equality. During the investigation, fundamental issues regarding the price system are raised. The significance of the pricing process for a socialist community is dealt with, and the interrelations of pricing and planning are discussed. The author believes both in the significance for a socialist community of the indications of the pricing process based upon free individual choice of occupation and consumption, and in the practicability of its adoption by such a community. Thus, while developing his own theme, he joins issue with three different schools of thought. First, with the scientific or technocratic exponents of an 'Age of Plenty', according to whom the problem of scarcity, and hence of pricing, will not exist in a rationally planned society. Second, with those socialists who deny, wholly or in part, the relevance of the categories of rent and interest in a socialist community. Third, with those economists who assert that socialism is an impossible ideal because under socialism all rational economic calculation would be impossible.

While the author's original purpose in this book was to make a contribution to pure economic theory, he found himself, in developing this theme, more and more obliged to take into account the purposes of economic activity and to consider the significance of such institutional devices as planning and the market in the light of these purposes. Hence he was led to keep constantly in mind the interrelations of economic factors with wider social (sometimes called political) factors: thus such fundamental concepts as welfare, freedom, and equality are here discussed, not only in their economic aspects but in their more general social aspects. It is inevitable that the author should have proceeded upon certain assumptions regarding social ends. It may therefore be made explicit at the outset that the present work is based upon the liberal and democratic assumption that the ultimate purpose of social and collective action is the enlargement of opportunity for the development of individual personality as far as this is compatible with the equal opportunity of all other individuals.

This book, like all products of human labour, whether material or intellectual, is the result of a social and not an individual process. Thus its author is deeply indebted for encouragement and inspiration to a great multitude of conscious and unconscious collaborators. Those who have helped him by their writings are mentioned in the bibliography. Those who have helped him by talk and discussion are so numerous that he cannot mention them all by name. He would like, however, to acknowledge the contributions of members of the Grangetown Advanced Tutorial Class (W.E.A.) in Economics of 1935–6. A special word of gratitude is due to J. D. Bernal and Lancelot Hogben for their endeavours to widen the author's intellectual horizon beyond the narrow perspectives of academic economics.

H. D. D.

25 August, 1939.

CONTENTS

CHAPTER I

INTRODUCTORY

1. The Economic Problem

THE fundamental purpose of all economic life is the satisfaction of human needs with resources that are limited in comparison with the needs clamouring for satisfaction. On the one hand are needs—needs for nourishment, shelter, entertainment, fellowship, solitude—complicated by infinite gradations in quality and variety, and by countless vagaries of individual taste and of collective fashion. On the other hand are the resources at the disposal of society—raw materials, sunlight in its protean manifestations, the time of human agents. These resources, either in their crude form, or combined and recombined into instruments of production, semi-manufactured goods, and finished goods, are requisite to the satisfaction of most human needs. Even the most intellectual and spiritual needs make some call upon material resources, or upon human labour-power, for their satisfaction: for paper, printing-machines, and typographers' labour; for masonry and timber, and the labour of architects and builders; for maple-wood and catgut, and the time of skilled fiddle-makers. These resources are scarce, relative to the possible needs for which they could be used. There may be enough rough cloth in the world to give every one a simple garment, but there is probably not enough to give every one all the sumptuous robes he may desire; moreover, the making of cloth takes its toll of the producers' time, which might otherwise be spent in leisure, or in other kinds of labour, satisfying other needs. Even if ultimate material resources were so abundant as to obviate any need for economizing them, human labour would be scarce in comparison with the multifarious purposes on which it might be expended. There are only twenty-four hours in the day, and everybody could use them all in work, without satisfying all their own or their neighbours' desires. But man must rest from labour in order to enjoy the fruits of labour; hence the demand for leisure competes with the demand for production, and time must indeed be carefully husbanded if the needs of man are to obtain anything like the greatest satisfaction of which they are capable.

The fundamental problem, then, of every economic society is the allotment of limited resources (including human labour power among the resources) to the satisfaction of needs (including the need for leisure), so as to secure the maximum of satisfaction. It is essentially a quantitative problem as well as a qualitative one. It is not only a question of what needs are to be satisfied, but to what extent, as compared with other needs requiring satisfaction; not only a question of what resources are to be made use of, but the proportions in which a given quantity of resources is to be divided among different uses, all yielding different and competing satisfactions. It is this quantitative problem that is the essential economic problem.

It is here that we must distinguish between technology and economics. The agronomist can tell us the most efficient method of growing wheat under given conditions, and, given the quantity of wheat desired, can tell us the quantity of land and labour required for the production of that quantity. He can tell us the same for the growing of cotton and the rearing of cattle. But the determination of the quantity of wheat, cotton, and meat required for a certain population, with certain tastes and standards of living, balancing the relative satisfactions afforded by wheat, cotton, and meat as against the quantities of land and labour required for their production—this is the problem of the economist. Similarly, the metallurgist can advise on the best methods of producing steel of a given quality, and on the quantitative relations between ore and coke, while the expert in structural steel-work can explain the advantages of steel for building purposes as compared with brick, stone, or wood; but the ultimate problems regarding the quantity of steel to be produced, considering its possible uses and the consumption of resources used up in its making, the allotment of the steel produced to different uses, the balancing of steel against alternative materials in various branches of construction, taking into consideration the resources consumed in the production of the various alternatives—these are all economic problems. We may say that the proper work of the economist begins after that of the technician has been done.

Any society must have a method of determining what and how much is to be produced, of choosing between alternatives and of achieving its ends with the greatest economy of means. The method of a capitalist society is the system of production for profit and exchange upon the market,[1] modified by monopolistic combinations of capitalists, by trade-unions and by such occasional and irregular intrusions of deliberate social intervention as tariffs, marketing-boards, railway-rate regulation, factory acts, social insurance, &c. The productive energies of society are continually being diverted by the motive of private gain into the channels in which they will yield most profit to those who control them— that is to say, the greatest surplus of selling price over cost of production. Meanwhile competition, even if imperfect, is tending to equalize selling price and cost. Therefore, in theory, since sale price is determined by the consumer's

[1] It is also the method of an economic system without large-scale production or large-scale marketing, but having private property and division of labour, in which goods are produced by small independent producers directly for a local market. This system is what Marx calls 'simple commodity production'.

effective demand, and cost depends upon the capacity of productive resources to satisfy demand in alternative uses, there should emerge the maximum satisfaction of needs with the minimum expenditure of resources. In reality this desirable result is attained only very imperfectly. Under capitalism, four causes contribute to falsify the readings of the price-index and hence to pervert the allocation of resources to production.

(*a*) The inequality of consumers' incomes systematically distorts the measurement of social needs. A rich man wanting a country cottage for a few week-ends in summer can outbid two farm labourers who need shelter all the year round; two cottages are thrown together to make one week-end dwelling and two bread-winners have to seek work elsewhere at grave risk of unemployment or else add a six-mile tramp to their already fatiguing labours.

(*b*) Another all-pervasive cause of the falsification of the price-and-cost calculus is monopoly. The 'invisible hand' which is presumed to maximize satisfaction operates only under conditions of perfect competition. But perfect competition is not a real entity; it is an abstraction born of the economist's urge to rationalize the working of the economic system. Even that degree of competition which, in John Stuart Mill's day, was enough to give the 'invisible hand' good scope for its beneficent work only exists during a period of exceptionally rapid technical development: it is a fleeting transitional phase between one period of monopoly (mercantilism) and another period of monopoly (imperialism). Monopoly is the natural offspring of competition. Once it is established, the presumption no longer holds good that the distribution of resources produced by the self-interest of private entrepreneurs corresponds to the maximum satisfaction of consumers.

(*c*) The meretricious modern art of publicity makes it often more profitable for the manufacturer to spend money in making people want to buy the things that he produces, rather than on producing the things that people want to buy. This tendency is reinforced by the inevitable ignorance of the consumer, called upon to discriminate between the properties of rival brands of tooth-paste, vacuum-cleaners, canned peaches, radio-sets, and artificial silk cami-knickers. It is often more profitable to advertise poor goods than to improve their quality.

(d) On the production side, money costs not infrequently fail to correspond to true social costs. Cheap goods can be made out of sweated labour; the costs of salvaging the human wreckage of industry being thrown on the relatives of the workers or on the general tax- or rate-payer. Costs can be cut by means involving the neglect of safety precautions, the pollution of the air by smoke, the contamination of rivers by noxious affluents, or the sacrifice of human life on the roads.

Nevertheless, the price-and-market system does give some sort of a solution, even though it be distorted and perverted by class privilege and exploitation, to the problem of the economic allocation of resources to the satisfaction of various and competing needs. However much this solution may be criticized, it is urged that some solution, even an imperfect one, is better than none.

2. SOCIALISM

(1) **General notion of socialism**. Ever since the early days of industrial capitalism, men have sought a remedy for its abuses and defects in some material reorganization of the economic system. In particular, the private ownership of the means of production has appeared to many reformers as the fundamental source of evil in the system. To some, such as James Mill and Henry George, it is the private ownership

only of land and natural resources; to others, such as Major Douglas and Professor Soddy, it is the private ownership only of credit, that is the source of evil; but to the majority, the private ownership of *all* non-human means of production—factories, railways, machinery, and raw materials, as well as land and natural materials, and credit—has appeared as a barrier to the full utilization of the resources of the world in the service of the needs of mankind. The author holds this last-expressed view. However important historically may have been the special role played by private property in land and minerals, or in credit facilities, as a factor in the evolution of class privilege, in the present stage of development of capitalism all forms of land and capital have become merged in a single mass of privately owned means of production. The concrete goods of which this is composed have become interchangeable with one another; their special nature—whether land, produced means of production, or intangible 'productive relations' such as credit—has become irrelevant. The ownership of a portion of this mass confers the right to appropriate a certain part of the income of society. If private ownership of productive resources is to blame for the disharmonies of capitalism, it is private ownership of *all* means of production, and not of land, or credit, or some other part of the whole, that must be set in order.

Nor, in view of the intimate interlocking of share-capital and loan-capital in modern business organization (especially that effected by holding companies, so that loan-capital controls share-capital and vice-versa), is it possible to establish a distinction, such as the theorists of 'National Socialism' do, between creative capital (*schaffendes Kapital*) and predatory capital (*raffendes Kapital*), and to make of the latter (generally loan-capital: hence the 'tyranny of interest'— *Zinsknechtschaft*) a scapegoat for the sins of the twain.

Once private property in land and capital is established, there is a constant tendency for its ownership to become concentrated in fewer hands, until a definite class of owners of means of production ('capitalists') emerges. The interests of this class are distinct from, and in many ways antagonistic to, those of the rest of the community. The class division between owners and workers begins.

The distribution of property tends to inequality and therefore the distribution of incomes derived from property tends to inequality. On the other hand, the distribution of incomes derived from work tends to be much less unequal. The reasons for this are legion. A few are:

(1) Owing to the diminishing marginal utility of income, the larger one's income the easier it is to save out of it or otherwise use portions of it for the purpose of adding to one's property. The marginal disutility of labour, however, increases steeply after a certain point. Thus, while it is progressively easier to add to a property-income, it is progressively harder to add to a work-income.[1]

(2) Owing to the working of the law of averages, the chances of total loss of capital diminish the greater the number of different portions into which it is divided for purposes of investment. The 'small man' cannot easily or cheaply spread his risks in this way, and is thus more subject than the big investor to loss due to the vagaries of the market. (This is particularly noticeable in the general depressions that, under capitalism, periodically devastate the market economy). If the 'small man' seeks safety in gilt-edged securities or in conservatively managed investment trusts, he has to put up with a distinctly lower rate of return than the big operator can get on his capital with equal safety.

(3) Exclusive market information and exclusive opportunities for investment on profitable terms are more likely to

[1] See the present author's *Institutional Revenue*, ch. v, § 26.

come to those who are already rich than to men of small
means. Similarly, employment at a high remuneration is
more readily obtained by those who are already well-to-do
or who are connected by birth, education, or social ties with
the rich than it is by poor men.

(4) Once a society has begun to be stratified into classes
on the basis of differences in income, the wealthier sections of
the community in general contrive to monopolize the educational machine so that the necessary training and equipment
for the better paid employments can only be acquired by those
who already belong to the higher income classes.[1]

All these (and other) influences are cumulative in effect.
There are, of course, counteracting influences, such as the
tendency of the rich to relative sterility, extravagance and
spendthrift behaviour (Veblen's 'conspicuous waste'), the
voluntary endowment of public institutions by the rich,
and progressive taxation. But the general tendency, in a
system of private free enterprise and private ownership of
the means of production, is towards greater inequality and
towards the stratification of society into antagonistic classes
on the basis of wealth and of the origin of wealth. While
minor divisions may be important, the division that domi-
nates social life is that between the owners and the non-
owners of the material means of production.

Socialism thus arises as the political objective of the non-
owning class. In order to diminish inequality of wealth and
to abolish the class stratification of society, socialists propose
to abolish private ownership of the material means of production. Some method must be devised of administering
the economic system after the expropriation of the existing
private owners. This is the problem of the economics of a
socialist community.

[1] See E. Ll. Lewis, *The Children of the Unskilled*; *Institutional Revenue*,
pp. 58, 156; and *Political Arithmetic* (ed. L. Hogben), chs. viii, ix, x.

(2) **Definition of socialism.** The definition of socialism that was generally accepted during the half-century between 1875 and 1925 is 'social ownership of the means of production'. Since that time the phrase 'planned production' has been tending to take its place. There is a close connexion between these two definitions. On the one hand, one of the chief advantages claimed for the socialization of the means of production is the elimination of the waste due to unplanned, chaotic, individualistic production. Individualistic production is co-ordinated, it is true, by the mechanism of price and the market; but it is subject to gross disturbances even in this sphere and it is fundamentally blind, purposeless, irrational, and incapable of satisfying many of the most urgent of human needs. On the other hand, so it is claimed by socialists, the planning of production is impossible on any basis less radical than the complete elimination of individual property rights in the means of production, at least in all the major branches of economic activity, and the transfer of these means of production to organs of collective economy. Only so can the community sweep away the secrecy, arbitrary boundary lines, vested interests, overlapping of functions, waste, and monopoloy that characterize private enterprise. One fundamental difference between socialism and capitalism will be the existence of an authority able to view the economic system as a whole and with power to make decisions involving the system as a whole. Another fundamental difference will be the fullest publicity of all relevant economic statistics throughout the whole system. All organs of a socialist economy will work, so to speak, within glass walls.

Socialism has also been defined *tout court* as equality of income[1] and, although few socialists would adopt this definition without reserve, socialism of nearly all schools has

[1] G. Bernard Shaw, *The Intelligent Woman's Guide to Socialism and Capitalism*, pp. 19, 49, 68, 94, 297, 343.

been held to imply equality in one or other of the following senses:

  (a) a greater approach to equality in the distribution of wealth;
  (b) equality of economic opportunity, in a more genuine sense than that of bourgeois liberalism;
  (c) distribution according to need rather than according to effort or product.

In effect, these three tend to the same result, since both equality of opportunity and distribution according to need would lead to greater equality of actual income than exists under capitalism, although not to an absolute arithmetical equality. Nor is the concept of greater equality unrelated to the definitions in terms of social ownership or of planned production. Since the most glaring inequalities of actual income and nearly all the inequalities of opportunity are based on the private ownership of land and capital, social ownership will almost certainly tend to greater equality. Also, since the object of genuine economic planning (as opposed to the sham 'planning' which, like so-called 'rationalization', is simply a euphemism for the restriction of production and the destruction of machinery organized by monopoly-capitalism) is to substitute a conscious and direct relation of production to human needs for a relation arrived at by an indirect mechanism through the unconscious pushes and pulls of innumerable private interests in the market, a true planned economy would approach to some extent the ideal of distribution according to need.

The formal definition of socialism that will be used in this book is as follows:

Socialism is an economic organization of society in which the material means of production are owned by the whole community and operated by organs representative of and responsible to the community according to a general economic plan, all members of the community being entitled to benefit from the results of such socialized planned production on the basis of equal rights.

This definition includes the three elements of

(i) social ownership of the means of production,
(ii) economic planning,
(iii) equality.

It purposely, however, leaves vague two points:

(a) how society is to work the productive equipment that it owns, whether through government departments, public utility corporations, national guilds, co-operative societies, or what not;
(b) exactly how the social product is to be distributed, whether according to service or need, whether in separate shares to individuals, or in communal supplies and services.

But it does explicitly rule out irresponsible private enterprise, and the continuance of any form of privileged income or of class inequality in the division of the social product.

(3) **Criticisms of socialism.** Criticisms of socialism have their fashions just as socialism itself appears from time to time in various guises. During the first half of the nineteenth century the Malthusian bogy was most consistently invoked by opponents of communistic schemes. It was held that population was always pressing upon the means of subsistence and that only private property coupled with individual responsibility for the support of offspring could prevent an increase of population up to the point of famine. Communism might establish equality, but it would be an equality of misery. As the *bourgeoisie* lost their fear of over-population, new arguments against socialism had to be found; and thus, until recently, the question of incentives

has occupied the front place in discussions on the possibility of collectivist socialism. It was held that socialism would lack the incentives to work and efficiency that under capitalism force men to give of their best in the service of the community—the magic of ownership, the ambition of making a pile, or, for those not fortunate enough to inherit or win an independent business command, the hope of promotion and the fear of dismissal. Socialism might eliminate exploitation, but it would be at the price of universal mediocrity and inefficiency. But this has not happened in such public enterprises as the Post Office, the B.B.C., and the Central Electricity Board in Britain; nor has it in the Soviet Union, where, under a collectivist economy, there have taken place an unprecedented rise in productivity and a spectacular outpouring of human energies and enthusiasm. Thus the 'incentive' argument appears less convincing. Accordingly, there appears in orthodox economic circles a new critique of socialism, more subtle and technical than the previous ones, based on the supposed inability of a socialist community to solve purely economic problems. It is admitted that such a community might acquire a mastery over technique not inferior to that achieved under capitalism; that new psychological incentives to do and give of one's best might be developed, as powerful as the love of gain or the fear of destitution; that, even though every child born were guaranteed a share in the resources at the disposal of the community, philoprogenitiveness would not necessarily bring the law of diminishing returns into rapid and fatal action; what is asserted is that, even with highly developed technique, adequate incentives to activity, and rational control of population, the economic directors of a socialist commonwealth would be unable to balance against each other the worthwhileness of different lines of production or the relative advantages of different ways of producing the same good. L. von Mises, in his

Gemeinwirtschaft[1] makes two definite charges against socialist economy:

(1) where the state is the sole owner of intermediate or instrumental goods there can be no price formation for
such goods, hence no rational reckoning of cost and
hence no rational economy;

(2) under planned economy the managers of industry can
have no discretionary power and no pecuniary responsibility for production; therefore, rational risk-bearing
becomes impossible.

The conclusion to be drawn from these two propositions
is that a socialist economy would have no guiding principles
and would, as soon as it lost any parasitic support that it
might get from comparison with neighbouring capitalist economies, degenerate into an affair of wild guesses and random
decisions.[2] One of the objects of this work is to refute this
criticism of socialism and to show that, as far as pure economics is concerned, a socialistic economy is at least theoretically possible.[3]

Another line of criticism, which was run in double harness
with the incentive arguments by such critics of socialism
as Mallock, and is paraded to-day by Mises and Gregory
alongside of the 'rational calculation' argument, is that
planned collective economy is inconsistent with any kind of
freedom of choice for consumers or freedom of employment for workers. This point, too, will receive attention in
this work.

[1] Translated as *Socialism*, 1936.
[2] For other critiques along these lines see F. A. Hayek, *Collectivist
Economic Planning*, B. Brutzkus, *Die Lehren des Marxismus im Lichte der
russischen Revolution*, G. Halm, *Ist der Sozialismus wirtschaftlich möglich?*
[3] For slightly different solutions of the problems see F. M. Taylor,
'Production in a Socialist State', *American Economic Review*, March 1929.
G. Morreau, 'De Economische Structuur eener Socialistische Volkshuishouding', *De Economist*, June, July–August, September 1931.

3. Planning

(1) General notion of planning. The words 'planned production' and 'economic planning' have been used in section 1 of this chapter. It is time to give a more precise definition to the concept. For the purpose of this book the following definition is adopted:

> Economic planning is the making of major economic decisions —what and how much is to be produced, how, when and where it is to be produced, and to whom it is to be allocated—by the conscious decision of a determinate authority, on the basis of a comprehensive survey of the economic system as a whole.

This definition emphasizes three characteristics of planned economy:

(i) conscious nature of economic decisions,
(ii) unity of control,
(iii) basing decisions on survey of economy as a whole.

Item (i) restricts the designation 'planning' to forms of deliberate conscious control of economic life. An economic plan involves more than an economic system or an ordered scheme of economic life. A pure market economy gives rise to an ordered scheme of economic activity, in the sense that definite laws of economic behaviour are discoverable in it; but the order that exists under it is not one that is consciously willed by any economic agent, it emerges as the resultant of the separate and independent wills of a large number of economic agents, each of which makes his decision in ignorance of all the others. Such an economy exhibits orders of a sort, but no plan.

Under (ii), the possibility of deputed or federal authority is not excluded, nor is the existence of a field of minor economic decisions that need not be made in detail according to plan, but simply fitted into the plan in their totality. In

the ultimate analysis, however, the responsibility for economic decisions must be single and undivided.

Under (iii), partial planning of particular industries and
enterprises is excluded. Planning must be general if it is to
deserve the word. However, we may apply the term planning
to schemes of economic control that deal with the broad
outline of economic activity, without regulating details, provided that, so far as they go, they treat the economic system
as a whole. Thus, schemes for deliberate control of the
price-level, of the proportion between consumption-goods
industries and capital-goods industries, or of the distribution
of the national income between different classes might all be
referred to as examples of economic planning.

In this connexion it is convenient to give more exact and
specialized denotations to certain terms in common use, to
wit: planning, rationalization, and scientific management.
The meanings of all three terms contain a common element:
the idea of rational co-ordination of means and ends. It
would be convenient, and would agree with common usage,
if we used the word planning to denote such rational co-
ordination in the economy as a whole, rationalization to denote rational co-ordination in an industry or group of industries, and scientific management to denote the same in an
enterprise or group of enterprises.

We must also distinguish planning from intervention.
Intervention involves some degree of deliberate interference
with the working of the free-market system of economic co-
ordination, but need not involve planning the system as a
whole. Intervention may be exercised by the State, as by
protective duties, quotas, marketing boards, factory acts,
minimum-wage laws, and regulation of the hours of labour;
or it may be exercised by private associations, such as trade
unions or manufacturers' associations, and take the form of
collective wage bargains, of price and output control, of

delimination of sales territory, and of other restrictive cove-
nants that modify the normal working of market equilibrium.
The point about intervention of this type is that, while it
modifies the conditions under which the market system
works itself out, it still leaves the ultimate result of the economic process to be determined by the mutual interaction
of a large number of independent economic agents. It does
not create a deliberate, conscious control of economic life.

It is clear that economic planning, in the sense in which
the word is used here, implies the unification of property
rights in the means of production. The powers of control
over the land and capital of the community that must be
vested in the planning authority will give the latter the effective substance of ownership. It may be that individual pro-
prietors of means of production may be allowed to retain
nominal titles of ownership; but, if so, this will amount to
little more than a vested right to receive certain incomes
secured on the general product of planned industry. Planning thus, by its nature, implies *unified* ownership of the
means of production. This does not of logical necessity
mean *public* ownership: we shall examine later whether there
are reasons for believing that, in fact, planning must involve
public ownership of the means of production.

(2) **Planning and socialism.** The terms Socialism and
Planning have been defined. It remains to examine the relation between them. Although socialism has been defined so
as to include planning, let us for a moment take it to mean
only public ownership and control of the means of production (better called collectivism) and consider whether it
necessarily involves planning. We must also consider whether
planning necessarily implies public (as distinct from unified)
ownership. In other words, can unplanned socialism or
planned capitalism exist?

(1) *Unplanned Socialism.* We can, in abstract theory, con-

ceive the transformation of an unplanned capitalist economy into collectivism in the following way: (*a*) all the separate enterprises existing under capitalism are converted into public bodies *without further unification or co-ordination*, in such wise that each trades on the basis of market prices as an autonomous concern, having no connexion, except through the market, with any other undertaking; (*b*) all rights of property in land and capital are transferred to the community in such wise that the latter appropriates the shares of the national income imputed to these factors by the process of price-determination in the market and redistributes these shares to its members as individual income. Such an economy would be unplanned collectivism. It is easy to see, however, that it would almost inevitably slide into a planned system. The separateness of the various enterprises and the mutual blindness of those who conduct them, while natural under private ownership, would be a highly artificial state of affairs under public ownership. The organs of public economy would have every reason for mutual consultation and publicity, none for separateness and secrecy. In particular, the organs responsible for the investment of savings and the creation of new capital would, by the very nature of their functions, tend to envisage their task from the viewpoint of the social economy as a whole, and thus become, whether they would or not, planning organs. Thus, unplanned collectivism, although logically thinkable, is unlikely to occur in practice.

(2) *Planned Capitalism.* Can a planned organization of economic activity be combined with private ownership of the means of production? As we have seen, planning involves a *de facto* unification of property rights in the means of production. Must this unification lead to public ownership and to the abolition of income from property, i.e. to socialism, or is it possible that a planned economy would

continue to hand over a large proportion of its total product
to a small class of rentiers? This question is so important
that a separate section has been allotted to its discussion.
The broad conclusions that emerge from the discussion are
that planned capitalism, although a possible form of economic organization, is unlikely to be durable, because of its
social and political consequences.

(3) **The consequences of planned capitalism.** It now
remains to consider the reasons which, in the present writer's
opinion, render impracticable any mixed system of public
and private enterprise or combination of planning with private property in the means of production. Mixed systems
may be divided into two classes. (1) Those of which unplanned private enterprise forms the essential basis and
fundamental pattern, but which have been extensively in-
vaded and infiltrated by various kinds of state intervention
in particular industries, such as public ownership, public
control of prices and profits (e.g. in public utilities), or tariff
privileges and subsidies from public funds granted to industries which remain in private ownership. (2) Those which
consist of a system of planning superimposed upon and co-
ordinating a system of private enterprise and individual
ownership. Into this class come the various projects of
planned capitalism, including the Corporate State in its
various forms, Sir Arthur Salter's Ordered Society,[1] Mr.
Harold Macmillan's Industrial Self-Government,[2] and Mr.
Walter Elliot's Bucolic Utopia.

(1) Intervention, whether in the form of state ownership,
of state control, or of fiscal manipulation, which is confined
to particular industries and stops short of planning the
national economy as a whole, suffers from all the defects of
unplanned economy and from some peculiar to itself. As in

---

[1] A. Salter, *Recovery* and *Framework of an Ordered Society*.
[2] H. Macmillan, *Reconstruction* and *The Middle Way*.

a completely unplanned economy it is liable to cyclical fluctuations and to unexpected variations in economic data. The
state, if it runs an enterprise, is simply one entrepreneur
among many, competing with the others in the capital market
and in the labour market. It is as much at the mercy of
fluctuations in the supply of capital as a private entrepreneur,
and in its relations with labour it is forced willy-nilly into
the role of the exploiting employer. This is the position of
the London Passenger Transport Board *vis-à-vis* its employees. In a capitalist society even a socialist government
has to consider the interests of rentiers and to resist 'unreasonable' wage demands from its employees. An example
of this is afforded by successive 'Front Populaire' governments in France. If the state does attempt any different
policy, it is as likely as not, working in an unplanned economy
in ignorance of many of the relevant data, to do things which
defeat its own ends. A case in point is the dilemma of a
socialist government in a capitalist state trying to deal with
unemployment under the stipulation, imposed by capitalist
interests, that it will not compete with potential private
enterprise and that it will do nothing to disturb 'confidence'.

Unless the state can consider the economic system as a
whole—i.e unless it plans—intervention is likely to do more
harm than good. As an example, we may adduce the usual
consequences of tariff protection: one industry is benefited
and a number of others are harmed. Moreover, such piecemeal intervention can rarely envisage the true objectives of
economic policy. Thus the natural attempt of the state,
dealing with unemployment in a fundamentally unplanned
economy, is to give help of some kind, financial or administrative, to declining industries and obsolete processes, thereby
prolonging their uneconomic existence, rather than to develop new and more efficient processes and new industries
satisfying hitherto latent wants.

Finally, the peculiar bane of all state intervention that falls short of complete socialism is political interference by sectional interests. Once the state deviates from the policy of *laisser-faire* (or more precisely from the individualistic minimum of intervention[1]) it immediately puts a premium on political corruption. It becomes advantageous for any compact economic interest to capture the machinery of the state and to use it to further its own private purposes. The tariff history of all protectionist countries[2] and the annals of economic imperialism[3] offer ample illustration of this.

(2) A completely planned capitalist economy[4] could avoid most of these difficulties. It would be free from the defects of piecemeal intervention. Through the glass walls of a planned economy the consequences of favouring one section at the expense of another could be clearly seen—so clearly seen in fact that inequalities of personal advantage, not based on functional differences of generally accepted utility, would soon cease to be tolerated in a politically democratic community. Moreover, the economic functions of the capitalist —the provision of new capital, the assumption of risk, the introduction of new materials and processes—that in an unplanned economy afford some sort of social justification for his existence would be wholly or largely superseded in a planned capitalism by the planning authority, leaving the capitalist as a mere rentier, a receiver of socially unjustified and therefore privileged income.

Thus a planned capitalist economy would come up against

[1] See H. Sidgwick, *Elements of Politics*, ch. iv; *Principles of Political Economy*, Bk. iii, chs. ii, iii, iv.

[2] F. W. Taussig, *Tariff History of the United States*.

[3] J. A. Hobson, *Imperialism*; V. I. Lenin, *Imperialism*; P. T. Moon, *Imperialism and World Politics*; L. Woolf, *Economic Imperialism*.

[4] Completely planned in the sense that the planning authority would be in a position to review the economic system as a whole, not in the sense that every detail of economic life must be regulated by it.

one almost insuperable difficulty. This is the division of the
product of industry, not only between the owning class and
the working class, but among different sections of the owning
class. As long as the market is the ultimate arbiter between
the claims of the different parties to the production process,
so long can the illusion be maintained that the division of
the product is governed by forces as impersonal and inevitable as those which govern the weather. Even in a society
where many industries are in fact carried on by the public,
but as isolated enterprises not part of a general social plan,
this illusion of inevitability may persist. But as soon as the
state, through a definite planning organ, makes itself responsible for the consideration of economic activity as a whole,
this illusion is destroyed, and the essentially social nature of
all economic relations is revealed.

If, under private enterprise or under unplanned piecemeal
state enterprise, the coalminers ask for an advance in wages,
they may be told that their demands cannot be granted
because they go beyond the capacity of the industry to bear.
If they ask why the industry cannot afford to pay higher
wages, they will be told that it is because the price of coal is
too low. If they ask why the price of coal is as low as it is,
they will be told that it is because the demand for coal is
small; and so on. But in a planned economy the whole
system of quantities, prices, wages, &c., is the result of the
deliberate decisions of a responsible planning organ. If
wages are too low in any one industry, it is the duty of the
planning organ to adjust prices and quantities produced, so
as to yield equal wages to work of equal skill, responsibility,
and difficulty in every industry. If, then, wages are low in
all industries, it is either because productivity per head is
low, or because factors other than labour are taking a large
proportion of the total social product. But the proportions
in which the social product is divided between labour and

other factors, while in an unplanned economy they are the apparently fortuitous result of the interaction of innumerable uncontrollable factors, are, in a planned economy, the result of decisions for which the planning authorities are directly responsible. The illusion of objectivity thus stripped from the process of income-formation, the non-wage elements in distribution will be seen clearly for what they always have been in essence—the fruits of exploitation (Marx's Surplus Value, Veblen's Free Income, my Institutional Revenue). Once this occurs, the pressure of the organized working class for a continually increased share of the social product, leading ultimately to a complete expropriation of the property-owner, can only be resisted by the destruction of the organized working-class movement and the abolition of all democratic institutions. In other words, capitalist planning can exist only on the basis of Fascism.

Not only the distribution of the product between labour and property, but also the division of the share of property among the various groups of property owners will be attended by a similar difficulty. In a planless economy, a ceaseless process of competition, modified by partial and usually temporary monopoly, allocates varying amounts of surplus value to one group and another in a manner that seems inevitable and 'natural'. Once planning is complete, the share of each section has to be determined by a deliberate decision of the planning organ. Unless the property-owning class is content to accept once and for all an allocation of shares in the surplus product according to the relative competitive strength of different sections at some definite moment before full planning was established, the planning organization will be the object of ceaseless attempts on the part of vested interests to seize control of it for their own profit. (Observe that this is equally true of national groups—e.g. British finance-capital as against French finance-capital—and of industrial groups within a country—e.g. export industries against home-market industries, capital-goods industries as against consumption-goods industries). It is in the highest degree unlikely that conflicting interests—whether national or industrial—within the owning class will acquiesce in such a stabilization of any particular *status quo*. On the international scale war and on the national scale organized political corruption will be the result. Planned capitalism will not only be a fascist society but a gangster-fascist society. A socialist society can avoid this difficulty by distributing the surplus product on a basis of equality. Capitalism, however, is based on the creation and preservation of privileged income for a particular class. Since its essence is the denial of equity, it is impossible for it to find any 'equitable' formula for the division of the social product either between Labour and Property or among the different sections of Property.

In this connexion it is interesting to note the objection made by defenders of the existing system to 'bringing economics into politics'. In truth, economics have been in politics all the time, but in a concealed form. What the supporters of capitalism object to is the making manifest of the economic implications of existing social institutions of property, inheritance, and educational inequality. They attempt to divert the workers' interest from fundamental social institutions—the true subject of politics—to the superficial inanities of party-political sham-fights. It is to their interest to prolong the illusion of a 'natural' economic order, working by impersonal and irresistible economic laws; it is to their interest to conceal the exploitation of the worker behind the veils of a system of objective market relations which allot wages to the worker and interest to the capitalist equally in the form of the price of a 'service'.

Of all forms of piecemeal nationalization or state-control, that of the banking system would come closest to setting up a planned economy at one stroke. Once the state was responsible for the conduct of the banking system it would be obliged to look beyond the purely commercial criteria of banking practice (reserve ratios, liquidity of assets, &c.) and consider demands for credit from a social-economic point of view. It would have to consider the balance of saving and investment, the proportion between consumption-goods and production-goods industries, the volume of speculative compared with productive transactions, &c. In other words, a state-controlled banking system would be obliged to consider the economic activity of the community as an organic whole; thus it would already be in embryo a planning organ. Ultimately, therefore, the nationalization of banks would make manifest that fundamental conflict of classes which is latent all the time in the system of market economy. This probably accounts for the fact that proposals for the nationalization of the banks arouse much more bitter opposition from the capitalist ranks than proposals for the nationalization of any other industry.

4. The Economic Problem Under Socialism

(1) **In general.** A socialist society will have to solve the problems that are solved in a capitalist society, however imperfectly, by the method of production for sale in the market at a price. Must it work out a brand-new solution *ab origine* for these problems, or may it make use of some of the machinery evolved during the period of petty commodity production that preceded capitalism and perfected under capitalism itself? In other words, the field of our investigation is the extent to which price and its correlates, money and the market, can be adapted to a planned socialist economy.

With regard to the significance of pricing for a socialist economy, socialists are divided into two schools of thought: those who hold that the individualistic assumptions behind the pricing process have no relevance for a socialist community, and those who hold that they have.

(a) The first school would reject in principle the notion that the demand schedules of individual consumers give any adequate indication of human needs. The most brilliant exposition of this view is probably Lancelot Hogben's *Retreat from Reason*.[1] It rejects the two corner-stones of individualistic economics: the doctrine that the individual knows best what is good for him, and the doctrine of the insatiability of human wants. It asserts rather that the basic needs of humanity can be ascertained better by scientific study than by offering people a choice of goods in the market-place, and that non-basic needs are the result either of class standards of consumption (Veblen's 'conspicuous waste' and 'pecuniary emulation') or of profit-mongering advertising campaigns, which multiply satisfactions without increasing satisfaction. If these views be accepted, social production will be carried out not in response to the indications of the market but according to a planned survey of human needs.

(A further point made by these theorists is that the normalizing of consumption, following on the scientific study of human needs, would make possible standardization in production to an extent previously unheard of, and thus reduce greatly the cost of satisfying those needs. In this way, it is hoped, the goods that are required for human consumption can be so few and so easily produced that they will become free goods and the economic problem as such will disappear.) Later (Chapter II, section 1 (3)) we shall examine the contentions of those who reject the concept of the insatiability of wants. Also (in Chapter II, section 1 (4)) we shall deal with the view that scarcity will be abolished, and economic calculations thereby rendered unnecessary, by

[1] See also the same author's 'Introduction' to *Political Arithmetic* and Lewis Mumford's *Technics and Civilisation*, ch. viii, sections 6 and 7.

technical progress in the future 'age of plenty'. Meanwhile, however, we shall adhere to the more orthodox views.

(b) The second school of socialists starts off with the liberal individualistic conception of welfare as consisting in the satisfaction of particular individuals' particular wants, interpreted by those individuals themselves by an act of deliberate conscious choice. It entrusts the satisfaction of those wants to a collectivist economic organization rather than to private enterprise, because it believes that collectivism can, when the distribution of income as well as the organization of production is taken into account, provide a greater aggregate of individual satisfaction than private enterprise can. A social order of this type may be called libertarian socialism. Adherents of this school desire socialism in order that they may establish, for the first time in human history, an effective individualism.

(2) **Pricing under socialism.** Whichever view, therefore, be taken of the process of satisfying human wants—whether we accept or reject the relevance of the individual's demand schedule—there remains the economic problem, the problem of disposing of limited resources so as to provide the maximum satisfaction of human needs, which needs are, if we interpret the word needs in its widest sense, capable of indefinite expansion. This implies that the economic organizers of the community must adopt some system of valuation. That is to say, there must be established a scale of relative importance (in other words 'value') among the different possible ends of economic activity; resources must be valued according as they contribute to these ends ('imputed value' of the Austrian School); the most advantageous uses of resources must be discovered and scarce resources must be husbanded ('costing' and 'principle of substitution'). According to the first school of socialists the alternative ends of economic activity will be comparatively few and will be

laid down by some authority acting on behalf of the community as a whole. According to the second school they will be determined by the individual preferences of millions of separate economic subjects; in this case the problem of balancing one man's preference against another's will arise.

Analogous to the problem of consumers' preferences for goods is that of workers' preferences for jobs. Here too, two solutions are possible. Either people can be allocated to different occupations in accordance with some objective test of capacity (e.g. by some development of industrial psychology) or they can be allowed to choose according to their own preferences. In both cases the fact that some kinds of labour are scarcer than others must be taken into account in the social cost-accounting scheme; in both cases it will be economically desirable to increase the supply of the scarcer types of labour. In the first case, however, the only problem will be the balancing of the cost of training against the productivity of the factor; in the second case an additional problem arises of offering inducements to workers to move into occupations where labour is relatively scarce out of occupations where it is relatively superfluous. A libertarian socialist community cannot dispose of human factors of production by administrative order as it can dispose of non-human factors. It must respect individual workers' preferences for one job over another.

In what follows we will assume a libertarian form of socialist community; not because it is necessarily the best or the only possible form of socialism, but because it raises in the most acute form the economic problem. If it is soluble under libertarian socialism, it is *a fortiori* soluble under authoritarian socialism.

The problem before a libertarian socialist economy is threefold. First, there is the measurement of demand, in order that production may be directed so as to yield the maximum of satisfaction. Second, there is the measurement of cost, in order that the satisfactions that are procured may be procured with the minimum expenditure of resources; the calculation of costs affords a criterion for deciding between alternative plans of production. Third, there is the problem of distribution—that of allotting to particular members of society definite shares in the goods produced.

In capitalist society[1] the price system solves, after a fashion, all three of these problems at once.[2] Thus the pricing process has a threefold function in the individualistic system, corresponding to the pricing of consumption goods, of intermediate goods, and of ultimate factors of production.[3]

(1) The pricing of consumption goods acts as a regulator of demand. Hence it (i) allocates already produced goods to consumers according to the scarcity of the goods and the intensity of the consumers' demand; and (ii) indicates the kind and number of goods that should be most worth while to produce in the future.

(2) The pricing of intermediate goods (and of ultimate factors of production) yields a measure of relative cost and hence acts as a guide to the worth-whileness of production, as well as to the best method of production.

(3) The pricing of ultimate factors of production affords an automatic method of distribution. By allowing owners of such factors to appropriate their economic value as personal income the value of the whole mass of the social product is allocated without residue and without

[1] Also under simple commodity production.

[2] Price also is a means of comparing physically and technically dissimilar goods, and hence of calculating a measure of aggregate production. This function of price is derived from those numbered (1) and (2) following. It will be discussed under heading (2), the pricing of intermediate goods. (See Chapter III, section 6).

[3] The phrase 'ultimate factors of production' is used to designate production goods (such as land and human labour) that cannot be resolved into other production goods.

deficit, among the collective producers of it, according to a process that, apparently, takes place independently of the wills and preferences of any individual in authority.

A socialist society that adopts the price system may also use the same device for all three purposes. If, however, the socialist community jettisons the system of sale at a price in a free market, then it will have to develop new machinery to deal with these three problems. It is possible that three different kinds of machinery will be necessary for these three separate purposes. In other words, there is no necessity in the nature of things that a device for the measurement of consumers' preferences should serve at the same time for the allocation of producers' shares in a collective product.

A socialist community might adopt the price system for function (1) only, or for functions (1) and (2), or for all three functions. That is to say, it might price finished goods and allow the consumer free choice of goods already produced at the prices fixed, but might adopt a completely separate and distinct method for the calculation of costs and a third system for the distribution of individual income. Alternatively, it might extend the pricing process to include a costing system based on imputed prices of intermediate goods and ultimate factors of production, while completely divorcing individual earnings from the value of factors of production. Finally, it might adopt the price system in its entirety, thus setting up within the socialist community a simulacrum of capitalist economy.

5. Some General Assumptions

We postulate an economic society of the Occidental (West European, North American, and Australasian) type, at a fairly high level of technological development. Economic self-sufficiency is not postulated. (Foreign trade under socialism is discussed in Chapter VII.) In this society we shall assume that private property is recognized in goods used for personal consumption but not in goods used for trade or for producing goods to be sold in the way of trade. Natural resources and instrumental goods are owned by the community, and all production is undertaken by organs of the community. (Later we shall consider the possibility of modifying the assumption that *all* production is socialized; see Chapter VI.) We shall assume the existence of a number of separate production units, grouped according to the nature of the product or the needs of the market into larger units, and these larger units into still larger units, and so in a hierarchy with a Supreme Economic Council (S.E.C.) at the head. (This need not preclude a multiformity of types of organization: government departments, autonomous commissions, national guilds, co-operative societies, and non-profit-making voluntary associations.) The S.E.C. will be provided with the appropriate organs for statistical research and control and will have powers of inspection and audit over the entire economic system.

We shall not, however, concern ourselves with the details of economic organization. It is tempting to draw a picture of a planned socialist system of industry—the constitution of the planning organs, the hierarchy of combines, trusts, and enterprises, the special organizations required for banking, transport, housing, agriculture, &c. But to do this would lead us away from our central topic, which is the part played by the price system in a socialist economy.[1]

---

[1] For a discussion of problems of economic organization the reader is referred to such works as B. and S. Webb's *Constitution for a Socialist Commonwealth of Great Britain*, G. D. H. Cole's *Principles of Economic Planning*, or *Britain Without Capitalists*.

CHAPTER II

CONSUMPTION GOODS—THE REGULATION OF DEMAND

1. SOCIAL NEEDS

WE shall take it as axiomatic that a socialist community must produce in order to satisfy the needs of its members. But, first, we must clarify this concept of needs. A socialist community must give a broader interpretation to the term 'needs' than does a capitalist economy. Broadly speaking, we may say that orthodox economic theory identifies needs with wants, and considers only such wants as can be expressed in terms of individuals' preferences for particular concrete goods or for particular services that are capable of being rendered to particular individuals. Closely related to this individualistic interpretation of needs are the concept of the insatiability of wants and the concept of scarcity, which latter may be said to be the leading idea of bourgeois economic theory.

(1) **Needs and wants.** The distinction between needs and wants is the distinction between the objective and the subjective. Needs are what we *really* require for life, efficiency, and enjoyment: wants are what we *think* we require. Obviously the method of selling goods for money on the market, especially if the process is backed by all the arts of salesmanship, lays emphasis on wants as distinct from needs. The assumption of the individualistic school of economists is that every consumer is the best judge of his own needs and that his own conscious want is a reliable guide to what will give him most satisfaction. This would be controverted by many, who point out that even in such elementary things as food the individual's conscious wants are no guides to what

is really wholesome, while in such matters as housing, public health, education, and insurance it is generally admitted that people will not buy in the open market as much of these services as is good for them. Hence arises the necessity of providing social services otherwise than through sale on the free market. It is suggested that many other things, such as food and some forms of recreation, should be provided in the same manner as the existing social services and on the same principle, that of some objective standard of need rather than the subjective velleity of want. Give people more money to spend and they will feed themselves on tinned goods, pickles, and cream buns. To raise their real standard of living, therefore, they should be provided with nutritious food whether they consciously want it or not. Thus runs the argument.

Thus there is a case for the intervention of a body of experts whose function is to mould the individual's schedule of wants into uniformity with his real needs. But in view of the resentment that most people feel when their conscious choice is interfered with, it would appear best that this intervention should take the form of persuasion rather than compulsion. The powerful engine of propaganda and advertisement, employed by public organs of education and enlightenment instead of by the hucksters and panders of private profit-making industry, could divert demand into socially desirable directions while preserving the subjective impression of free choice. If the meretricious but effective arts of the salesman and the publicity expert were placed at the disposal of impartial and disinterested bodies of experts—dieticians, architects, heating engineers, textile specialists, orthopaedists, psychologists—what an improvement in the standard of food, houses, clothes, footgear, and toys would result!

(2) **Communal and individual consumption.** The existing system of production for the market emphasizes 'commodities'—i.e. concrete goods destined for individual

consumption or particular services rendered to particular individuals—rather than human needs (or even wants) in general. Now many needs are satisfied by such individualized commodities. Every one needs his own particular tooth-brush. Human feet are so little standardized that A's shoes are not kind on B's corns.[1] Cricket bats, musical instruments, books, and bicycles (or motor-cars) are individual things that soon acquire an individual relation to their user. In all these instances there is a strong case for the satisfaction of needs through individual provision of concrete goods and services. A very large number of needs whose satisfaction requires the use of scarce resources are individual needs, in the sense that they are felt by individuals, that their intensity varies from one individual to another, and that their satisfaction requires that the individual should have the power of disposal over specific goods. To the last statement there are many exceptions—parks and museums are instances of an important class of exceptions—but a vast number of needs do call for individual disposal. A communally provided beef-steak, tooth-brush, pair of trousers, book, or bicycle must be actually in my possession before it can satisfy my needs. In some cases, such as the beef-steak, I must have the power of absolute disposal, even unto destruction. In others, such as the tooth-brush, and the trousers, I require exclusive control over the whole period of its employment. In others, such as the book and the bicycle, a right of temporary disposal will sometimes satisfy my needs, but I must be able to get the particular book or bicycle that suits me—not any book or bicycle will do. In these cases, it is not social need but individual need that requires satisfaction even in the

---

[1] The application to shoe design of one-tenth of the skill and effort nowadays devoted to selling shoes and creating fashionable novelties, lines of sales talk, &c., might well abolish corns and other foot troubles within a generation.

most communistic society. Granted that no individual exists except as a social being, and that all individual needs arise within a social framework, nevertheless the need when it arises is the need of an individual and requires for its satisfaction individual power of disposal over goods.

But many human needs are of a different kind. Without relapsing into the nonsensical (and fascistically tendentious) belief in a super-personal entity capable of experiencing satisfaction apart from the individuals composing it, we may subscribe to the view that many individual needs can be satisfied better (or can only be satisfied) by a certain set of social relations, involving in some cases the entire social economic system, rather than by the provision of concrete commodities. The desire for leisure can only be satisfied by an economic system in which work is deliberately planned so as to allow of short hours. The desire for country walks and scenery cannot be satisfied (except for an aristocratic minority) by providing each individual with a private park and woodland; but it can be satisfied by collective action on a national scale with regard to the utilization of land. The desire for children and a normal family life can be satisfied to a certain extent by the redistribution of income in consonance with family needs, each family being left to spend its income on commodities as it thinks best; but far more effective, up to a certain point, is planned social effort in the matter of housing, medical services, domestic help, and the collective supervision of children in order to guarantee to their mothers a certain minimum of free time.

It thus appears that there is an important distinction to be made between two categories of goods and services. On the one hand there are such goods and services as satisfy essentially collective needs—such as security and order, beauty in the city and countryside, public health, education—and on the other there are such goods and services as satisfy essentially individual needs. In the first category may also be included many needs, such as a minimum of food, clothing, and shelter, which are strictly speaking individual, but which, being relatively unspecialized and common to the bulk of mankind, may possibly be more easily supplied by collective provision than by individual provision. This will leave in the other category the relatively more specialized needs which vary from person to person and which only the individual concerned can adequately estimate in intensity or balance against the intensity of other needs. Consumption thus falls into two main divisions. We will call the first the division of communal consumption,[1] and the second the division of individual consumption.[2]

(3) **The insatiability of wants.** If we think of the satisfaction of human needs entirely in terms of individual consumption, we are likely to magnify the importance of 'commodities' and to conceive of satisfaction entirely in terms of the number and variety of such individually consumed goods. Thus arises the concept, basic in orthodox economic theory, of the insatiability of human wants: the idea that, however many goods an individual is provided with, it will always be possible to make *some* addition to his welfare by adding to the stock of goods in his possession; that, even if satiety has been attained in one department of wants, others remain to respond to the stimulus of novelty, so that the point of satiation with *goods in general* is never reached.

[1] The division of communal consumption does not correspond exactly to what are called 'social services', since some social services (e.g. social insurance) take the form of money payments made to individuals, who then enter the market as individual demanders of goods (see Chapter IV, section 5).

[2] Note the distinction between communal and individual *consumption*, as defined above, and socialized and private *production* (see Chapter VI, section 1). For the latter, I use the terms socialized and private *sectors*, following the soviet terminology, while for the former, I use the terms *divisions* of communal and individual consumption.

If, on the other hand, we think of the satisfaction of human needs entirely in terms of communal consumption, we may be tempted to reject this concept of the insatiability of human wants. It can be argued very plausibly that the majority of the wants whose satisfaction keeps busy the productive resources of society at the present day are factitious wants, the result either of competitive standards of expenditure in a class society or of high-pressure salesmanship impelled by the desire for profit. It is obvious how capitalist enterprise in the consumption-goods industries stimulates the production of articles serving ephemeral and fantastic wants (the numerous industries battening on women's fashions in clothes and cosmetics illustrate this point). Even in the case of genuine needs, capitalism multiplies varieties beyond all necessity, and stultifies freedom of choice by making intelligent choice impossible. Moreover, capitalist enterprise, having embodied much skilled labour and other resources in the production of superfluous goods, proceeds to utilize more labour and material resources in the task of selling what has been produced. The great bulk of the effort spent in salesmanship, of the skilled printing and other work involved in advertising, of the floor-space, glass, and concrete devoted to elaborate show-rooms—the bulk of all this represents one waste caused by another waste. As a general rule, the more useless the commodity the more effort is wasted on pushing the sale of it. Moreover, even if we set aside wants obviously ephemeral and fantastic, and variety that is hypertrophied to the point of being meaningless, a very large part of the wants that are satisfied by the goods produced in a capitalist society are not real human needs at all, but are wants based on what Veblen calls 'conspicuous waste'.[1] Things are desired not because they serve some purpose of convenience or comfort or beauty, but simply because they

[1] Th. Veblen, *Theory of the Leisure Class*.

are expensive and their possession is a mark of social superiority—in a society stratified by pecuniary wealth. Illustra-
tions of this are the use of platinum in jewellery in spite of
its dull appearance (it is significant that the quantity of
platinum that the market will buy falls as the price falls—a
reversal of the normal law of demand), the high rents of
uncomfortable and badly appointed flats with a 'good ad-
dress', the demand for old furniture that is good neither to
use nor to look at, and the racket in limited editions of books.
In such cases it is pedantry in the economist to talk of
scarcity as determining the price: it is the price that causes
the scarcity.

A society that was free from these factitious wants arising
out of competitive display and competitive salesmanship
would find it very much easier to organize the satisfaction of
the genuine human needs that remained. The goods serving
these needs could be standardized much more than at present
by the elimination of trivial and meaningless varieties without
sacrificing any real freedom of consumers' choice. Suppose,
for example, that the skill and energy that is spent in designing new models of motor-car or radio, with slight variations
in order to make people discontented with their last year's
model or in order to make them think there is some essential
difference between A's product and B's, were pooled in one
organization instead of being dissipated over several mutually secretive and antagonistic establishments; suppose further that they were set to work, first in analysing what the
consumer really wants (as distinct from what he can be made
to think he wants), second in designing a small range of
models embodying these desired properties, each of which
would be technically the best possible in its line, and third
in organizing the production of the selected models on as
large a scale and as cheaply as is technically possible: can it
be doubted that goods of the highest quality could be turned

out in quantities that would enable every family, perhaps every individual, to possess one? Probably many goods—almost certainly the staple foods, and possibly some articles of clothing and furniture—could become free goods; but it is somewhat extravagant to suppose that all goods could be multiplied up to the point of satiety of the needs that they served.

Some element of scarcity, and hence *some* necessity for choice, would remain. House-room and garden-space cannot be indefinitely increased and, even after ample allowance had been made for the needs of children, people would have to choose between increased living accommodation and other desirable things. Even were all elements of ostentation absent in the design of clothes and furniture, some people's desire for these commodities would outrun the community's power to produce them as free goods. Moreover, even the most drastic simplification and standardization could not eliminate all varieties in design. Differences in purpose would still necessitate differences in design. It is impossible to imagine *the* motor-car or *the* wireless set: there must be a range of different powers and sizes. As soon as such a range is produced it is necessary to compel the consumer to choose which article he will have: it would be uneconomic to provide one of everything for him.

Moreover, tastes differ, even in the most simplified community: one man would prefer a big garden to a motor-car, another would prefer a grand piano to a radio set. To multiply up to the point of satiety a narrow range of standardized goods for mass consumption would mean renouncing the opportunity of producing some other goods, satisfying other wants, less widespread perhaps, but still more intensely felt than those satisfied by the less urgently desired units of the mass-produced goods. That is to say, some at least of the recipients of a standard motor-car issued free to all citizens might prefer that the time and labour embodied in it might have been embodied instead in an astronomical telescope or a chest of viols.

Human enjoyment may be active or passive: in the one case, an individual actively *does* something—makes a chair, plants a garden, plays a musical instrument, or climbs a mountain; in the other case, he simply lets himself be amused —by radio, cinema, musical comedy, football match, or light novel[1]—or passively enjoys the pleasure of mere possession, as the rich vulgarian with a gallery of old masters or a library of first editions that an agent has got together for him. It is characteristic of satisfactions of the first type that, in general, they require less in the way of material equipment than satisfactions of the second type. For this reason, an economic system based on private profit-making fails to develop active enjoyment as fully as it might be developed, while it stimulates all forms of passive or acquisitive enjoyment to the full. Moreover, in many cases, the equipment needed for active enjoyment can conveniently be provided as means of communal rather than of individual consumption (public libraries, swimming baths, sports grounds, parks of culture and rest, and workers' clubs with their provisions for games, dancing, study, and hobbies).

Thus, it is reasonable to suppose that, under socialism, active enjoyment would be stimulated much more than it is at present and therewith the tendency to the multiplication of ephemeral toys and pastimes would be lessened. Nevertheless, there will probably remain some craving for passive enjoyment and the acquisition of personal property: moreover, in most cases even active enjoyment requires a certain

---

[1] I am not suggesting that it is impossible that any one of these occupations may be the occasion of a genuine *effort* of understanding and appreciation, in which case it enters into the category of active enjoyment. But, in most cases, it is a form of passive enjoyment.

minimum of some sort of gear, personally owned and used—woodworking tools, a garden in which to grow things, the books that a student needs constantly at hand—and thus we cannot suppose that even under socialism, at least within a measurable period of time, the need for 'commodities' (in the sense of goods provided for individual consumption) will entirely disappear, nor that the productive resources of even a socialist community will be so enlarged that none of these commodities will be 'scarce' in the economists' sense of the word.

But even if we accept the possibility of satiation, so far as individual wants are concerned, the spectre of scarcity is not yet exorcized, and the economic problem as such will not be eliminated. Even if individual wants are satisfied by a limited quantity of consumption goods, requiring for their production a comparatively small part of the community's available resources, the possibility of an almost indefinite extension of collective activities requiring material resources—such as scientific research, artistic production, athletics, public buildings, and communal pageantry—will continue to exemplify the insatiability of wants and will raise in a new form the old problem of alternative ends. In scientific research alone it would be possible to draw up a quite reasonable programme of investigations, likely to result in immediate benefit to humanity, which would absorb all the resources of the community above a bare subsistence level. Once it is decided that the whole programme cannot be undertaken at once, the question of priority arises. The resources available for research become scarce and must be economized.

(4) **The age of plenty.** It is necessary to deal with the contentions of those who claim that economic calculations will be unnecessary in the 'age of plenty' which modern technical invention will usher in, or would usher in were it not for the resistance of financiers (usually conceived of as

in some way opposed to the genuine industrialists) aided by the obscurantism of economists. Many writers, such as Lewis Mumford,[1] Lancelot Hogben,[2] and the technocrats, consider that standardization and mass-production methods will make it possible to increase the supply of all commodities up to the point of complete satisfaction of all needs—in other words, that all goods will become free goods.

One argument to the contrary, that founded on the insatiability of wants, has already been considered in the previous sub-sections. Another is that technics alone will never produce an age of plenty, since the absence of a way of relating technical means to the needs whose satisfaction is desired may easily dissipate the means in wasteful forms of production, so stultifying the potential age of plenty at the outset. Further, one factor of production will never cease to be scarce, but will on the contrary become more scarce; its use will, therefore, have to be economized more imperatively as productivity advances. This factor is human labour. As productivity advances, the value of human labour increases proportionally (or even more than proportionally) with the income per head of population. Hence emerges the necessity of a strict economic accountancy applied to labour and to all goods into the production of which a high proportion of direct labour enters. Under this heading come:

(1) *Personal services.* Apart from menial domestic service, which an equalitarian society will eliminate, either by mechanization of the home or by people learning to do their own domestic work, there are a variety of services such as those of sick-nurses, restaurant waiters, hairdressers, drivers of hired cars, &c., which, with the rise of the remuneration of those who render them nearly to the level of professional salaries, will become relatively extremely expensive.

[1] L. Mumford, *Technics and Civilisation*, ch. viii, sections 6–7.
[2] L. Hogben, *The Retreat from Reason*.

Some, like sick-nursing, will probably be organized almost entirely in the communalized division of consumption—the private nurse will become as rare as the private tutor, the private chaplain, or the private orchestra of musicians. Others will be eliminated by mechanization—the cafeteria will displace the restaurant waiter, and the chambermaid will perhaps be replaced by such arrangements as H. G. Wells foreshadows in his *Modern Utopia*.[1] But hairdressing is not yet mechanized, nor can public-service vehicles entirely take the place of hired cars. The people who perform work of this type will probably acquire the status and pay of professional workers in a class society, and their services will cost their fellow citizens correspondingly dear. It is important to note that, however cheap private cars become in a mechanized socialist community, a taxi drive will still be fairly expensive.

(2) *Distributive, clerical, and transport services.* These inevitably make up a considerable part of the cost of any finished consumption good—i.e. the good as ready for the actual consumer. As the cost of manufacture is reduced so the cost of checking, handling, wrapping, &c., will increase relatively. These processes can be simplified and rationalized, in part they can be mechanized, but the human element will always remain and must be paid for.

(3) *Goods that cannot be produced by mechanical means.* The production of some goods cannot be reduced to mass production methods; such goods will remain relatively scarce even in a socialist society. It is conceivable that some very important foodstuffs come into this category. While the production of many vegetable substances can, given suitable material conditions, be mechanized in a high degree (wheat is an example), animal husbandry seems to call for a considerable expenditure of human labour per unit of product. Hitherto, the urban population of the high-wage regions of

[1] H. G. Wells, *A Modern Utopia*, pp. 107-8.

the world have maintained their high standard of life at the expense of underpaid and overworked peasant farmers or agricultural labourers. If cowmen are to work an eight-hour day and be paid at the rate of skilled mechanics, beef and milk are going to become comparatively scarce goods.

These considerations suggest the possibility that, in an equalitarian economy which had attained a very high level of technical efficiency, human labour might be so scarce compared with other factors of production that costing might be based on it alone. If, furthermore, equal educational opportunities and occupational mobility levelled out the distinctions between labour of different kinds, labour might come to be costed on the simple basis of time. In this way the costing system of the socialist community would gradually come to be based upon the Labour Theory of Value.

2. THE ESTIMATION OF NEED

Thus we have seen that even a socialist community must proceed on the assumption that human needs are insatiable. As soon as it begins the task of organizing the processes of production so as to satisfy the needs of its members, it comes up against the fundamental economic fact of scarcity. In plain language there is not enough to go round. To whatever heights of efficiency the productive organs of society are raised, however abundant the yield of products, the wants of the consumer are insatiable and will always tend to race ahead of the production of the means of satisfying them. A few of the simpler needs may be satisfied fairly easily with a limited supply of staple goods, but all the more will the more complex and individually specialized wants assert themselves. Since it will never be possible to satisfy *all* needs, a choice must be made among them. A choice must be made of what goods are to be produced, and, when they have been produced, some equitable and efficient method must be devised of getting them into the hands of those consumers who most need them.

There are at least six possible methods of allocating goods to consumers: they all involve to some degree the estimation of the intensity of social need for a good or service. These are:

(1) Rationing.

(2) Soliciting Consumers' Opinions.

(3) Advisory Bodies of Consumers.

(4) A Representative Assembly.

(5) Experts' Opinions.

(6) Choice at a Price on a Free Market.

(1) **Rationing.** Rationing is the simplest method of apportioning goods to consumers, although it is a very rough-and-ready solution of the problem of estimating social need. Rationing is a brusque refusal of the right of choice to the individual consumer. In an emergency, when supplies of absolute necessities are scarce and hard to replace, rationing may be justified, but it has no place in the economics of a community that has the means to produce and distribute abundance. (In a capitalist order it may be resorted to in a time of scarcity when the unimpeded working of the price system would mean that the rich would overbid the poor for the necessities of life. It is then not so much a way of apportioning goods as a palliation of inequalities of purchasing power.) Rationing is least inappropriate when applied to bare necessities, since differences between individuals' needs are probably less important in the case of necessities than in the case of other things. The extension of a system of rationing to the multiplicity and variety of consumption goods available under conditions of normal productivity would involve enormous difficulties. What should a single ration consist of? As long as it is only a question of prime necessities of a simple type, each ration can consist of an identical collection of

objects—so many pounds of bread, sugar, meat, potatoes, and so on, so many yards of cloth and pairs of standard boots. But as soon as more elaborate goods begin to be issued, how is the ration to be made up? In the case of books, for instance, each citizen cannot receive one copy of every book published, unless the rationed number of cubic feet that makes up his dwelling is nearly as large as the British Museum Library. Some system of book-tokens would have to be instituted. In the case of clothing, so many yards of cotton or woollen fabric would have to be equated to so many yards of silk, one pair of silk stockings issued in lieu of more than one pair of lisle. Thus the concept of the relative value of goods would emerge. Possibly even the market itself would emerge, surreptitiously. Just as in the war-time army the teetotal soldier, unless unusually conscientious, bartered his rum ration for cigarettes or bully-beef, so one can imagine the more frivolous citizenesses of a rationed socialist society exchanging their book-tokens for their more serious sisters' issue of silk stockings.

But over and above these difficulties, rationing suffers from the disadvantage that, even if it can allot goods already produced, it can afford no guiding principle for deciding what should be produced in future. By assuming the previous existence of a stock of goods that simply have to be issued somehow to consumers, instead of allowing the kind of goods that come into being to be dictated by consumers' preferences, it commits in an egregious form the fallacy of putting the cart before the horse.

(2) **Soliciting consumers' opinions.** To some extent individual variety in taste and desire can be allowed for by obtaining the opinion of users of goods and services, by personal interviews, questionnaires, newspaper ballots, &c. While useful as an adjunct to other methods in eliciting consumers' views on quality, variety, convenience, &c., this

method suffers from the fatal defect of not being quantitative. If the consumer prefers A to B, but if A costs more than B in the sense of absorbing more scarce resources in its production, is it worth while making A rather than B, and if so how much A compared with how much B? It must be possible to balance the 'how much more' of preference against the 'how much more' of cost. Moreover, this method is incapable of dealing with the case, which must be regarded as normal, in which the desire for a good outruns the technical and administrative means available for its satisfaction: in other words, it does not take into account the fundamental fact of scarcity. Ask people to express preferences for goods, without tying them down to the inexorable limits of a fixed quantum of disposable purchasing power, and they will express desires for far more goods than their collective labour can ever produce. Even as an indication of a simple order of preference, without endeavouring to assess quantitatively the intensity of preference, this method is essentially unreliable owing to this element of irresponsibility in the mentality of consumers.

(3) **Advisory bodies of consumers.** An advisory body of consumers (consumers' council) appointed for the purpose of sifting and formulating consumers' preferences may give more reliable results than a canvass of unorganized opinion. A body of consumers that has been appointed or elected for other purposes, such as local administration (see no. 4) or as the managing board of an organization supplying goods according to the decision of the market (a consumers' co-operative society), is more likely to give reliable indications than an *ad hoc* consumers' council, with no other and more responsible functions to fulfil.

(4) **A representative assembly.** Where a supply of goods or services is to be given to a determinate body of people (residents in a certain area, members of a certain occu-

pation) the quantity and quality of these services may be determined by a representative body chosen by and from the whole number of the beneficiaries, and the cost of the goods or services defrayed out of the aggregate income of the body as a whole. Thus the assembly will be an administrative organ, financially responsible for its decisions, and not a merely advisory body. In this way responsibility and a certain adjustment of value to cost will be secured. But the experience of individualist societies suggests that this sense of responsibility is strengthened if the members of the consuming body receive some part of their income in a freely disposable individual form, and if they are made in some way to realize that an increase in their collective consumption as a group must be balanced by a reduction in their consumption as individuals. This could be achieved if the remaining portion of their income was regulated by the price-and-market method. This is achieved under individualism by the familiar devices of public finance (taxes, estimates, budgets, &c.). Under socialism, public finance ceases to be a thing apart and becomes part of the normal economic process. The method of representative assemblies is thus complementary to that of individual choice at a price (no. 6).

(5) **Experts' opinions.** The method described above suffers from the disadvantage that, while an increasing number of social services are of a highly specialized type involving expert knowledge (e.g. health and medical services, education, transport, prevention and detection of crime), the representative assembly is usually composed of ordinary members of the public devoid of expert knowledge in all these branches of applied social science (in fact the more representative it is the more it should be so composed). This has led to the view that such services should be controlled by experts. Let the doctors decide on what health services are necessary, the teachers draw up the educational programme, the sanitary

engineers plan the sewers, the police commissioners decree universal finger-printing, the dieticians control our food, and the publishers give us the books we ought to read. To a very great degree this is sound. By all means let the experts say how their own service is to be carried on and decide the details of policy. But it is unsafe to leave to the expert the decision of how far the service is to be developed, and what proportion of the total social income should be allotted to its cost. Left to himself each expert will draw up an admirable plan for his own department, but the aggregate costs of all the plans will absorb more than the total available social income. Some one must co-ordinate the experts. A super-expert? No, the common man, for whose welfare all the experts exist. The representative assembly, as described under (4), will be able to receive and discuss the experts' reports and plans, examine their estimates, and then allot the available funds.

(6) **Choice at a price on a free market.** Free choice of goods, at a price that equates demand and supply, allows each consumer a maximum of freedom in consumption combined with the maximum regard to other consumers' needs and preferences.

It enables a double process of adjustment to be effected. (a) As between different commodities entering into the consumption scheme of a single consumer, it enables him to compare the relative attractions of the commodities, taking their scarcity into account as mirrored in their relative prices. Then, as relative scarcity, and so price, of certain goods changes, the consumer can substitute one good for another and effect other adjustments of the relative quantity of different goods consumed. (b) As between different claimants for limited supplies of a single commodity, it allocates the available supply in accordance with consumers' own estimates of the intensity of their needs (modified by their income-levels).

It has the further advantage not only that it allocates goods to consumers but also that it serves as an indication of what goods are most worth while to produce. Unlike the five methods described up to now, it can be articulated with the measurement of costs of production. (See Chapter III, sections 2 (3), and 4 (1).)

The sale of goods in the market, at a price, necessarily implies the use of money—not necessarily, of course, full-value metallic coins of specific weight and fineness, but some form of undifferentiated, freely disposable, impersonal purchasing power. How it gets into the consumers' hands in the first place we shall inquire in the chapter on Distribution (Chapter IV). How its issue is to be regulated and its purchasing power controlled, we shall inquire in the section on the General Price Level (Chapter VIII, section 3). We shall simply assume its existence, and, provisionally, that it consists of metallic or paper tokens each representing a definite number of units of fixed purchasing power in terms of finished goods.

A compromise between rationing (no. 1) and the price-and-money system (no. 6) would be the issue to consumers, in definite quantities, of tokens of different kinds, available only for the purchase of specific kinds of goods. Thus a man's income might consist of a certain number of food-tickets, of clothing coupons, of notes accepted only by the municipal authorities in payment of house-rent, of book-tokens, of coupons exchangeable against theatre or concert tickets, of mileage-books available on the community's railway, motor-coach, and steamship services, and so on. This method would give greater flexibility than simple rationing but less than the free market, since it would not permit the individual to shift the relative proportions of his income spent in procuring different kinds of satisfaction. Of course, if the tokens were transferable, a rate of exchange between, say, food-tickets and book-tokens, would be set up, which would simply restore the conditions of the free market, with small but probably irritating inconveniences.

The chief objections that have been made to the method of the free market are:

(*a*) As an index of social need it is distorted by inequalities in individual demanders' incomes. Upholders of the existing system are wont to compare the direction of production by price on the open market to a continuous general election held under a meticulously accurate form of proportional representation. They omit to press the comparison further and point out that, so long as inequalities in individual income persist, the election is conducted with plural voting of a most exaggerated type. Nevertheless, if the inequalities of distribution could be abolished or reduced to negligible dimensions (see Chapter IV, section 4), the free exercise of effective demand by consumers on the market would give a very representative and sensitive index of consumers' real preferences. Under these conditions there could be no objection from socialists to the extension of price and the free market to the allocation of consumable goods and the direction of production over a very wide range of social economic life. In a society which had secured virtual equality in the distribution of income, free choice of goods at a price would result in an allocation of goods to consumers very closely in accord with their needs, or, at any rate, with their wants, that is to say, their own individual estimates of their needs.

(*b*) Estimates made by one individual of the intensities of his own wants fail to take into account the fact that the consumption of some goods affects other members of society besides the consumer. In the case of some goods, such as high-powered motor-cars, cocaine, or noisy wireless sets, their consumption reduces the utility enjoyed by other people. In the case of other goods, such as higher education, physical exercise, or private houses of pleasing architectural aspect, their consumption increases the utility enjoyed by other people. These effects on other people's welfare are not taken into account in the money-offers made on the market by the consumers of these goods. In such cases, the free-market method can be modified by suitable taxes and subsidies, designed to weight the individual's personal estimate of worth-whileness with a correcting factor which would represent the interests of the other parties involved.

It would seem, then, that of the methods of estimating demand enumerated above, two are especially adapted, one to the division of individual consumption and one to the division of communal consumption. The method of free choice at a price should be adopted for the first, and that of the representative body for the second. (As auxiliaries to both of these recourse may conveniently be had to some or all of the other methods—direct solicitation of consumers' views, advisory bodies, and experts' opinion.) The economic activities of the community thus fall into two main divisions. On the one hand, there is the production of goods and services to satisfy the demands expressed by individual purchasers in a market. On the other hand, there is the provision of goods and services free of charge to all members of society, as the result of a decision based on other grounds than market demand, made by some administrative economic organ of the community as a whole.

3. The Division of Communal Consumption

(1) **Its range.** We must particularize more closely the goods and services that are to be included in the division of communal consumption. Three kinds of provision for human needs come under this heading.

(i) Goods and services that are individually consumed and

that might therefore be supplied through the market, but which the community decides to supply communally. Many services such as education, cultural amenities, roads, water-supplies, domestic heating and lighting, local transport, postal services, insurance against various kinds of misfortune, accident and loss, *may* be provided by individual purchases at a price in the market (or by specific charges assessed on a definite consumer or group of consumers), or they *may* be provided by a levy on the total social income. Some kinds of material goods, also, may be provided communally, in the same way as these immaterial services are provided. Some existing social services are of this type, e.g. milk and free meals for schoolchildren, surgical appliances and spectacles supplied through the National Health Insurance, &c. Several conditions may be suggested for the selection of goods (including services) to be provided communally for individual consumption. (*a*) The good must be such that an increase in its consumption is calculated to add to social welfare. (*b*) It must be of such a nature that it is unlikely to be used wastefully if provided without payment. (*c*) It must not be too directly competitive with goods sold in the individualized division. These are necessary conditions. If they are fulfilled other circumstances may be suggested which would strengthen the case for communal provision. The method of the free market is inapplicable to many of the most important social services—open spaces and public amenities generally, education, health and medical services—either because, as in the case of open spaces, making a charge for admission is an intolerable nuisance; or because, as in education and health services, people will not pay voluntarily beforehand for what they are only too glad to have once they have it; or, as in the case of medical services and many other services for relief in cases of emergency, because people do not envisage the emergency and provide for it beforehand; then, if they are required to pay for relief at market prices, their whole scale of preferences is turned topsyturvy. In these cases, therefore, and also in many others where the trouble of making individual charges and the consequent book-keeping, issuing and checking of tickets, salaries of pay clerks, money collectors, inspectors, &c., is large compared with the revenue received, the method of the free market is unsuitable, and communal provision is indicated. It may reasonably be expected that in a socialist community many things now provided through the market would enter the circle of the social services. There seems to be no reason why bread, milk, simply cooked meals, clothing of a plain standardized type, and many other things should not be provided as free unrationed issues, leaving the more luxurious and varied qualities to be provided in response to market demand.

(ii) Goods and services that are communally consumed and that must therefore of their very nature be communally supplied. Such are defence; the maintenance of internal order; the administration of civil justice; many public health services; the inspection of factories, food and drugs, water-supplies, sewers, &c. The cost of these services, that is to say the cost of armaments, the construction and erection of offices, public buildings, the salaries of the police, of the army and navy, of judges, ambassadors, many civil servants, the ministers of state and the president (or other ceremonial head of the state), must be a charge upon the general resources of the community.

(iii) Satisfactions less definite in character than goods and services, which cannot be divided or graduated among individuals but which must be enjoyed to the same extent by all or none. They, like the second category of human needs, involve preferences which cannot be expressed by any mechanism of individual choice in a market, since they are preferences for one pattern of social life as against another pattern of social life. Liberty (for the consumer or the worker), equality, security (of occupation or income), stability of social relations, the amenities of town and country, the opportunities of bringing up children under favourable conditions—all these are satisfactions to the enjoyment of which the 'all or none' principle does most certainly apply, at least within the bounds of one territorial community. (It is possible that a socialist world might consist of a number of territorial communities enjoying a large measure of administrative independence and free to experiment collectively in patterns of social life.[1]) In this category comes the choice between more leisure in the form of shorter working hours and the product of more work, the choice between more rapid technical progress with its resultant insecurity of occupation and less rapid progress with greater security, the choice between ruralization and urbanization, and many more choices of an all-or-nothing character. These cannot be balanced by the method of individual calculations of less or more, but must be solved by the collective decision of some central authority.[2] This point will be returned to in Chapter IX, section 2.

(2) **Its delimitation.** The drawing of a line of demarcation between the divisions of individual and communal consumption is, as in the individualist economy, a matter of social policy rather than of strict economic calculation. According to the principles of the Austrian school of economists, resources should be allocated between these two divisions so that the marginal utility of resources used in communal consumption should be equal to the marginal utility of resources used in individual consumption. But, since there is no such

[1] See W. Beveridge, *Planning Under Socialism*, essay on 'My Utopia'.
[2] See 'The Social Significance of the Theory of Value', § 3, by E. F. M. Durbin, *Economic Journal*, December 1935.

thing as the marginal utility of resources in general—only to a determinate economic subject—this formula has significance only if applied to a particular individual. If we can identify a large group of individuals in society whose utility position we can describe as typical, then we can restate the formula in terms of the marginal utility of resources to any one such representative individual. This approach to the subject reveals its theoretical difficulties. Moreover, in the absence of any means for measuring the marginal utility of an operating table in a hospital, of a fume cupboard in a University chemical laboratory, or of a rock garden in a public park, this theory is of little practical use. It will probably be difficult in practice to find any method better than the rough and ready adjustments of public finance in an individualist society.

The practical problem, however, would be simpler in a socialist community than in a capitalist one, for two reasons:

(i) In the first place, owing to inequalities in income and differences in the standard of living, it is impossible, even theoretically, in capitalist society to allocate resources satisfactorily between communal and individual consumption. Gross inequalities in individual income render the marginal utility of resources spent in the free market an almost meaningless concept; differences in the standard of living make the marginal utility of resources used in communal consumption very different to persons of different social classes; it is impossible to make an economic balance. Under these circumstances, the process of allocation becomes not an economic but a political process; power and not welfare determines the issue. Thus, under capitalism, when a democratically elected body votes social services, the forms of economic allocation merely conceal a struggle between the haves and the have-nots; hence the complaints of injustice and corruption which are voiced by all parties to the transaction. In a fundamentally equalitarian community, on the other hand, there would be differences of individual taste, but no great differences between the standards of living of different classes. In such a community, therefore, the allocation of resources on the marginal utility principle as between individual and communal consumption would be theoretically possible. In practice, any representative body of men, whatever the details of the method of their selection, might be trusted to arrive at a decision in the matter that would give substantial satisfaction to the majority of people. The representative body might be chosen by lot. (This is the application of the principle of the jury.) But we are used to the process of democratic election, and this process, purged of the disorders engendered in it by class divisions and by the vested interests arising out of the private ownership of business, is probably the best for the purpose. This argument suggests the necessity for the establishment in any socialist commonwealth, however much addicted to the rule of experts and specialists in their own fields, of democratically chosen assemblies, occupational, regional, and national, which would have the ultimate decision upon the broadest issues of economic planning.

(ii) The other reason is that, with all production carried on by organs of public economy, many of the obstacles that now exist to an extension of social services would be swept away. In a private-profit economy the scope of such communal provision is seriously limited for two reasons. (*a*) The competition of public enterprise diminishes the profit margin, and so discourages private enterprise. (*b*) The provision of goods and services free by the public diminishes some consumers' money-demand for goods and services of the same or a similar type provided by private enterprise. If the community provides milk for schoolchildren or houses for slum-dwellers on the basis of objective indications of need (such as malnutrition or a high tuberculosis rate), the machinery for supplying milk or houses to all other consumers is put out of gear. Hence the ridiculous situation that, when public works are undertaken for the relief of unemployment, the more useless the works the less they interfere with 'recovery'.[1]

A more difficult problem than the allocation of resources between the two divisions would be that of the allocation of resources between different communal uses. The same methods of budgeting and of making appropriations and the same methods of audit and control as obtain in the public finance of capitalist states will have to be applied here, improved perhaps in detail, but not in essence.

In addition to providing free of charge things like museums, schools, baths, hospitals, parks, sports grounds, &c., the community might consider it desirable to promote the consumption of some goods that could not economically be provided free, such as useful and instructive literature, travel in search of work or in the course of study, certain kinds of surgical equipment, &c. The best way would be to vote a definite subsidy out of the division of communal consumption and then pay it over to the appropriate productive organization in aid of cost of production. In the same way the consumption of some things that were considered socially undesirable but could not conveniently be prohibited, such as alcoholic beverages, could be checked by a tax whose proceeds would contribute to the cost of communal consumption.[1] In this way it would be possible to adjust

[1] During a transitional stage, while production was temporarily at a low level and before equality of income had been achieved, it might be considered desirable to check certain forms of consumption as diverting resources to socially unnecessary ends. Thus a tax might be imposed upon silk underclothing, elaborately prepared food, frivolous entertainment, and house-room above a certain standard of space per person. In a fully developed socialist society there is no reason why these commodities should not be provided as well as any others in response to the effective demand of the consumer-citizens.

quantitatively the extent to which certain forms of consumption could be controlled in the social interest, instead of relying on the clumsy all-or-nothing machinery of free issue or prohibition.

It is possible that such a system as is here described would in time, by the gradual expansion of communal at the expense of individual consumption, evolve into a condition of complete communism. Even at the present stage of economic productivity there are great possibilities of extending the communal provision of goods and services. Why should not transport within an urban area such as Birmingham or Leeds be a free service? Why should not the local telephone service be as free to all as it is in some countries to residents in an hotel or boarding-house? Why should not letters, at least within the country, be carried free? Consider the saving effected by cutting out the printing and punching of tickets, the emptying of coin boxes, the sale and cancellation of postage stamps, &c.

A wealthy community such as Great Britain or the United States could surely afford to maintain public dining-rooms at which a plain but nourishing meal would be served free of charge to all comers. It would not be a charity soup-kitchen but a place to which the director of a trust or a popular novelist might go as readily as a simple labourer. Those who wanted something more luxurious could still indulge their fancy in a restaurant where more dainty and more varied food was sold at a price. In populous places there could be stalls at street corners where a cup of tea or coffee and a slice of bread and butter could be had for nothing by the passer-by.

In time standardized suits, boots, and underwear might be issued free from local clothing stores, especially if the forecast of a recent scientific writer is realized, of making 'from cellulose materials such as wood, by direct chemical and mechanical methods, a light and porous material which could be moulded or pressed into clothes without spinning, weaving, or tailoring. As such clothes could hardly cost more than a few pence, laundering would be superseded.'[1]

(3) **Its cost.** The cost of all goods provided in the division of communal consumption must be defrayed by a levy on the general resources of the community. This levy will differ from that made for similar services in an individualist community in that it can be made on the undivided social product instead of by taxes on portions of the social product that have already been individually appropriated.

Thus, what is usually known as public finance will become an integral part of the economics of a socialist community. Certain technical problems in taxation will, however, assume a very different aspect in a socialist economy. For example, in a community where incomes are roughly equal, problems of the incidence of taxation on persons of different income-levels (e.g. the choice between direct and indirect taxes) are unlikely to give rise to serious conflicts of opinion. On the other hand, the allocation of the cost of services as between national, regional, and local areas will remain of impo⁻tance. For in a socialist community, no less than in an individualist one, economy in the use of resources will be promoted if the cost of amenities and services of purely local interest are defrayed out of the social product of the local population concerned. The same applies to groups of persons organized on a basis other than local—such as occupational. If social services come to be administered largely by trade unions, as in the U.S.S.R., the whole body of persons engaged in an industry will dispose of a certain proportion of their aggregate income by communal decisions in the same way as municipalities and counties do to-day.

[1] J. D. Bernal, 'Science in Industry', in *The Frustration of Science* (ed. D. Hall), 1935.

The prices at which labour and materials will be reckoned in the costing of social services and the rate of interest charged will be those determined in the division of individual consumption (see Chapter III, section 4 (1)). In the valuation of services that are used only in the communal division, such as those of teachers, research workers, and (perhaps) doctors, the same difficulties will be found as are found to-day in analogous cases. They must be equated roughly to services requiring similar skill, responsibility, or training in the production of goods for the market. According to strict economic theory, an error is involved here, since the cost of such services will be determined entirely by the use of these services in the division of individualized consumption. However, the error is unlikely to be serious unless (*a*) the services are highly specialized *and* mobility of labour is restricted, or (*b*) the division of communalized consumption expands until it includes the major part of all production.

4. THE DIVISION OF INDIVIDUAL CONSUMPTION

The pricing of consumption goods. We have seen that a considerable part of the national income of a socialist community will consist of goods and services sold at a price to members of the public, who are free to buy as much or as little as they choose of each kind of commodity at the price at which it is offered. (See section 2 (6) of this chapter.) We must now consider, therefore, price formation in the division of individual consumption. With regard to the pricing of consumption goods, no difficulty, at any rate in theory, need be found. The shopkeeper-state can sell goods at a price to its citizen-customers and, according to their response, regulate the quantity and quality of goods that it supplies. We will assume the existence of retail selling agencies, having in their hands stocks of goods for sale to the public. These agencies may be general shops for the sale of many kinds of goods, like co-operative stores and department stores; or they may be for the sale of one particular kind of goods, such as bicycles, wireless, or books. They can experiment, by raising and lowering prices or by varying qualities and designs, exactly as capitalist retailers do. How their stocks are replenished we shall inquire later.

In the case of goods whose supply is seasonal (such as strawberries) or is not under the control of the productive organs of the community (such as antiques, works of art, out-of-print books, services of celebrated actors and singers, &c.) the rates of supply must be taken as given quantities, independent of the retailers' control. The selling agencies will then adjust their prices so as just to clear their stocks, raising the price when stocks fall short and lowering it when they accumulate.

In the case of the majority of goods, however, the rate of supply can be affected by the decisions of the productive organs of the community. Instead of one variable, price, that is susceptible of deliberate adjustment, we have two, price and quantity, that can be adjusted. The principles of rational economy require that in such a case the price and the quantity disposed of should be varied until the quantity is as great and the price as small as possible consistent with the condition that the selling price just covers cost. (In what sense precisely 'cost' is to be understood we shall consider later in Chapter III, section 4.) The most convenient way of effecting this is for the productive organs to produce according to the orders of the selling agencies. The latter will then vary their orders according to the state of demand. Two procedures for accomplishing this end seem feasible. One is for the selling agencies to vary their prices so as to keep their stocks at a minimum, but to increase their orders as the selling price rises and decrease them as the price falls. Losses would be avoided by reducing sales, profits would be absorbed by increasing

sales. The other procedure is for the selling agencies to sell
at cost (or cost plus a small margin to cover contingencies),
rather as the co-operative societies tend to do to-day, and to
regulate their orders according to the rate at which their
stocks were exhausted. They would endeavour to keep their
stock of each particular good at a certain definite figure, and
increase or diminish their orders according as the good sold
quickly or slowly. In either case the productive organs of
society will deliver fresh supplies against payment at an
appropriate price (determined as in Chapter III, section 4 (1)).
These prices will enter into the costs of the selling organizations. The latter will be so conducted as to reduce to a minimum the margin between cost and sale-price; the small
surplus which they make, after deduction of casual losses and
perhaps small bonuses on turnover, will either revert to the
community as a whole or be paid back to consumers as a
dividend on purchases.[1]

The general principles of price-determination here laid
down will not preclude the possibility of fixing the prices of
some goods (especially services) at definite figures, subject to
revision only over long periods, and leaving demand to adjust
itself to the price. This is the method adopted at present with
regard to postage and telegraph rates; railway, bus, and tram
fares; railway freight rates; port dues; and fees for various
legal and administrative services. It is not, however, capable
of being generalized for all commodities. Such fixed prices
are only compatible with economic equilibrium if they are
exceptions to the general rule of free price-formation.

This method of determining prices is essentially one of
trial and error, and it requires for its successful carrying out
that the process of selling goods be decentralized into a large
number of autonomous trading bodies between which there

[1] For price-formation in a socialist economy see Cassel, *Theory of
Social Economy* (2nd ed.), ch. iii, § 15.

will exist a sort of competition. It will be suggested, why not centralize the determination of prices in some sort of central statistical office?

It is true that the rule-of-thumb methods described above are capable of being much improved and gaining in precision and rapidity of adjustment by a proper use of statistical data. On the basis of its experience with changing prices and quantities the statistical service of every sales agency would be able to draw up a demand schedule for each type of good sold. (Indeed, the construction of demand schedules both for consumption and production goods will be one of the most important duties of the statistical services attached to selling agencies, productive organs, and the S.E.C. itself.) Theoretically, the task is a very difficult one, since the demand for one commodity is not a function of its price alone but of the prices of all other commodities.[1] (Joint demand and composite supply are special cases of this general proposition.) Practically, the task could be solved, to an approximation sufficiently close for the guidance of the managers of industry, by taking groups of more closely related commodities (composite supply or joint demand) in isolation from other groups. Under capitalism, demand schedules are apt to exist in the realm of faith rather than in that of works,[2] but with the greater publicity and fuller statistics of the socialistic economy they would become much easier to draw up.

The information so obtained and made available throughout the economic system (together with much other statistical material) would be of the greatest use to the managers of the various selling agencies and productive organs; it would enable them to adjust prices and quantities with much greater accuracy than is attainable nowadays and would speed up the

[1] Cf. G. Cassel, *Theory of Social Economy*, ch. iv, § 16, pp. 139–47; L. Walras, *Éléments d'économie politique pure*, p. 162.

[2] See, however, Henry Schultz, *Theory and Measurement of Demand*, and the literature quoted therein.

process of achieving equilibrium; but it is unlikely that it would enable the trial and error method to be superseded entirely. The statistical determination of demand schedules will be a valuable aid to the managers of the various selling agencies, but it will not relieve them of the task of quasi-individualistic price-determination. This matter will be discussed in more detail in Chapter III, section 4 (1), pp. 104–5.

CHAPTER III

PRODUCTION GOODS—THE MEASUREMENT OF COST

1. THE CONCEPT OF COST

IN the production of the goods and services that ultimately satisfy human needs (consumption goods), various things are used up. Human labour and raw materials are embodied in goods as they are produced, together with a proportionate amount of various kinds of indirect labour and of the wear-and-tear of machinery, buildings, and other fixed plant. The raw materials used in industry are either naturally occurring materials in a state of nature, or they have undergone some intermediate processing and represent a mixture of natural materials and the wear-and-tear of fixed plant. Further, since the surface of the globe is limited and since different portions of it are suitable in varying degrees for the activity of human beings and for the extraction of raw materials (differences in fertility or convenience of situation), certain portions of land acquire scarcity; their use in production becomes an element in cost, generally referred to as rent. Machinery, buildings, and other fixed plant can be further resolved into human labour, raw materials, &c. Ultimately, all goods produced can be resolved into a combination of human labour, natural materials, and land. These we may term the ultimate factors of production, while partly manufactured raw materials, machinery, buildings, and other produced means of production may be called intermediate goods. The ultimate factors and intermediate goods alike may be styled means of production or production goods.

Now, means of production are scarce relative to the almost unlimited possibilities of consumption that they can be used to satisfy. In fact it is the scarcity of means of production that is responsible for the scarcity of consumption goods. If scarce means of production are used for producing a given quantity of consumption goods, they are not available for producing other consumption goods. They constitute the *costs* of the goods in which they are embodied. In a rational economy, costs are the ultimate measure of economic scarcity. They afford an index of the relative worth-whileness of producing different kinds of goods or combinations of goods and of different ways of producing the same good or combination of goods.

The cost of a given consumption good or combination of goods is thus measured by the quantity of production goods used up in making it. Now, rational economy consists in the use of scarce means of production so as to produce the maximum satisfaction at the minimum cost. This involves two things: (*a*) when the production of an extra quantity of goods is under consideration, the cost of the additional product must be balanced against the satisfaction yielded by it; (*b*) when alternative methods of producing the same good are available it must be possible to measure and compare the costs incurred by the alternative methods and to choose the method that involves the least cost. Therefore, a method of measuring and calculating cost must be devised.

2. METHODS OF CALCULATING COST

Two methods have been suggested of computing cost upon a basis not involving the price system. They are based upon technical, rather than upon economic, considerations. Although they are, in the writer's opinion, seriously defective from the point of view of rational economic calculation, they are logically self-consistent. These two methods are by labour-cost and by energy-cost. There remains, as a third method, the computation of cost according to the price system.

(1) **Labour-cost.** The cost of goods may be reckoned as proportional to the quantity of labour expended in their production, both directly and indirectly. Indirect labour-cost is the labour-cost of raw materials, &c., used up in production, together with an appropriate share of the labour-cost of maintenance and replacement of machinery and of the labour-cost of general economic and political administration. According to this method, raw materials in their natural state (i.e. upon which no labour has been spent) and the uses of land will not be taken into account; nor will any interest charges appear, depreciation of machinery being a simple fraction of the total labour-cost of the machine (e.g. on a machine costing 10,000 man-hours and having an estimated life of 10 years the depreciation charge will be just 1,000 man-hours per annum). Quantity of labour is difficult to define. Labour-time is a first approximation: not necessarily the actual time spent on a job, but the time that would be spent by a normal worker under normal circumstances using standard equipment ('socially necessary labour-time'). The real difficulty is that labour is not homogeneous. It exists in different forms (navvy's labour, typist's labour, physician's labour) having different concrete uses and not perfectly interchangeable. A labour-force composed of ten typists and ten doctors will not dig as many cubic feet of earth as twenty navvies; nor will ten navvies and ten typists be as effective in combating an epidemic as twenty doctors, although, perhaps, one typist, three navvies, and sixteen doctors would be a still more effective group. We are here driven to consider the use-value of different kinds of concrete labour and to take into account their relative effectiveness. But their relative effectiveness differs according to the type of labour that is chosen as the basis of comparison. At one time effectiveness in growing food, at another time effectiveness in setting up a lathe or winding a dynamo may be the standard, and the

same worker may be graded differently by different standards. What is the standard? There is no single and universal standard. Since all kinds of labour are not equally available, it seems that not only use-value but also relative scarcity must come into the process of valuation of different kinds of concrete labour. In practice, an hour of (say) a bus driver's labour does not count as equal to an hour of (say) a bus conductor's labour. As Marx says:

'Skilled labour counts only as simple labour intensified, or rather as multiplied simple labour, a given quantity of skilled labour being considered equal to a greater quantity of simple labour. Experience shows that this reduction is constantly being made. A commodity may be the product of the most skilled labour, but its value, by equating it to the product of simple un-skilled labour, represents a definite quantity of the latter labour alone. The different proportions in which different sorts of labour are reduced to unskilled labour as their standard are established by a social process that goes on behind the backs of the producers and, consequently, appear to be fixed by custom.'[1]

But this reduction of qualitative differences to quantitative differences involves a process of valuation. In exchange economy the ratio between one hour of one kind of labour and one of another is the ratio between the *value* of the net product of an hour's work of the marginal worker in the one trade and the *value* of the net product of an hour's work of the marginal worker in the other. In other words, it depends on the relative scarcity of labour power in the two trades and on the relative utility of their products. In a non-exchange economy three possibilities are open: one is to adopt and stereotype the values of a previously existing exchange economy; another is to adopt, for converting different kinds of labour into simple socially necessary labour-time, empirical coefficients based upon some non-market estimate of relative

[1] K. Marx, *Capital*, vol. i (trans. Aveling and Moore), pp. 11–12.

social value; the third is to charge all labour up to cost at the same rate irrespective of the kind of work. The first solution is so obviously an irrational makeshift that we will not consider it further, except to note that it is a pitfall that a socialist commonwealth might easily fall into in its early days. The second solution raises the very difficult question of how to measure relative scarcity and social utility without the measuring-rod of price. It opens the door to the making of purely arbitrary estimates by irresponsible authorities. The third method is the logical result of the labour-time theory. (Note that the reckoning for purposes of social *costing* of one hour of every worker's time at the same rate does not necessarily involve the payment of equal hourly *wages* to all workers.) The only deviation from the principle of equality of labour-time that would be consistent with the strict labour-time system would be the addition to the hourly rate of skilled labour of an amount corresponding to the extra *cost*, measured in labour-time, of training that worker. E.g. suppose that a doctor's training lasts 10 years longer than that of an unskilled labourer and uses up 3,000 man-hours of instructors' time. Suppose, further, that on the average a doctor's working life is 30 years, or 60,000 working hours, then it would be justifiable to increase the hourly rate at which doctors' labour was costed by $\frac{3,000}{60,000}$ or 5 per cent. But this method takes into account only the *cost* of special training. It makes no allowance for the *scarcity* of particular aptitudes (or, more accurately, for any degree of scarcity of aptitude in excess of what corresponds to the cost of training).

The principle of reckoning labour-time to cost at a uniform rate makes it impossible to make a proper economic comparison between two ways of doing a thing that differ only in the amounts and kinds of labour used; e.g. if there are two methods of producing a given product: in one way, M_1, x_1

hours of labour of kind A and y_1 hours of labour of kind B are employed and in the other, M_2, x_2 of A and y_2 of B, it may be that $x_1+y_1 < x_2+y_2$ while $ax_1+by_1 > ax_2+by_2$, where a and b are coefficients proportional to the economic value of an hour of A's labour and of B's labour respectively.[1] In such a case a reckoning according to pure labour-time will make method M_1 seem preferable to M_2, while a reckoning according to economic costs will make M_2 seem preferable to M_1.

The non-reckoning of interest means that although the use of fixed capital is taken into account as stored-up labour, in so far as it is used up in the production process, neither the total quantity of fixed capital relative to labour nor the length of time during which such capital is in the course of giving out its stored-up labour enters into the calculation of cost.

For example, if there are two goods, A and B, and the production of A involves 500 hours of direct labour plus 500 hours of stored-up labour while the production of B involves 800 hours of direct labour plus 200 hours of stored-up labour, both goods will be reckoned as costing 1,000 hours and consequently as being equal in cost, no account being taken of the additional amount of stored-up labour involved in the production of A. Or again, suppose that there are two goods B and C, both of which take up 800 hours of direct as against 200 hours of stored-up labour, but that the stored-up labour used in producing B takes the form of one month's use of a machine costing 24,000 hours of labour which lasts for 10 years, while that used in producing C takes the form of one month's use of a machine costing 12,000 hours of labour and lasting for 5 years; then B and C are reckoned as of equal cost in spite of the fact that the production of B involves the use of twice as large a stock of stored-up labour as the production of C.

[1] Computed by the value of their respective marginal products in alternative occupations.

It is interesting to note that cost accounting in terms of pure labour-time is appropriate to two phases of economic development at opposite poles to each other. One is a state in which mechanical aids to production are unimportant relative to human labour and in which, consequently, the supply of human labour is the chief factor limiting the creation of wealth. The other is a state where the use of mechanical aids has been developed to the full—to the point of capital saturation—when once more labour is the only scarce factor of production (see Chapter II, section 1 (4)).

(2) **Energy-cost.** The cost of goods may be reckoned as proportional to the quantity of energy (reckoned in physical units as foot-pounds, kilogram-metres, kilowatt-hours, calories, therms, or what not) embodied in them. This system of costing has been suggested by H. G. Wells,[1] by Professor Soddy,[2] and by Howard Scott[3] and the group calling themselves Technocrats, but its full implications have never been worked out. Strictly applied it would involve the ignoring of the use of land and raw materials in their native condition. (Extracted raw materials, of course, would be costed according to the energy expended in getting them.) Human labour would be costed according to the energy-cost of the physical maintenance of the human body considered as a machine. Fixed capital would be reckoned as stored-up energy, and be charged to cost as it is used up, but, as in the case of labour-cost, the time-element would be ignored, i.e. interest would not enter into energy-cost.

The defects of this method of costing are similar to those of costing according to labour-time. In particular, it ignores the varying degree of *scarcity* of different kinds of labour, since scarcity is not necessarily proportional to energy-consump-

[1] H. G. Wells, *A Modern Utopia*, ch. iii, § 2.
[2] F. Soddy, *Cartesian Economics*, p. 12.
[3] H. Scott, *Introduction to Technocracy*, pp. 47–8.

tion. Thus, neither method measures true economic cost in the sense of the relative scarcity of the means of production. By neither method is it possible to compare properly different methods of production entailing the use of different kinds of concrete labour. Both methods ignore the scarcity of naturally occurring raw materials, of land, and of stored-up past production embodied in instruments of production.[1]

(3) **Price as a measure of cost.** If consumption goods are priced according to the scarcity principle, the goods entering into their production can be priced in the same way. Giving the name 'cost' to the sum of the prices of all the production goods used up in the making of a given consumption good, we can say that it will be worth while offering such prices for production goods as will make the cost of a consumption good not more than its price. Thus given the prices of consumption goods, there can be derived from them the demand prices of any given quantities of production goods. The demand for consumption goods determines price, which is imputed back to production goods and then is reflected forward again to consumption goods in the guise of cost.

One fundamental principle of economic equilibrium under the price system is that the selling price of every good should equal its cost as imputed from the prices of other goods. If a good sells above cost, it is being kept artificially scarce—the consumer is being deprived of satisfactions that might be provided by resources that are now yielding less satisfaction in other employments. If a good sells below cost, the consumer is obtaining a certain satisfaction by the use of resources that would, in other employments, yield greater satisfaction. Costing is therefore linked naturally to the

---

[1] In general, those socialist theorists who propose to base cost on some 'objective' measure, independent of the market valuation of individual goods, ignore rent as well as interest. See section 3 (1) of this chapter.

process of price-determination according to scarcity and consumers' preferences.

Where, as in a developed exchange economy, many production goods enter into the making of one consumption good (joint demand) and where many different combinations of production goods can be made to yield the same result (composite supply), the demand price for a given production good is equal to its marginal net product. The net product of a production good may be defined as the price of the additional product obtained by the use of one additional unit of the production good. The marginal net product of a production good is its net product at the margin of employment, i.e. at the point at which all available quantities of the production good are taken into use. As the available quantity increases, the marginal net product falls, partly because of the falling price of the consumption goods, due to increased abundance, partly because of the diminished physical productivity of increased quantities of one kind of production good combined with an unchanged quantity of others. Thus the equality of price with marginal net product means that price falls as quantity increases—in other words, the price of a production good is a measure of scarcity just as is the price of a consumption good.

In a position of equilibrium the following conditions are fulfilled: all means of production are fully utilized; prices of all goods are equal to cost; if alternative methods of production are possible, that one is chosen which yields the product at least cost; and, finally, a production good capable of alternative uses (i.e. in composite supply) is so distributed between different uses that its marginal net product in each use is equal to the same quantity, namely, to its price.

In this way, prices can be established for all production goods; first for intermediate goods and ultimately for ultimate factors of production—i.e. human services and natural resources. Thus labour power and natural resources can be reduced to a common standard of comparison by the price system.

But these ultimate factors of production are not the only elements that must be taken into account in a rational system of costing. When labour, land, &c., are combined to form intermediate goods, two processes occur. (1) There is a storing-up of ultimate factors of production over a period of time. A mass of intermediate goods represents a stock of resources held through time, the use of which involves more than the use of the ultimate factors of production: it involves the use of an accumulation of such factors (in Böhm-Bawerk's phrase, 'roundabout methods of production'). At any given moment the quantity of accumulated resources is limited or scarce: hence the use of them involves a cost, called by economists interest. (2) The creation of a mass of intermediate goods involves the fixing of resources in a form which has only one specific use (or a narrow range of specific uses). Once fixed in this form, they are useless for any other purpose. Technical changes in the processes of production or changes in the desires and tastes of the community, intervening since the production of the intermediate goods was begun, may destroy or diminish the usefulness of the intermediate goods in question. Hence arises an element of uncertainty; and the holding of stocks of means of production involves, therefore, a further element of cost. By the devices of a rate of interest and of a charge for uncertainty (both analogous in nature to a price), these further elements in cost can be reduced to comparability with labour power and natural resources. Thus all elements in cost are welded into a closed and self-consistent system by the method of pricing. In no other method of costing can these results be achieved. (See section 3, sub-sections (2) and (3), of this chapter.)

In the ultimate analysis, costs in an exchange economy are the values of the alternative opportunities for production that are foregone when the decision is taken to make the particular good with the resources in question.[1] Cost is the expression and the measure, in terms of price, of the ultimate economic fact of scarcity.

3. SOME SPECIAL CATEGORIES OF COST

The methods of calculating cost according to labour or energy suffer from the defect that it is impossible for them to take into account the use of land and natural resources, the time-factor in production (i.e. the use of a stack of accumulated resources, held over a period of time), and the element of uncertainty. As soon as it is required to take these elements into account, it becomes necessary to find a common measure for them and for labour-time or mechanical energy, as the case may be. Although arbitrary equivalents might be set up by an economic planning authority in a non-exchange economy, they would have no real significance. The only way in which they can be brought to a rational common measure is by the process of pricing in a market. We must therefore proceed to the examination of the part played in a rational costing system by (1) Land (including natural resources), (2) Time, (3) Uncertainty. In other words, this is the problem of Rent, of Interest, and of the hitherto unnamed element in social cost which is the price of Uncertainty-Bearing, and which we shall call Uncertainty-Surcharge.

(1) **Land—rent.** Owing to differences in physical yield and convenience of location between different sources of power and natural products, it is necessary to undertake production

[1] See F. von Wieser, *Natural Value*, bk. v; E. v. Böhm-Bawerk, *Positive Theory of Capital*, bk. iii, ch. 10; bk. iv, ch. 7; P. Wicksteed, *Common-sense of Political Economy*, vol. i, p. 380; H. J. Davenport, *Economics of Enterprise*, chs. vi and viii; G. Cassel, *Theory of Social Economy*, ch. iii, § 12, pp. 91–3; H. D. Henderson, *Supply and Demand*, ch. x.

at different rates of real cost to satisfy the same need with physically similar goods (e.g. wheat of identical food value grown on fertile and on poor land; coal of equivalent calorific value from mines of unequal difficulty in working). Under these conditions an increase in output can only be provided at an increase in real cost (whether this be measured in labour-time or in energy-units). Moreover, in the case of different branches of production, increased output will involve different rates of increase of cost—what we may call the cost-gradient will be different. The production of some goods can be indefinitely extended at constant cost. In their case there is no doubt as to the right principle of valuation. Their value is proportional to the average cost of production. But how should a good be valued that is produced under increasing costs? The natural answer is: At average cost. But this fails to take into account that, if there are two kinds of goods being produced at the same average cost, one with a high cost-gradient, the other with a low (or zero) cost-gradient, then an increase in the output of the former will involve greater expenditure of labour-time (or energy) than an increase in that of the latter. To be able to balance against each other the effect on the total expenditure of labour-time (or energy) of increased production of different goods, given a certain rate of production already undertaken, goods should be valued according to their marginal costs of production, not their average costs. (These coincide in the case of goods produced under conditions of constant cost.) But this leads at once to the emergence of a form of surplus value. In the case of goods produced from sub-marginal sources of supply, the difference between their cost and their value (i.e. between their actual cost and the cost of production of similar goods at the margin) is a surplus value, identical with Ricardian rent (whether or not it is appropriated by private owners of natural resources).

Under market economy this surplus is naturally imputed to the site; so that the superior field, mine, &c., is supposed to 'earn' a rent. If a site is capable of alternative uses, then the rent which it can 'earn' in its different uses is an indication of its relative superiority in these uses. Its owner then has a pecuniary incentive to use it in the way in which it is most productive.

If goods are valued according to the cost of the marginal portion of supply, then, even under any of the arbitrary systems of costing mentioned above (labour or energy), a surplus would emerge which could be treated as rent. If, however, goods were valued according to their average cost of production (which is usually the method favoured by the proponents of arbitrary systems of costing), then rent will be absorbed into cost. The question whether or not rent should be reckoned as a separate entity is thus seen to be identical with the problem whether goods should be valued according to marginal or average cost of production.

Two consequences flow from not including the rent of land in the computation of cost. The first is that the measure of cost is distorted. The second is that it is difficult to allot parcels of land of different quality to their most appropriate use.

(a) As stated above, the true cost of increasing the supply of a good will be under-estimated if the good is produced under conditions of increasing costs. There will thus be an over-investment of the community's resources in the production of such goods as compared with goods produced under constant or diminishing costs.

(b) Under the second head it must be noted that the charging of a rent for the use of land is the way by which, in a market economy, land is forced into its most productive use. It may be argued that a similar result could be achieved in a planned economy by ascertaining the productivity of given parcels of land under given forms of cultivation and calculating, by means of the calculus of variations, which combination of uses would give the maximum yield. In order, however, to calculate the maximum yield it is necessary to express the different products of land in terms of a common denominator, i.e. in terms of their values. But unless the comparison was made on the basis of their *marginal* and not of their *average* returns, incorrect results would be obtained. Therefore, since marginal returns must in any case be determined, the use of rent as a device for ensuring the optimum use of scarce natural resources seems to be justified. Furthermore, the use of economic rent as a device for allocating land and natural materials to their most productive uses fits in conveniently with a decentralized economy in which a large measure of autonomy is allowed to separate enterprises.[1]

(2) **Time—interest.** (*a*) *Capital and interest.* We must next take into account the influence of time in production. To obtain a given rate of physical output a certain quantity of physical resources must be held in the form of intermediate goods (machinery, buildings, stocks of raw materials, and goods in process). These intermediate goods represent a certain storing of resources in time, since the machinery, materials, &c., now being used in the process of production are the result of past processes of production. The average length of time that elapses between the first steps taken in the chain of production and the delivery of the finished product may be called the period of production.[2] Most methods of increasing the physical productivity of a given quantity of

---

[1] For the pricing of land under socialism see Cassel, *Theory of Social Economy*, ch. vii, § 29, p. 289; also Henderson, *Supply and Demand*, ch. vi, § 5: for natural materials see Cassel, *op. cit.*, ch. vii, § 30, pp. 293–4.

[2] An alternative expression for this quantity is the ratio of the community's *stock* of means of production to its *flow* of finished consumption goods (see G. Cassel, *On Quantitative Thinking in Economics*, p. 22). Note that this expression implies the possibility of expressing both the

resources (including land and human labour) involve the utilization of these resources in ways which produce a greater physical product but at a remoter period of time—in other words, a lengthening of the period of production. For instance, machinery increases the product of labour; but, in order to make the machinery, labour must be diverted from some other line of production to machinery-making. Now, different uses of the ultimate factors of production may be classified in the order of the remoteness of their ultimate benefit (in other words, in order of the length of the period of production in each particular use). If we assume that in a rationally ordered scheme of production the uses of ultimate factors of production that yield immediate benefit are preferable to those whose benefit is deferred, we must devise some quantitative method of estimating this preference. Moreover, we must be able to balance a greater yield at a more distant date against a lesser yield available sooner.

An economic community, based on division of labour, must divide its economic activities between provision for the needs of the present and the maintenance and extension of the equipment that makes possible provision for the needs of the future. The proportion in which it so divides its resources is the result of a balance between the 'productiveness' of material equipment and the 'prospectiveness' of the members of the community.

In an individualistic economic system the rate of interest is the regulator of its capital-structure. Interest arises in market economy as a payment made for the use of means of production during time. In its simplest form it is a discount on future values (or an agio on present values) so that the value of a finished good tends always to exceed the sum of

stock and the flow in terms of a common unit, in other words, the possibility of valuation. See also J. Marschak's 'Note on the Period of Production', *Economic Journal*, March 1934.

the values of its constituent factors by an amount which is proportionate to the time taken up in production. If interest be reckoned on the value of all intermediate goods used in production for the time during which they are locked up in the productive process, this surplus is absorbed and value tends to be equal to cost. In the idealized individualism of the Austrian school the rate of interest is determined by the interaction in the market of millions of individual time-preferences, just as the prices of goods are determined by the interaction of millions of individual marginal utilities. In the real system of capitalism individual time-preferences are overshadowed by the action of banks and by the strategic reserve policy of company directors.

A socialist community that attempts to guide production by the preferences of individuals expressed in the market must make use of the device of a rate of interest, for two reasons. One is for costing purposes, since otherwise there will be relative over-production of goods whose manufacture involves *relatively* more time-consuming methods than the average. The second is as a rationing device, to allocate between the various branches of production the resources available for the satisfaction of future needs. Thus, the marginal productivity of capital goods will establish, at any given moment, a definite relation between the quantity of resources so available and the rate of interest that just allocates them without deficit or excess. But in the absence of a free market for savers there is no means of deciding, on individualistic principles, what quantity of resources should be saved. This decision will have to be taken by the planning authority on behalf of the community as a whole and will be, from the liberal individualistic point of view, arbitrary. (See Chapter IX, section 2 (2)).

To illustrate the problem of interest in a socialist community let us take the case of a railway that has to cross a

piece of high ground. Either it may be built in the open with
two steep slopes, or it may be constructed with deep cuttings
and a tunnel. The first way involves greater cost in operation
than the second for the whole time that the line is open: the
second way involves a greater expenditure of labour and
materials at the time of construction. How can the authority
planning the railway balance the extra annual cost of operation against the additional once-and-for-all cost of construction? If the additional construction-cost is only five times
the extra annual operation-cost, it is almost certainly worth
while to build the tunnel. If it is a hundred times more, the
tunnel is almost certainly not worth while. Projected works
can be classified according to the number of 'years' purchase'
that they require. It is obvious that the community should
undertake first those works in which a present outlay saves
a large annual cost before proceeding with those that effect a
less saving. Equilibrium is obtained by pushing the investment of resources up to the same number of years' purchase
in all lines of production. The community must decide upon
a certain number of years' purchase (in other words a rate of
interest) and apply it as a touchstone to distinguish between
feasible and unfeasible undertakings.[1]

Of course it would be possible to use the marginal productivity of capital as a sieve for sorting out worth-while
projects (rationing function of interest) without actually
charging it into the price of goods (cost function of interest).
But, as already remarked, this would result in a relative over-
production of goods whose production involves a higher-
than-average ratio of capital to labour.

[1] G. Morreau (op. cit.), who does not admit the propriety of including
interest in the cost-reckoning of a socialist economy, proposes to discriminate between different uses of capital resources according to the
quantity of consumers' surplus which they yield. This is an interesting
suggestion; but it is open to the objection that no one has yet shown
how to determine an objective measure of consumers' surplus.

Unless interest is taken into account in the computing of cost, it will appear equally preferable to produce either of two commodities in each of which the same quantity of labour and land is incorporated, although in the case of one of them the expenditure may be spread over a hundred times the period of time that it is in the other. The community will be led to spend its resources on schemes that will only produce consumable goods after centuries, while in the meantime it will suffer penury.

To compute a rate of interest, each undertaking will have to start with a certain capital, based on an inventory and valuation of actual capital goods. Extensions of capital will take the form of investments or loans made under the control of the S.E.C. from a central fund. Each undertaking will draw up several alternative plans of activity on the assumption that interest is 6, 5, 4, 3, &c., per cent., the schemes at the lower rates being naturally more extensive than those at the higher rates. On the basis of these schemes it will be able to draw up a schedule of its demand for capital at different rates. The S.E.C. can then construct an aggregate demand schedule for capital to be employed in the whole of industry. This will, in fact, be a schedule showing the marginal productivity of different quantities of resources applied to capital formation.[1]

Two procedures can now be followed, according as to whether quantity of accumulation or interest-rate is to be taken as the independent variable. (i) In the first case the S.E.C. will fix the amount of capital that is to be raised; then the ruling rate of interest for the current accounting period

[1] The objection may be made that it is not legitimate to aggregate the demand schedules of single enterprises into one social demand schedule, on the grounds that each individual demand schedule is dependent on the actual rate of interest. This is a valid objection theoretically, but it could be got over practically by the process of successive approximation (see footnote 2 to p. 83; also pp. 99–100, 102–3).

will be determined by the schedule of marginal productivity of capital. (ii) In the second case the S.E.C. will fix a certain rate of interest; this will determine the corresponding quantity of capital to be saved out of the total social income during the year. In either case, the rate of interest, however arrived at, will be used for all accounting purposes (interest on original capital of enterprises and trusts, interest on short-period balances, depreciation, insurance, hire-purchase contracts, &c.). Capital will be supplied to undertakings in accordance with their original demand schedules.[1, 2]

(i) If the amount to be saved is to be taken as the independent variable, then the most appropriate formula would be that of F. P. Ramsey[3] 'the rate of saving multiplied by the marginal utility of money should always be equal to the amount by which the total net enjoyment of utility falls short of maximum possible rate of enjoyment'. It may be objected that the practical application of this formula involves the numerical determination of utilities. Nevertheless, this problem might not prove to be insoluble in a community where individual incomes are approximately equal, given free choice of consumption and the sale of consumption goods at a price in the market. If it can be solved, even approximately, a rate of saving can be determined, and then from the aggregate demand schedule of the socialized undertakings a correspond-

---

[1] In the foregoing it is not assumed that any capital is supplied by voluntary individual saving. It is all provided by a levy on the undistributed social product, in accordance with a decision of the S.E.C. Individuals may save, in the sense of postponing consumption; but this is not envisaged as a source of capital.

[2] If either the demand for or the supply of capital is changing rapidly, the error involved in aggregating demand schedules will be appreciable. In this case it will be necessary to establish a provisional rate of interest, then to allow the different organs of collective economy to re-contract with each other on the basis of this provisional rate, and so to draw up their final demand schedule for capital.

[3] 'A Mathematical Theory of Saving', *Economic Journal*, Dec. 1928.

ing rate of interest can be found. Changes in productivity and demand will then be reflected in changes in the rate of interest.

(ii) If interest is to be taken as the independent variable, what principles should be followed in deciding upon a rate of interest? If Cassel's argument in the *Nature and Necessity of Interest* is valid, then the rate of interest depends on the duration of human life. In an ideal individualist community accumulation would proceed, and interest fall, until the number of years' purchase of a perpetual income had risen to something short of the average duration of the adult portion of human life.[1] Here it is true that the socialist community cannot determine the exact figure with the accuracy of individual investors, balancing the attractiveness of perpetuities against that of life annuities. Still, no extreme error in valuation will be incurred if the S.E.C. accumulates until the rate of interest falls to say 2 per cent. and then keeps the rate of interest steady. The reason why 2 per cent.—50 years' purchase—is chosen is that it corresponds to the duration of adult human life. On the assumption that a socialist community should be longer-sighted than the individual investor, the rate of interest might ultimately be lowered to 1 per cent.—corresponding to 100 years' purchase (three generations) respectively. If the tempo of technical invention increases or if public taste becomes more changeable, the amount of new capital to be raised in a year will increase; if invention or changes in taste fall off, the amount to be raised will diminish.[2]

[1] See also Cassel's *Theory of Social Economy* (Benn ed.), vol. i, pp. 241-5.
[2] For the problem of interest in a socialist society see F. von Wieser, *Natural Value*, bk. ii, ch. 6; bk. iii, ch. 3; also pp. 142, 163, 206; E. v. Böhm-Bawerk, *Positive Theory of Capital*, bk. vi, ch. 10; G. Cassel, *Theory of Social Economy*, ch. vi, § 26; H. D. Henderson, *Supply and Demand*, pp. 14–16, 130; H. D. Dickinson, *Institutional Revenue*, Appendix to ch. iv. For a different view see M. Dobb, *Political Economy and Capitalism*, ch. viii and Note to ch. viii.

The question is often discussed: Why should not the socialist community accumulate capital until the rate of interest fell to zero? In the writer's opinion, this would be quite impracticable. As the rate of interest fell, there would be a rapid increase in the number of uses of capital that would, under modern technical conditions, become worth while. At zero interest, the demand for capital would absorb so high a proportion of the social income that the real time-preference of the members of the community would rise steeply. If, then, the S.E.C. were to reflect their preferences correctly, it would have to reduce the volume of collective saving and re-introduce a rate of interest in order to ration the available capital.

(b) *Long-term and short-term capital.* The provision of capital to industry falls under two heads, long-term capital and short-term capital, corresponding roughly to the distinction between fixed capital and circulating capital.

(i) Long-term capital is represented by the buildings, plant, machinery, and other durable physical equipment of industry. Every undertaking will be capitalized at a value corresponding to the cost of reproduction new of its fixed capital, and will be required to pay interest at the current rate on this capital to the organization next above it in the hierarchy of collective enterprises. (This could be effected formally by the issue of debentures, to be held by the controlling organization. Increase of capital equipment would be accompanied by an issue of new debentures, diminution of capital by a cancellation or writing-down.) New fixed capital would come out of the Social Fund[1] and would be issued by the Investment Board on the basis of the schedules drawn up by the various organs of collective economy.

The possibility of a loss of capital must be dealt with. This may be due to a variety of causes, such as diminution in the importance of the particular branch of the social economy,

[1] See sub-section (4) of this section; also Chapter IV, section 5.

rapid technical change, physical destruction, or sheer mistakes of judgement. If an industry or trade declines in importance, as brewing might if people became more abstemious, the capital sunk in it must simply be written off. Technical change, if not too rapid, should be covered by allowances made for obsolescence and risk; but violent changes in technique (such as the supersession of existing means of lighting by the invention of 'cold light') would necessitate a drastic writing-off of capital assets. Similarly, physical loss should be covered by insurance; but catastrophes such as earthquakes, floods, conflagrations, and acts of war must also entail writing-off. Finally, decisions of the planning authorities (the S.E.C. and of minor organs) may prove to have been unwise, and their reversal will involve abandonment of capital investments. In all these cases the fact should be recognized that the community's wealth has diminished by the amount of the resources that have been sunk in enterprises that will yield no return in the future. There should be kept a capital account of all the community's assets (including non-industrial ones such as public buildings and institutions devoted to communal consumption) and the total of this should be kept as closely as possible in correspondence with the actual facts.

An important problem in the theory of costs arises in connexion with this matter of writing-off capital rendered obsolete by technical change. In balancing the economic advantages and disadvantages of a new process, to what extent should the loss of capital sunk in the old process be considered? Competitive private enterprise cannot afford to do this. If a new process appears, every firm hastens to adopt it (or one like it), since it realizes that if it does not its rivals will and that it will in consequence be handicapped in the competitive struggle. On the other hand, public bodies and monopolistic private firms usually try to delay the adoption

of innovations until the old capital equipment is at least
partly worn out. (Consider, e.g., the attitude of many municipalities owning gas and tramway undertakings towards electric
lighting and omnibuses.) Undoubtedly the competitive system produces a high rate of technical progress, but is it
socially justified? The answer seems to be that it is, and that
a socialist economy should in this matter imitate competition.
'In economics bygones are forever bygones.' Capital sunk in
a process represents social resources, the product of past
labour and sacrifice, locked up in an irrevocable form. Its
value to the community is not what it *has* cost but what it
will yield (its quasi-rent in Marshall's terminology). If
society can produce the same result by other and better
means, the value of the old means is already potentially lost.
New resources, not yet immobilized in means of production,
should flow into the most productive uses. The productivity
of these uses depends on the demand for their products as
compared with the sacrifice of current, fluid resources.
Present resources, not past resources, are what count. Thus
it seems that the value of sunk resources should be ignored
in deciding on the worth-whileness of new processes.

The case of labour, however, is different from that of non-
human resources. Here again bygones are bygones, and the
fact that certain workers have acquired specialized skills that
are to be rendered unnecessary by new methods should not
weigh in the balance when decisions are being taken about
the introduction of new methods. But the fact that the community owes these men the opportunity to fit themselves to
take part again in social production should weigh in the
balance. Hence the cost of re-training displaced workers (or
pensioning those too old to be re-trained) and other costs of
transfer, such as those of transport and rehousing, where the
transfer is geographical as well as occupational, should be
debited against new methods and processes.

(ii) Short-term capital would be supplied by the socialized banking systems. All organs of collective economy would keep a current account with the Central Bank; they would be debited with the value of all materials bought and wages paid, and they would be credited with the value of all goods and services sold. Since production is normally undertaken in anticipation of demand, this would mean that every undertaking would have a permanent floating overdraft at the bank equivalent to the value of resources locked up in the process of production. The undertaking would pay interest at the current rate on this overdraft, thus taking the time-lag of production into account in the system of socialist costing.

Institutions serving the division of communal consumption (such as hospitals, schools, libraries, &c.) should follow similar methods. They should keep capital accounts which would be written up or down to correspond with the actual value of their fixed assets. Their revenue and expenditure would be checked by the bank in the same way, interest being charged on the net balance (if negative) or paid on the net balance (if income anticipated expenditure).

In the course of time the Central Bank and its agencies would probably come to exercise the function of a general accounting, checking, and controlling organ, keeping track of the progress of goods in process of manufacture through their various stages, of the quantities of goods in stock at all stages, &c. Any delay in the movement of goods along the road to ultimate consumption would be reflected in a rise in the demand of the various undertakings for short-term credit.[1]

(c) *Consumption capital*. One way in which the fruits of stored-up labour ('waiting') can be used is in the creation of

[1] For the role of the Gosbank of the U.S.S.R. in checking the execution of the Plan by the various organs of collective economy see L. E. Hubbard, *Soviet Money and Finance*, chs. v and vi.

durable articles of consumption, like dwelling-houses, swimming-baths, grand pianos, motor-cars, household furniture, wireless receivers, gas or electric stoves, vacuum cleaners, washing machines, refrigerators, &c. Under capitalism the use of these commodities tends to be restricted to those who can afford to lock up resources in durable means of consumption over a period of time, i.e. the rich. However, even under capitalism, private enterprise has undertaken the provision of dwelling-houses on hire (without which the poorer consumers would not be able to find house-room), and the provision of other durable goods on the basis of hire or hire-purchase has begun to develop.

It is clear that, if a socialist community wishes to promote the use of such amenities, it will, in the absence of large individual incomes, be obliged to provide them in some way other than outright purchase. In the case of swimming-baths, sports grounds, libraries, and many other amenities, provision through the division of communal consumption will be best. Where, as in the case of pianos, motor-cars, wireless, &c., individual consumption is most convenient, such consumption will have to be facilitated by appropriate methods of hire or hire-purchase. It is probable that the consumption of these goods could be extended and that many other amenities, now almost exclusively the privilege of the rich, could be brought within the means of the less well-off by the development of hire services.

There is no reason why the consumption of durable goods should not be facilitated by advances to consumers out of the capital funds at the disposal of the community. In the case of houses it is generally admitted that this is desirable. In Britain and in most European countries, municipal and other local authorities build houses and rent them to householders: in Australia and New Zealand the state makes advances on mortgage to individuals who wish to acquire a house or a farm. There is no reason why this should not be extended to durable consumption goods in general. As in the case of houses, either the goods could be owned permanently by the community and let out on hire to the consumer, or they could be sold to the consumer on the instalment plan, the community advancing a proportion of the purchase money against proper security.

The usual objections to instalment selling are absent or of diminished weight in a planned economy, where the fluctuations in individual income are less than in an unplanned economy, and where the financial organs of the community can keep a watchful eye on the aggregate amount of consumer indebtedness and take care that no more than a reasonable proportion of consumers' future income is pledged for the payment of instalments. On condition that the schemes of payment provide for the extinction of the debt well within the lifetime of the commodity bought, instalment selling makes possible an increase of durable, as compared with ephemeral, satisfactions in the average individual's scheme of consumption.

With regard to consumption loans, other than those destined for the acquisition of durable goods, the propriety of making public provision is more doubtful. A properly organized system of social services and of publicly owned insurance should eliminate all ordinary cases of sudden need for a loan. Nevertheless, since cases might arise in which an individual experienced a sudden need for disposal over a sum of money, due to causes not covered by insurance or the ordinary social services, some organization for making loans on security should exist. If every adult citizen had a current account with the State Bank, some development of the existing overdraft system would suffice; otherwise something in the nature of a publicly managed pawnshop or *mont-de-piété* would be required. Since private property in land and production goods would not exist, the only property available to be pledged as security for a loan would be in the form of durable consumption goods.

This would create a use for accumulated resources that would compete with the use of the same resources in the form of industrial and distributive capital. The demand for the hire of durable consumption goods would have to be added to the demand for capital in the form of production goods, in order to arrive at the aggregate demand schedule for capital, and hence to determine a rate of interest for the socialist economy. This rate of interest would have to be applied in reckoning the appropriate charge for the use of goods under hire and hire-purchase agreements. It would also be applied to pure consumption loans. In this case, however, interest would be only a small part of the charge made by the public to the borrower; most of the charge consisting of insurance against risk and costs of administration.

(d) *Temporal variations in interest.* Different rates of interest may be appropriate for different points of time in the future. If the real income per head of the community is going to rise appreciably within the next ten years, the community will be able to afford a more generous scale of provision for the future, and hence calculate with a lower rate of interest, ten years hence than it can now. Thus, while it would be in accordance with the *present* relation of needs and resources to charge interest at, say, 4 per cent. on a capital outlay made in the current year, it might be appropriate to charge 3 per cent. on an outlay made five years hence and $2\frac{1}{2}$ per cent. on one made ten years hence. In this way a compound interest table by double entry might be drawn up, in which the interest on £100 would depend not simply on the number of years for which the investment ran, but also on the particular year at which it started. In this case only the rate of interest for the current year could be determined on the basis of actual bids from the organs of public economics. The rates of interest for future years would have to be determined by more or less arbitrary deductions from (or in the case of declining real income per head, additions to) the current rate. These deductions or additions would not be completely arbitrary, since (i) they would be based upon fairly reliable estimates of the future course of production, and (ii) they would be continually checked by a process of trial and error. The greatest element of uncertainty in these calculations would probably be the influence of technical discovery and invention upon the future demand for capital and hence upon the future marginal productivity of capital.[1]

(e) *Geographical variations.* It is possible that the rate of interest, however arrived at, would not be uniform throughout all parts of a socialist commonwealth. If the latter included regions at greatly different levels of economic development (China and Central Europe, for example) a uniform rate of interest would drain off all investible resources from the more developed region to the less developed. This is, of course, precisely that movement of resources which is necessary to establish economic equilibrium and also that which would maximize the social product; but too rapid a progress in this direction might be undesirable. The S.E.C. would have to divide the entire community into regions of approximately similar economic development and establish an appropriate rate of interest for each. It would plan a certain transference of resources from the more to the less developed regions, but less than that which would immediately equalize the yield of capital. The exact magnitude of the transferences that would be made yearly from the more to the less developed

---

[1] The problem discussed in this paragraph was raised by Mr. Maurice Dobb in an article 'Problems of a Socialist Economy' (*Economic Journal*, Dec. 1933) and in his book *Political Economy and Capitalism*, ch. viii.

regions and the number of years over which the process of equalization should be spread could not be determined on purely economic grounds. It would involve judgements of a social character and would require to be considered as part of the conscious planning of economic life (see Chapter IX, section 4 (1)). The ultimate object would be the establishment of a uniform rate of interest over the entire territory.

(3) **Uncertainty—uncertainty-surcharge.** Some of the risks to which economic life is subject cancel each other out if a sufficient number of cases are taken; by the statistical rule of averages, they yield in the aggregate a precisely calculable certainty. Such risks are those due to wind and weather, to human carelessness or folly, and to the hazards of fire and of the sea. These can be, and usually are, insured against. A socialist community would have even greater opportunities than an individualist one for the extension of the principle of insurance. But certain risks are not destroyed by aggregation: these are the uninsurable risks and constitute true economic uncertainty.[1]

In a socialist community, it might be held, there should be no question of economic risk: economic planning should eliminate it. This is true of many kinds of risk. It is true of risks due to the simultaneous action of a number of entrepreneurs ignorant of each other's decisions. But in any economy where free choice is permitted to consumers and to providers of services and where any progress in technical knowledge occurs, an element of uncertainty is bound to exist.

Economic uncertainty is of two main kinds. The first kind is due to the 'anarchy of production' under capitalism. In each part of the economy entrepreneurs are taking, without mutual consultation and without exact knowledge, decisions about output and prices which affect the decisions of other

[1] See F. H. Knight, *Risk, Uncertainty, and Profit*, chaps. ii and vii.

entrepreneurs. Each one is ignorant of what the others are doing, or, at the best, makes uncertain inferences from unreliable (and frequently deliberately misleading) indications. It is no wonder that market requirements are now under-, now over-estimated, that production is subject to violent fluctuations, and that a great deal of uncertainty reigns throughout all fields of enterprise. Where entrepreneurs are engaged in complementary processes, things are bad enough; but when they are actively competing the anarchy of production becomes a real chaos. One has only to think of the retail distribution of coal or milk, the anarchy in the streets during the period of 'pirate' competition with the L.G.O.C., the chaos of the coal industry and of the Lancashire cotton industry. This kind of uncertainty would be abolished by social ownership and planned production.

The second kind of economic uncertainty, however, is that which is inherent in all production in anticipation of demand, such as characterizes a highly developed economic system. Production in anticipation of demand involves uncertainty for two reasons: first, the possibility of changes in the methods of production; second, the possibility of changes in the wants that production is undertaken to satisfy. The first involves the risk that new ways of satisfying old needs may diminish or destroy the usefulness of resources that have been invested in the old ways (e.g. the improvement of road transport diminishes the usefulness of railways). The second involves the risk that new needs or changes in the relative order of urgency of old needs may call for a diversion of resources to new uses that leaves some resources underutilized (e.g. the growth of the cinema leaves theatres half empty: a change-over in consumption from beer to chocolates will diminish the usefulness of brewery equipment). Uncertainty of this kind would still exist even in a socialist economy.

Since the degree of uncertainty will vary as between one branch of production and another, any economic choice (whether of the individual consumer or of an organ of collective economy) will be a choice between economic alternatives involving uncertainties of different degrees. A rational calculus of economic costs must reflect this fact. This means that to the elements of cost already described—wages, rent, and interest—an additional charge must be made, adjusted according to the degree of economic uncertainty involved in the particular branch of production.

To this proposal it may be objected that the greater part of economic uncertainty can be avoided by proper planning and that the residue should be shouldered by the socialist administration as part of the inevitable overhead of social economy. But the fact that a certain amount of uncertainty is inevitable is no reason why it should be borne by the community without charge. If a consumer desires a particular commodity whose production involves uncertainty, whether due to technical change or to the fickleness of demand, there is no reason why he should not have it, but he should be made to contribute to the social costs incurred as the result of uncertainty.

As has been already stated, unavoidable economic uncertainty is due to two causes: (a) technical change in methods of production; (b) fickleness of consumers' demand.

(a) Uncertainty due to changes in methods of production could be charged for by an addition to the rate of depreciation of machinery and plant over and above the rate calculated on the basis of physical durability and of the current rate of interest. In other words, not physical but technological obsolescence will be allowed for. This is in accordance with present-day capitalist practice, especially in industries where technical progress is very rapid and where depreciation rates of as much as 50 per cent. are met with (in other words a process is not considered worth employing unless its net proceeds are sufficient to repay its capital cost within two years). In fact, it would not be too much to say that depreciation has ceased to have any connexion with the physical life of fixed plant and has become (where it is not merely a device for cooking balance-sheets) an element in cost corresponding to what has been here called 'uncertainty-surcharge'.

(b) Uncertainty due to changeableness of demand is likely to arise chiefly in the provision of goods and services where the incalculable and frivolous element of consumers' preference is most marked, such as in the supply of clothing (men's and women's), amusements, sports, games, toys, and novelties generally. The most efficient statistical service in the world will not make it possible to predict, without a large margin of uncertainty, whether spots will be more popular than stripes next season, how a new film or musical play will go, what will be the reception of a novel, a gramophone record, or a mechanical 'Mickey Mouse'. In the minds of many people who think that planning can eliminate uncertainty lurks the idea that uncertainty may be abolished by abolishing consumers' freedom of choice. But this is like cutting off one's feet in order to keep one's socks from wearing out. The economic organization of a socialist society should exist to satisfy human needs: variety and choice are human needs no less than so many calories of food and so many square metres of floor-space. Therefore a socialist society should aim at providing a variety of gratifications and at permitting the ultimate consumer to choose freely between alternatives. (This does not mean to say that the economic organs of a socialist community should deliberately foster caprice. It could give the general public opportunity to make experiments in the art of consumption without reproducing the capitalist world's elaborately organized futility of luxury and fashion industries. It need not have an exclusive clique of dress designers conspiring to reshape women's waists, shoulders, and bosoms every six months in order to make all the clothes sold last season unwearable; nor need it work up through press and cinema a sudden and hectic enthusism for a craze like mah-jong or yo-yo, in order to sell the necessary equipment at ten times its cost price.)

On the other hand, variety and freedom of choice involves the risk that goods may be unsold or saleable only below cost; this is a waste, and waste must be paid for. It is only fair that the social cost of this waste should be borne by those persons on whose behalf it is incurred, that is, by the consumers of categories of goods whose demand is liable to more than average fluctuation. This could be effected by a surcharge depending on the degree of uncertainty involved in the provision of goods or service. Unless uncertainty is taken into account in social costing there will be a tendency to devote too many resources to branches of production where there is only a small chance that the product will be wanted.

Goods would be divided into categories according to the fluctuation of demand, ranging from staple foodstuffs and standardized machine-parts, upon which no uncertainty-surcharge would be made, up to those articles of luxury for which the demand was particularly capricious, upon which the heaviest surcharge would be laid.

The calculation of a surcharge for uncertainty is, in general, a more difficult task than the determination of a rate of interest, since it has to be done for each line of production separately. In the individualist community it is largely a matter of guesswork, that is to say unconscious judgement, based on old-standing habit and a mass of assimilated experience. The socialist community would for a time make use in the same way of the 'hunch' or 'flair' of the trained manager of industry, but it might in time evolve a statistical treatment of uncertainty based on the frequency distribution of sales and of price changes.

(4) **The Social Fund.** It should be obvious that these categories of rent, interest and uncertainty-surcharge, &c., are merely accounting prices: they are not paid to any actual landowner, capitalist, or risk-bearing entrepreneur, they form no part of any individual's income. The social product is composed of elements that can be distinguished analytically as the return to labour, land, waiting, and uncertainty-bearing; but as regards distribution, it forms a single undivided fund out of which individual shares may be carved out on any desired principle. The economic return to labour may be paid to the individual labourer: this is a point that we shall take up later (Chapter IV, sections 2 (5) and 3 (1)). It is definitely against the fundamental principle of the socialist commonwealth to pay rent or interest to any individual landowner or capitalist: there will be none to receive such an income. Society as a whole will own and manage the means of production, produced and unproduced, and as a whole will appropriate the product. Rent, interest, uncertainty-surcharges, and any surplus of the nature of profit will be paid into a fund, which we may call the Social Fund, into which also will go any part of the product of labour that is not paid to the individual worker as wages. We shall consider later (Chapter IV, section 5) the purposes for which payments will be made out of the Social Fund.

4. PRICING OF PRODUCTION GOODS—COSTING

(1) **Elements of costing system.** On the basis of the orders sent back by selling agencies the manufacturing organizations will be able to draw up demand schedules for their products. In the case of composite demand they will aggregate a number of different demand schedules.[1] In the case

---

[1] See note on p. 82.

of joint supply they will have a separate demand schedule for each product. If the proportion in which the joint products are obtained is invariable these can be simply aggregated to obtain a demand schedule for the total output. If the proportions are variable, a problem is presented which is mathematically soluble, given enough observations; this is to determine for each rate of output the proportions of the joint products for which the total receipts would be a maximum.

Each productive organization will be able to offer a price for the goods that it uses in the process of manufacture. In general, these goods will be in joint demand; therefore their prices will not be independent. Most of them, also, are in composite demand. The problem of valuation is complicated but not impossible. Thus demand schedules can be established for goods of higher order and, finally, for the ultimate factors of production (parcels of land of known area and quality, definite quantities of minerals and other natural resources, and certain numbers of workers registered as willing to do certain jobs—we need not at present discuss the method of their recruitment or assume any connexion between work and pay).

The quantities of these ultimate factors are known. We will assume provisionally that they are fixed. Then for each factor the S.E.C. will fix a price, which, according to the demand schedule, will just ensure its full employment. Let the costs of production be calculated on the basis of these figures. Then the productive organizations will slow down or stop the production of those goods whose demand price is below the cost price and will expand the production of those goods whose demand price is above cost. Moreover, the various productive agencies will find it possible, on the basis of possible alternatives in methods of production, to substitute one factor for another, thus modifying their demand for such factors. Ultimately, by a process of successive approximation, a true economic price for each factor will be established, which can then be used for costing purposes wherever the factor is used. In this way the costs are imputed from the demand for the marginal product and then deputed back to all other products. Also, at the same time and by the same process, factors of production will be so allocated to different uses as to bring in equal returns at the margin of employment.

So far we have not considered the supply of factors of production; or, rather, we have assumed its fixity. In the case of natural resources the supply is fixed, or at least independent of market changes. (The available quantities of land or minerals may be altered by scientific discovery or exploration, but are not *directly* responsive to changing intensities of demand.) The supply schedules of different kinds of labour depend on the policy of the community with regard to distribution.

Three policies with regard to distribution are possible:

(i) The payments made to the individual labourer may be based on some principle entirely independent of the economic value of the labourer's services. In this case the supply of each kind of labour is independent of the demand for its products: it is just the number of people that choose, or are ordered, to engage in that kind of work. The price of labour is in this case simply an accounting price that has no necessary relation to the actual income of the labourer, but it is the price which is relevant to the calculation of labour-cost. Each worker would be rated at a certain price, and this price would be used in calculating costs of alternative processes, in considering a transfer of the worker from one job to another, &c.; but it would not be his 'wages' in the sense that he would receive it as his personal income.

(ii) As an intermediate case, the payments made for labour

may depend on its value without coinciding with its value. There will then be a distinction between the money paid to the worker and the accounting price of labour, but there will be some relation between the value of labour and the number of workers offering themselves. (See Chapter IV, sections 2 (5) and 3 (1).)

(iii) The community may decide to distribute part of its income as wages for work done. In this case, each worker may be paid as wages the economic value of his services, as determined above, and the number of workers seeking work in each kind of occupation will then be a function of the price offered. In this case, supply schedules can be drawn up for each kind of labour. Mrs. Wootton has pointed out (*Lament for Economics*, pp. 229–32) that the problem of costing will be very much easier if the worker is paid in wages the economic value of his services than if the labour market is an 'imaginary' one as well as the capital market. In particular, the task of weighing against each other the different methods of production involving different combinations of labour and capital will be greatly facilitated. Moreover, such a procedure will be simple. Only one set of accounting prices will be necessary instead of two: wages and value of labour will coincide.

Whichever policy with regard to distribution be adopted, there will emerge a price for each of the ultimate production goods. These are land and natural products, and the different kinds of concrete labour. Two more things are necessary to a complete costing system. These are an allowance for time spent in production (interest or discount) and an allowance for uncertainty in the form of a surcharge above the normal rate of interest or depreciation. The principles to be followed in the determination of a rate of interest and of uncertainty-surcharges have already been discussed (section 3, sub-sections (2) and (3) of this chapter).

Prices of factors of production having been determined, a rate of interest and uncertainty-surcharges having been fixed, the S.E.C. would have all the necessary data for establishing a general system of costing and control throughout the productive machine. It would be possible to balance the relative advantages of competing methods of production and to compare the worthwhileness of spending resources on alternative lines of production. The principle of substitution would have full application.

In this way, however arbitrary the prices at first assumed, a set of prices can ultimately be established in consonance with the principles of scarcity and substitution. If factors of production are priced too high, some of them will be unemployed. If too low, the demand for their use will exceed their supply. Thus, by adjusting prices of ultimate factors until all are just fully used, the first stage of equilibrium will be achieved. Then those factors whose price has fallen will be substituted for those whose price has risen. Thus a further series of adjustments will take place. This is the second stage. Then, by applying the principle of cost to finished and intermediate goods, it will be seen that some are priced above cost and others below cost. As the prices of the ones are reduced and those of the others raised, factors of production will be absorbed into the making of the former goods and extruded from the making of the latter. This will entail a further series of adjustments, making the third stage. This completes the process, if the supply of ultimate factors of production is taken as fixed. Where the supply of the ultimate factors is variable, this can be taken into account in a fourth stage, and further substitutions effected. (These stages are logical, not temporal. In practice all four types of adjustment would be carried on simultaneously.) Thus ultimately an equilibrium will be arrived at in which full force will be allowed to consumers' preferences (as reflected in the prices of finished goods), technical conditions of production, and producers' preferences (as reflected in the supply of labour at different rates of pay). It would be possible to establish such a system, even starting from a condition of economic chaos (such as might result from a war or from a violent revolution) in which all rational accounting had been abandoned. Moreover, if there is any such thing as a position of economic equilibrium inherent in the original situation, the adjustments, after the first, will be in a series of descending magnitude. The first will be the most disturbing and difficult, and afterwards the process will become progressively easier and converge to a definite end position. Thereafter small adjustments will be sufficient to keep the system in equilibrium, except in the case of major technical innovations or of big changes in consumers' taste. (See Chapter IX, section 4 (1) and (4).)

In view of the possibility of gains and losses due to unforeseen changes in demand, it would be best to price goods at a small margin above cost and to apply the surplus to an equalization fund for each undertaking. All surpluses over a certain percentage of annual turnover should revert in some way to the community as a whole. Perhaps it would be convenient to divide it up, part going to the organization next above in the hierarchy (thus ultimately into the Social Fund), part being used by the undertaking for small additions to plant that would not need borrowing from the general capital fund, part perhaps being divided among employees in the form of a bonus, and part perhaps being divided among consumers as in the consumers' co-operative movement. (See Chapter IV, section 5.)

It can be shown that it is mathematically possible to determine, from data that are practically obtainable, the quantities and prices of a number of consumption goods and of the factors of production that combine to make them. It seems, therefore, that the whole process of price-determination could be resolved into a set of simultaneous equations, or, since only small deviations from an already established equilibrium need be considered, into a problem in the calculus of variations. Given, at each end of the chain of production, a free market for finished goods and for productive services, the prices and quantities that would exist if the intermediate goods were sold in a market, could, theoretically, be determined.[1]

The suggestion has therefore been made by the present writer[2] that, once the economic system of socialism has been set going, it would be unnecessary to create in this way within the framework of the socialist community a sort of working model of capitalist production, but that it would be possible to deal with the problems mathematically, on the basis of the full statistical information that would be at the disposal of the S.E.C. It is, however, unlikely that the method of trial and error would be replaced entirely by centralized price determination, based on the solution of thousands of simultaneous equations. The reason is not so much the difficulty and delay of solving the equations: at a cost of much less than what is wasted under capitalism in salesmanship, advertising, secret commissions, and other 'frictions', the S.E.C. could set up a machine capable of solving two or three thousand simultaneous equations. The reason is that the data themselves, which would have to be fed into the equation-machine, are continually changing. The conditions of demand and supply and the technical conditions of production are not static. They cannot be ex-

[1] Cf. Marshall, *Principles of Economics*, Mathematical Appendix, Note XXI; G. Cassel, *Theory of Social Economy*, ch. iv, § 16; E. Barone, 'The Ministry of Production in the Collectivist State' (published in *Collectivist Economic Planning*, ed. by F. A. von Hayek).

[2] H. D. Dickinson, 'Price Formation in a Socialist Community', *Economic Journal*, June 1933.

pressed in terms of fixed coefficients that can be determined once and for all; they can only be described by dynamic parameters subject to perpetual alteration. To determine these parameters requires continuous observation of the primary data of the market. The economic organs of the community will be engaged all the time in gathering these data and in reporting them to the statistical organs of the S.E.C. Since this is so it would be easier to give them at the same time the task of making the necessary adjustment of prices and quantities. The statistical determination of demand schedules would then take its proper place as an aid to, and not as a substitute for, the pedestrian method of trial and error. Even so, the statistical service of a socialist community might very well undertake the task of establishing the numerical values of the constants in the Walrasian equations of equilibrium.

(2) **Average cost or marginal cost?** One point that must be considered is whether, in those cases where cost varies with output, average cost or marginal cost should be the basis of price-determination.[1] Where goods are produced under conditions of increasing costs, average cost is too low, and marginal cost seems to be indicated.[2] Where diminishing cost is the rule, marginal cost gives a price that does not enable all the costs of production to be covered. Professor Pigou suggests that the social interest would be best served by pricing all commodities according to their marginal cost, subsidizing the production of diminishing-cost goods out of taxes on increasing-cost goods.

Variation of cost with output is of two kinds, long-period and short-period variation. The long period is defined as the

---

[1] For a discussion of this point see Pigou, *Economics of Welfare*, Part II, ch. xi, and Appendix III; and Robinson, *Economics of Imperfect Competition*, chs. ii, iii, vii, ix, x, and xi.

[2] See section 3 (1) of this chapter.

period during which the organization and technical equipment of industry can be adapted to the scale of output chosen; the short period as the period during which variations of output take place with organization and equipment unchanged.

(i) In the long period, variation of cost with scale of output is due to two causes: (a) changes in the supply price of factors of production, (b) changes in the efficiency of industrial organization, with changes in the volume of production. Broadly speaking, the price of a factor tends to rise the more of it is used, thus changes under (a) always involve rising cost with increasing output; while changes under (b) are of the type of economies of large-scale production,[1] and thus involve falling cost with increasing output. Hence increasing costs and diminishing costs are not exactly converse phenomena.

In case (a) above, the argument of section 3 (1) of this chapter applies, and justifies the equating of price to marginal cost. Since, in this case, marginal cost is above average cost, there arises a surplus of price above cost, in other words, rent. Thus, if price be based on marginal cost, rents are imputed to all factors of production whose supply is not perfectly elastic.[2]

In case (b) above, costs fall slowly as output increases. Thus marginal cost is somewhat above average cost. The policy of equating price to marginal cost will therefore lead to accounting losses (negative rents). Since these losses depend on permanent long-period circumstances, they will have to be covered by permanent subsidies. Thus the marginal-cost price policy entails the payment of subsidies to all productive organs enjoying economies of large-scale production.

---

[1] The difference between internal and external economies vanishes in a planned economy.

[2] If these rents are included in cost, average cost including rent becomes equal to marginal cost excluding rent.

Against these subsidies can be set the rents imputed to scarce factors in industries of type (a); but there is no reason to suppose that the aggregate sum of subsidies and of rents respectively would just balance.

(ii) In the short period, variation of cost with output is due to the fact that equipment and organization are properly adjusted to the scale of production only at one point (normal capacity). For outputs above this point, cost rises steeply and marginal cost is much greater than average cost. For outputs below this point, cost falls fairly steeply and marginal cost is considerably less than average cost. The principle of pricing goods at short-period marginal cost would mean that plants operating below their normal capacity would sell their products at prices well below average cost and would require substantial subsidies;[1] while plants operating above their normal capacity would sell their products at sharply enhanced prices and would make substantial accounting profits. In the one case, low prices, by stimulating demand, would raise output towards capacity; in the other case, high prices would choke off demand to a point compatible with short-period technical capacity.[2]

Under private enterprise, competition, if allowed to operate freely, tends to approximate price to marginal cost in the case of increasing-cost goods and to average cost in the case of diminishing-cost goods—in other words, to whichever species of cost is the higher. Thus only positive rents emerge.

If the S.E.C. decided to base its costing system on marginal rather than on average cost for all types of products (diminishing-cost goods as well as increasing-cost goods), the problem

---

[1] This is particularly likely to be the case where the minimum technically efficient plant in large, as in heavy industry and in most public utilities (e.g. railway transport, electricity generation, and postal services)

[2] See E. F. M. Durbin, 'Economic Calculus in a Planned Economy' *Economic Journal*, December 1936, and A. P. Lerner, 'Statics and Dynamics in Socialist Economics', *Economic Journal*, June 1937.

would arise that, in the case of goods produced under diminishing costs, aggregate receipts would fall short of aggregate costs (in other words, negative rents would arise) and all goods of this kind would need a subsidy. This situation might be met by the establishment of a Marginal Cost Equalization Fund, into which would be paid all positive rents arising from increasing-cost goods and out of which would be paid subsidies to maintain the production of diminishing-cost goods. It must not be assumed that the two sets of payments, incoming and outgoing, would balance. Under modern technical conditions, diminishing costs are far commoner than increasing costs. Therefore, the Marginal Cost Equalization Fund would be permanently in debit and its net outgoings would have to be met out of the Social Fund (see Chapter IV, section 5).

(3) **Divergence between social costs and individual costs.** Socialist costing could do what individualist costing cannot do—eliminate or greatly reduce the divergence between marginal social net product and marginal individual net product.[1] Ignorance of economic opportunities would be eliminated by the publicity of a planned economic system. Cost of movement of resources would be considerably reduced and many movements of resources could be made unnecessary by knowledge and foresight. In the calculation of costs allowance could be made for the items that are not included in capitalist costing and that bring about the divergence between the socially most desirable output and that which is most profitable to the individual firm. Thus the incidental benefits or disbenefits that an industry or undertaking renders to others or to the general amenities of the community could be taken into account in the form of deductions from or additions to the cost of production. Examples of divergence between social and individual cost are: inade-

---

[1] See Pigou, *Economics of Welfare* (3rd ed.), Part II, ch. i–x.

quate development or wasteful use of land and durable instruments of production in the hands of lessees; unemployment caused by sudden changes in industrial methods or equipment; pollution of the air by smoke or chemical fumes; the addition to social costs, in the form of hospitals and police, due to high-speed motoring or to the consumption of intoxicating liquors. In these cases, social costs are incurred that are not fully charged to the consumer. In other cases, social benefits are conferred that are not fully compensated by a pecuniary return. Examples are: afforestation, soil-conserving methods of agriculture, the laying out of parks and open spaces, the making of roads and other transport facilities, and practically all expenditure on education and research. Furthermore, the wasting of resources that occurs under free competition, due to ignorance, duplication, and overlapping of effort, and lack of standardization, could be eliminated, without the reduction of output and consequent mal-distribution of resources that is the almost inevitable concomitant of capitalist monopoly.

5. Economic Calculation under Socialism

We must now deal explicitly with Ludwig von Mises's chief objection to socialism (and indeed to any form of planned economy). Mises holds that economic calculation is impossible under socialism, since 'where there is no market there is no price system, and where there is no price system there can be no economic calculation'.[1] Elsewhere in the same book he expresses the same proposition in other words:

'Once society abandons free pricing of production goods rational production becomes impossible. Every step that leads away from private ownership of the means of production and the use of money is a step away from rational economic activity. . . . Without calculation, economic activity is impossible. Since

[1] L. von Mises, *Socialism*, p. 131.

under Socialism economic calculation is impossible, under Socialism there can be no economic activity in our sense of the word.
. . . It would no longer be possible to speak of rational production.
In the absence of criteria of rationality, production could not be
consciously economical.'[1]

Again, referring to proposals (such as those of the present
work) to solve the problem of economic calculation under
socialism by the creation of an artificial market for means of
production, he states that

'it is not possible to divorce the market and its functions in regard
to the formation of prices from the working of a society which is
based on private property in the means of production and in
which, subject to the rules of such a society, the landlords, capitalists and entrepreneurs can dispose of their property as they think
fit. For the motive force of the whole process which gives rise to
market prices for the factors of production is the ceaseless search
on the part of the capitalists and the entrepreneurs to maximize
their profits by serving the consumers' wishes. . . . It is only the
prospect of profit which directs production into those channels
in which the demands of the consumer are best satisfied at least
cost. If the prospect of profit disappears the mechanism of the
market loses its mainspring, for it is only this prospect which
sets it in motion and maintains it in operation. The market is
thus the focal point of the capitalist order of society; it is the
essence of Capitalism. Only under Capitalism, therefore, is it
possible; it cannot be "artificially" imitated under Socialism.'[2]

As will be seen from the quotations given, Mises takes up
a number of slightly varying positions. One moment it is
pricing in general that is impossible under socialism.
Another moment he admits the possibility of pricing consumption goods, but considers it impossible, in the absence
of independent, privately owned enterprises, to extend the
process to production goods. According to this view (which

[1] Ibid. p. 119.   [2] Ibid., pp. 137-8.

is the one which he most consistently upholds) it is in the pricing of production goods (which involves among other things the problem of costing) that difficulty is alleged to occur. In Austrian terminology, the real problem of socialist economics is not so much that of pricing as that of imputation. At other times it is the absence of the profit-motive that is the main point of the charge against socialism. This argument merges with that based on the impossibility of true entrepreneurship under socialism, which will be dealt with later (Chapter IX, section 3).

Mises's argument appears to involve a somewhat obvious *non-sequitur*. It identifies the price system with the market, and the market with the existence of separate enterprises and of private ownership of production goods. This involves a confusion of the essential nature of price with its historically and institutionally qualified manifestation. Mises's assertions can be resolved into the following propositions:

(1) Rational economic activity requires the pricing of all goods, production goods as well as consumption goods.

(2) Pricing requires the existence of a market.

(3) A market requires the existence of independent owners of the goods exchanged.

Accepting, for the sake of argument, the first proposition, we must first inquire what is involved in the notion of a price, or rather what is the minimum of conditions which a price must fulfil in order to satisfy the conditions for rational economic activity. On reflection it would appear that the conditions to be fulfilled are: (a) that with a definite physical quantity of every specific category of goods is associated a numerical equivalent or coefficient, whose magnitude is a function of the scarcity of unit quantity of the good relative to the wants whose satisfaction is dependent on it; (b) that these coefficients may be used as a measure of the economic equivalence of goods of different kinds, as in the comparison of qualitatively different collections of goods, the substitution of one means of production for another, or the computation of costs; (*c*) that the system of numerical coefficients is coherent and self-consistent. Now these conditions are fulfilled by any 'coefficients' attached to goods and adjusted (if necessary by trial and error), subject to the following rules: (i) at every stage of production output is to be extended up to the point at which the prices of the goods produced are equal to the sum of the 'coefficients' of the constituent elements; (ii) those methods of production and those combinations of constituent elements are to be preferred which make a minimum the sum of the 'coefficients' of the constituent elements; (iii) available supplies of ultimate production goods (goods of highest order) are to be just exhausted by the demand for them at the current 'coefficients'. If these rules are followed by the planning authorities, the 'coefficients' will be prices fulfilling the conditions enumerated above. Regarded from this point of view, the association of price with private ownership, free enterprise and the free market is an historical accident, not a logical necessity.

Let us assume that the organs of a socialistic economy adopt any arbitrary set of coefficients attached to specific categories of goods and operate with them according to the principles of price-reckoning under fully competitive capitalism: i.e. computing costs, substituting in order to minimize cost, and extending production until selling price falls to cost. Then, if in any particular case the right price had been hit upon by accident, the available quantities of the good would be just exhausted without leaving unused stocks or unsatisfied demands. Otherwise, stocks of some goods would be exhausted before all demands at that price had been met, and stocks of other goods would be left unused upon the hands of the productive organs. In the former case the price would have to be raised and in the latter case lowered. The price of any factor of production would be too high, just right, or too low, according as the available supplies were incompletely utilized, just drawn into employment, or insufficient for current demand. Consequential readjustments would then have to be made throughout the productive system, a fresh revision of prices would then be necessary, and so on. Thus by a process of repeated approximation a set of prices would emerge which would correspond to the real scarcities of the different goods and permit a rational calculation of costs and substitution-equivalents.

Even if these arbitrary coefficients adopted as a starting-point of a system of collectivistic pricing were absolutely arbitrary (e.g. numbers taken out of a table of logarithms and applied at random to the items in a mail-order catalogue), it is claimed that by a process of trial and error a consistent and rational set of prices would finally emerge. But they would probably be chosen so as to correspond in some degree to the actual scarcities of the goods that they were attached to; that is to say, they would not be absolutely arbitrary, but they would not be quite rational. Examples of such semi-arbitrary prices would be labour-values, prices taken over from a previous capitalist era, prices current in capitalist exchange in a neighbouring country, &c.

The system of prices for production goods so obtained would dovetail with the market for consumption goods at the one end and the market for productive personal services at the other. The prices at which consumption goods were offered for sale would be based on the prices of the goods entering into their production (costs of production), and would thus relate individual demand to the scarcity of the resources available for satisfying it. The remuneration offered for personal services would be the prices of these services, and thus the individual worker's preference in the choice of occupation would be related to the intensity of the

consumers' need for his services.   Thus the acceptance of
the first of Mises's propositions (that a price system is necessary for rational economic activity) does not necessarily imply
the acceptance of the other two (that pricing requires a market and that a market requires independent ownership).   In
fact, exchange of a kind, viz., the establishment of ratios of
equivalence between goods, can exist independently of the
market; and a market of a kind can exist independently of
private ownership.[1]

As to the essential nature of price, Cassel, who in his
Theory of Social Economy treats price as the measure of
scarcity,[2] shows a deeper insight than the writers of the
Austrian school.   The function of price, according to him,
is to choke off demand down to the point at which the available quantity of the good is just, and only just, allocated
among demanders.   If price is too high, some of the available
supply will be left over; if price is too low, there will not be
enough to go round.   We thus have a criterion for the correct-
ness of any given price.   Once the price of any one good A is
established, it becomes a point of departure in the determination of all the prices of other goods.   If A is used for the production of other goods, its price becomes an element in their
cost.   If A is produced by means of other goods, its price
becomes one of the elements determining the demand for
them.   If A is complementary to or competitive with other
goods the same is true, with the addition that substitution
becomes possible between A and its co-goods, and the extent
of this substitution is determined by the prices of the goods,
established on the basis of scarcity.

For historical and institutional reasons, we associate price

[1] See also A. P. Lerner, 'Economic Theory and Socialist Economy',
Review of Economic Studies, October 1934; and E. F. M. Durbin, 'Economic Calculus in a Planned Economy', *Economic Journal*, December
1936.
    [2] G. Cassel, *Theory of Social Economy*, ch. iii (especially § 12).

with individual enterprise and exchange on the market, but the essential character and function of price exists wherever a definite numerical relation is established between unit quantities of different kinds of goods and where the numerical coefficient attached to any given good is functionally related to its degree of scarcity. It is thus independent of any particular organization of the market. Mises has confused the *essence* of the pricing process (the application of the scarcity principle) with the particular *form* under which it is manifested in the capitalist economy (the market and private ownership of production goods).

6. Price as a Means of Equating Dissimilar Goods

Physically similar goods can be added together to give a total. Three tons of coal and six tons of coal are nine tons of coal. Two chairs plus three chairs of the same design are five chairs. So a figure can be given which represents the physical volume of production and by means of which different productivities can be compared. A mine that turns out 5,000,000 tons of coal per annum is more productive than one which turns out 4,000,000. But as soon as we attempt to add together dissimilar things trouble starts. What is the sum of two tables and three chairs? Is an output of 3,000,000 tons of coal+1,000,000 tons of iron ore greater or less than one of 2,500,000 tons of coal+1,500,000 tons of iron ore? Above all, how can we calculate an index of aggregate social productivity or of productivity per head when the total includes such dissimilar items as chairs, coal, railway engines, dish-cloths, and gramophone records? Things not too dissimilar can be reduced to a common denominator in terms of some common property; coal of different qualities, peat, and wood can be reduced to calorific power; tables and chairs can be compared on a basis of materials or labour; various textile products can perhaps be brought to a common measure; but the more heterogeneous the collection of goods, the harder this is. The two boldest efforts in this direction are the use of labour-time or of mechanical energy as a common denominator of goods of diverse sorts.[1]

Since the end of production is use, it would appear that the common measure of diverse goods should be their use-values. Under capitalism price is an inadequate measure of use-value, since the expression both of demand and of supply is distorted by inequality in means, monopoly, immobility of resources, vested interests, &c. But in a socialist community, price would be a fair working measure of social use-value, and so physically dissimilar goods could be compared on the basis of their relative prices. In fact no other basis seems to be possible.

There is, however, an apparent contradiction in this method, due to the so-called paradox of value, whereby as the physical volume of output rises the value per unit falls, and finally (at least in some cases) the aggregate value falls, in such a way that real wealth and value move in contrary directions. This contradiction can be resolved by the use of suitable index-numbers of production, or by measuring the volume of production in terms of the aggregate values of goods at a stable price-level. Methods of calculating index-numbers of aggregate volumes of production are described by I. Fisher in his *Making of Index Numbers*. (Generally speaking, corresponding to every index-number of general prices there is an index-number of production.) The general principle underlying all these index-numbers is that, while the different goods in a heterogeneous collection are compared on the basis of their *relative* market prices, an increase in the total quantity of goods is accompanied by an increase in the index-number. Thus, if the number of goods were reduced to one,

---

[1] See section 2 (1) and (2) of this chapter.

the index-number would be proportional to the physical quantity of that one good. If a collection of goods were *uniformly* increased in quantity, say by a 10 per cent. increase in the quantity of each good, then the index would increase by 10 per cent. If a collection of goods increases *irregularly*, some goods by more and some by less, then the increase in the index-number is the weighted mean of the different increases (different index-numbers differ in detail according to the method of weighting adopted). If a collection of goods change in such a way that some of the goods increase and some decrease in quantity, then the index-number is the weighted mean of a number of positive and negative quantities: it will show an increase or a decrease according to whether increases or decreases predominate in the collection. Often different methods of weighting will give different results, so that with the same data one index-number will register an increase and another a decrease.

In spite of the difficulties (more theoretical than practical) in the way of constructing index-numbers, some sort of index-number based on relative prices is the only way of obtaining a measure for the magnitude of a collection of heterogeneous goods: shoes, ships, sealing-wax, cabbages, and chromo-lithographs of kings.

CHAPTER IV
DISTRIBUTION OF INCOME—ALLOCATION OF LABOUR

1. INTRODUCTORY

THE socialist community has organized the production of goods. It must now proceed to organize the distribution of the product. Since the means of production are owned and operated by organs of the whole community, the entire product is at the community's disposal, to allocate as in its collective wisdom it thinks best. But the whole product of industry is not available for consumption: a deduction must first be made for new capital accumulation (what in an individualist society is called savings, or, more accurately, investment).[1] The remainder, the net consumable product, must then be divided into two portions, corresponding to the divisions of communal and individual consumption. Since the free market has been adopted for the latter division it is clear that, in order to establish equilibrium in the price system as a whole, the amount of purchasing power or aggregate money income distributed to individuals during any given period must be equal in the aggregate to the sum of the prices of goods offered for sale in the division of individual consumption during the same period. (See Chapter VIII, section 2.)

In the method of distribution of individual income to its citizens a socialist community would have a certain range of choice. It might choose precisely equal distribution, or a system of money allowances based on presumed needs, or a system of paying the worker according to the economic value of his labour, or a mixture of all three methods. To persons whose habits of thought have been formed in the environ-

[1] See note 1, p. 83.

ment of capitalism the third will appear the only feasible method of distribution. Such persons should reflect that, even under capitalism, the second method is in use, although to a very limited extent, e.g. in the form of old-age pensions.

In a socialist system there is no essential connexion between the value of labour and the payment of a sum of money to a labourer. For purposes of accurate costing it is necessary to know the value imputed to human effort from the ultimate consumption goods in which it is embodied; but this might be used for accounting purposes only, each worker being rated at a certain figure for purposes of time-sheets and transfers from one job to another. Under the system of cost accounting developed in the previous chapter, an economic value will be imputed to various concrete kinds of labour-power as well as to land and natural resources, and the services of produced means of production. It is clear that the return to labour might be dealt with in the same way as the return to natural resources and waiting: that is to say, it might all go into the Social Fund. Thus all earnings would be pooled and divided up on some principle other than that of imputed value, such as that of equal incomes for all, or that of payment according to need.

The principle of distributing personal income on a basis of making equal provision for equal need would result in a system of roughly equal payments to all adults, with graduated allowances to children, modified perhaps by additional payments to individuals whose needs are abnormal (e.g. expectant and nursing mothers) or whose occupations require special facilities or make special demands (a manual labourer needs more food than a sedentary worker, a novelist or artist more opportunity for travel than the average person). Its effect will be very similar to that of the method of exact mathematical equality and very different from that of the method of paying labour according to its imputed economic value. The advantage of the equal payment system is that it satisfies mankind's deep-lying sentiment of justice. The main disadvantage of such a system is that it deprives the community of the very useful method of regulating the supply of labour to different occupations by means of changes in the remuneration offered. If accompanied by free choice of job, it will lead to great scarcity of labour in some occupations and to a redundance in others, as compared with the social need for such labour. If not accompanied by free choice of job, it will defeat one of the chief ends of a socialistic re-organization of society: economic freedom for the ordinary worker. It will also introduce considerable difficulties into the problem of social costing.

2. The Allocation of Labour between Occupations

How then can the supply of labour be regulated so as to direct the labouring power of the community to various occupations in accordance with social needs? Five methods may be suggested.

(1) **Compulsory allocation of tasks.** This is the method of military organizations and is also resorted to in great civil emergencies, such as floods, famines, and earthquakes. For ordinary times it is too repugnant to the common man's sense of freedom to be practicable. Moreover, as any one knows very well who has had experience of military organization, especially in work of a non-military kind, it is incapable of maintaining a steady rate of efficient work, and it inevitably breeds evasion and fraud. Finally, it is of a hit-and-miss type. Under it there is no possibility of comparing different workers' fitness for alternative occupations. A characteristic example of the sporadic application of this method was seen in the U.S.S.R. some years ago when, on the occasion of a transport crisis, a decree of the Commissariat of Labour went forth that any one who had ever

worked on the railway and was now in a different employment was to be dismissed from his present job and must report himself within a week to the nearest railway station. Among the persons so conscribed for railway service there would probably be many who had found congenial work in other industries at which they had become efficient and socially useful, while on the railway they might be unskilled labourers; whereas there would be many persons not affected by the decree who would be fitter for railway service, and who would serve more willingly. To this method of regulating the supply of labour apply objections similar to those which apply to the method of rationing for the supply of consumption goods. Like rationing, it is clumsy and incapable of fine adjustment, destructive of freedom, and tolerable only in cases of grave emergency.

(2) **Moral suasion.** It might be possible, by exhortations and slogans, posters of the 'King and Country Need You' type, and other appeals to a sense of civic duty, to elicit the necessary supply of labour and direct it to the desired quarter; but enthusiasm so generated, although it may suffice to tide the community over an emergency, soon cools off, and the efforts so evoked will quickly become as slack and intermittent as those provided under a system of compulsion. In the U.S.S.R., although slogans and exhortation by speeches and newspaper articles are still much used and although special tasks are still achieved by means of subbotniks (voluntary work on rest-days), nevertheless the main emphasis is now being laid on more concrete forms of suasion —badges of honour, extra funds for social amenities in the factory, and more wages for individual workers.

(3) **The raising and lowering of qualifications for entry.** Just as at the present time an excess of medical students (an excess, that is to say, from the point of view of the medical profession's privileged standard of living rather

than that of the health needs of the community) is countered by raising the standard of examinations for medical degrees, so a strictly equalitarian socialist community could raise the minimum standard of competence required from the aspirants to the most eagerly sought-after occupations. A rush of enthusiastic would-be aviators and dramatic critics could be countered by a stringent process of selection that would reject all below the standard of a Kingston Smith or a William Archer. This method has, however, its limitations. For one thing it is uneconomic: it will result in an unnecessarily high degree of competence being exacted in the more attractive occupations and a serious shortage of even moderately efficient people in the less attractive ones. For another thing it does not work equally well both ways; one can scarcely meet a *dis*inclination to enter a given profession by *lowering* standards. If the discipline and unpleasantnesses of hospital life deter incipient nurses, it would not be very practicable to recruit the profession from people who had failed to pass the entrance requirements of the cardboard-box making industry. Nursing must be made more attractive. This brings us to the fourth and fifth methods.

(4) **The offer of non-pecuniary incentives.** It would be possible to vary what Marshall calls the 'net advantages' of different occupations relatively to each other, so as to attract workers into some and deter them from entering others, while still preserving equality of pecuniary remuneration. Money earnings are not the only incentives that can induce workers to prefer one job to another. The relative attractiveness of different jobs could be adjusted in various ways, such as by varying the amounts of leisure, privileges, or the insignia of honour attached to different occupations. Also appeals to public spirit, to the desire for adventure, or to the spirit of emulation (personal or professional) in achievement rather than in money earnings (what in the

U.S.S.R. is called socialist competition) might be a potent way of achieving a desired allocation of labour without unduly stressing inequality in personal earnings.[1] In this connexion it is worth remarking the development in the U.S.S.R. of titles, such as 'People's artist' or 'honoured author', and of orders of economic chivalry, such as the Order of Lenin, the Order of Labour, &c.

(5) **The offer of pecuniary incentives.** The last method to be described is the method characteristic of exchange economy (petty commodity production and capitalism). It is to offer to the worker, in return for productive services, definite quantities of general purchasing power (money) at rates which vary with the intensity of the demand for his services. This means, in other words, that the remuneration offered to the worker corresponds to the imputed economic value of his services. It need not necessarily equal the latter, but would rise as it rises and fall as it falls. The adoption, at any rate in part, of the system of paying each labourer according to the value of his labour would simplify the tasks of recruitment and transference of labour as well as the problem of labour discipline. In this case free choice of occupation would be compatible with an allocation of labour in accordance with the economic needs of the community, labour being attracted by higher earnings to places where it was in demand and being warned off from unwanted occupations by a shrinkage in earnings.[2] The advantages of such a system are, in the first place, its flexibility and, in the second place, the scope it gives to individual taste and preference. If more of a certain kind of labour is required, the wages offered for it can be raised until the necessary supply

---

[1] See the present author's article on 'The Economic Basis of Socialism' in the *Political Quarterly*, Sept.–Dec. 1930.
[2] For wages under socialism see Wieser, *Natural Value*, bk. iii, ch. vii; bk. iv, ch. x; also Cassel's *Theory of Social Economy*, ch. viii, § 38.

is forthcoming. No one is forced to enter the trade: those who do are those who, at the new rate of pay, prefer that occupation to others. In the case of the Russian transport situation just mentioned, the offer of a higher rate of pay plus a bonus to ex-railwaymen on re-engagement would have elicited an adequate supply of suitable labour without taking men from jobs in which they had acquired a higher degree of skill or become endued with greater responsibility than would be required from them in the railway service (on the assumption that skill and responsibility were paid for in other occupations, too).[1]

Under this method, which more than any other promotes freedom of occupational choice, the human effort required in production is hired by the community under contracts of service, freely entered into by its citizens. The proceeds of these contracts form part of the purchasing power at the disposal of citizens (i.e. of their income), and will be called Wages.

This method of regulating the supply of labour through the payment of wages and salaries may be combined with some of the other methods. Thus it would be possible also to alter the non-pecuniary attractions of different callings, to revise the entrance qualifications required for an occupation and to appeal to a sense of public spirit and civic duty. In fact all ways could be used except that of forced labour— and even this would be held in reserve by a socialist society (as by any other society) for grave public emergencies.

[1] It is interesting to observe the development of money wages in the Soviet Union. After a period during which equality of wages was aimed at (though never fully achieved), a phase has now been entered marked by definite and deliberate differentiation of wages on the basis of individual output or effort, of the social utility of the work, and of the relation of the supply of labour to the demand for it in the occupation. Even orders of economic chivalry are now accompanied by money pensions. The most recent drive towards increased efficiency of labour, the Stakhanovite movement, is characterized by very high individual earnings for workers who achieve high output or otherwise do good work.

3. Wages Under Socialism

(1) **Methods of payment.** Assuming that the method of wages is adopted, the next point that arises is: whether wages should be equal to the economic value of labour-power, or should merely be variable in the same direction. We have seen (Chapter III, section 4 (1)) that, once the principle of absolute equality is abandoned, there are very good reasons for paying the whole economic value of labour as personal wages, except perhaps in a few special cases.[1]

Once the principle is admitted of paying to the worker, as wages, the economic value of his services, there seems to be no valid reason in principle for objecting to any particular system of wage payments.

Time-rates, piece-rates, bonuses on output to non-process workers and other methods of payment by results all may have their part. Premium-bonus systems of the kind that cuts the earnings per piece as the output rises should be banned, since they are contrary to the sound economic principle that the faster the worker works the less use per piece he makes of the time, space, and machinery with which he works, and that, consequently, the higher is the value of his work *per piece*. In any case, careful time-study should remove all cause for rate-cutting.

Piece-rates obviously must be fixed by some quick and simple workshop procedure. Here a combination of the specialist on the managerial side (Taylor's 'time-boss' and 'rate-boss') with the men's representative of the shop-steward type should provide the elementary mechanism; but there must be appeal to some higher arbitral body, which will also have the function of laying down general principles of rate-fixing. Scientific methods of job-analysis and motion-study, together with an absence of profit-seeking on the part

[1] See, however, section 5 of this chapter.

of the management, should make rate-fixing easier than it is in most industries to-day.

A standard working day should be fixed for manual workers and non-responsible brain-workers. The three-shift (with eight-hour working day) or four-shift (with six-hour working day) system, where it can be introduced, economizes fixed plant. Every worker should be guaranteed regular days of rest (not necessarily all workers on the same day) and annual holidays with pay. Overtime should be paid at higher rates, as an economic inducement to the productive organs to avoid it, and if the worker is required to work on his normal rest-day such work should be penalized by still higher rates. But careful planning of production ought to reduce overtime and work on rest-days to a minimum. Instead of extra pay to compensate for work involving special hardship or danger (e.g. so-called 'dirty money' in boiler-scaling, and allowances for hot or cramped places in mines) it would be better to offer shorter hours, or extra holidays on full pay. Extra pay sometimes tends to create a vested interest in overtime or in bad working conditions.

The fixing of an actual rate of wages for any given kind of work or of a piece-rate for a given job will have to be effected by methods not essentially different from those in use at present. Some form of collective bargaining between the organs of collective enterprise, representative of the citizens' interests *qua* consumers, and the trade unions, representative of the citizens' interests *qua* workers, will have to be established. It is difficult to say in advance which will be better: a system resembling the British type of Conciliation Board, composed entirely of representatives of the parties themselves, except for an impartial chairman appointed by mutual agreement; or a system resembling the Australian Arbitration Court, which is a permanent and professional judicial body, before which the parties present their respective cases according to a quasi-litigous procedure. There is also room in any system of collective bargaining for the expert professional administrator of the Ministry of Labour type.

The general principles that any arbitral organ will have to apply in problems of wage determination are the following: (1) a shortage of labour in any particular job affords a prima-facie case for raising the standard wage; (2) unemployment in any particular job affords a prima-facie case for lowering the standard wage: (3) the net advantages (wages, hours, holidays, public esteem, &c.) of any occupation should be as near as possible the same as those in any other occupation calling for the same degree of hardship, skill, and responsibility; (4) differences in hardship, skill, and responsibility should correspond to differences in net advantages. Principles (1) and (2) correspond to short-period influences, principles (3) and (4) to long-period influences in the supply of labour. Where short-period and long-period indications are in conflict, the former should receive priority.

(2) **Regional variations in wages.** The possibility of variations in the basic rates of wages in different regions must now be considered. These may exist in three cases: (a) according to variations in the cost of living, (b) according to variations in the relative supply of labour, (c) according to variations in the efficiency of labour.

(a) The first case is parallel to the differences between wage rates in different towns sanctioned by many British trade unions. Not only might different basic rates be sanctioned by a socialist community as between one town and another or as between town and country but also as between different regions of the socialist territory, where the latter included great varieties of climate and physical features. To give equal net advantages to workers in Naples, Tromsö, Solingen, and Stalingrad would involve the adjustment of money wages to the different costs of various foodstuffs, to the cost of housing under conditions suitable to the locality, and to the opportunities for sport and culture. (The actual calculation of basic rates would entail the difficulties known to compilers of index-numbers in comparing expenditures on qualitatively different collections of goods.)

(*b*) Where the S.E.C. desired to promote the economic development of an under-populated region, it might very well fix for it temporarily a scale of wages that would give the worker net advantages above the average for his trade and grade, in order to promote voluntary migration thither. In the same way, labour might be persuaded by low basis rates to move out of relatively over-populated areas.

(*c*) Where the socialist community included peoples of very different cultural levels and where the economic value of their work varied considerably, it would be impossible to establish the same basic wage rates for all of them. Although every effort would doubtless be made, by education and investment of new capital, to bring the backward elements up to the same level of industrial efficiency as the rest of the population, it would be necessary, as a temporary measure, to sanction lower rates of wages for them than for the more advanced elements. If, for instance, the British Empire became a union of socialist republics, it would be a long time before the same real-wage scale could be applied to Indian and to Canadian workers. A low basic rate in a given region would, of course, tend to promote emigration; but if the average level of industrial efficiency in the region were low, few emigrants would be able to hold their own among the more advanced peoples amongst whom they settled. That efficient individuals should do so would be all to the good. But it would be necessary for the S.E.C. to make special plans for the raising of the efficiency of the backward people as a whole in order to achieve a maximum of economic welfare throughout the community.

In the two latter cases, (b) and (c), deviations from equality of real wages are indicative of a failure to reach equilibrium. It should be the policy of the S.E.C. to bring about equilibrium as soon as possible and so to remove the need for such inter-regional inequalities.

Closely akin to the subject of regional variations in wage rates is that of regional variations in the hours of labour. Differences in the real standard of living, due to causes (b) and (c) above, may connote, not only variations in real wages, but also variations in the workers' relative urgency of demand for leisure and for the fruits of labour. (See Chapter IX, section 2 (3).) In such cases local variations in hours of work should be permitted, as tending to maximize real satisfaction. Here again, since the ultimate object of the S.E.C. should be to equalize the standard of life of different portions of the community as quickly as possible, these variations should be smoothed out in the course of time.[1]

(3) **Changes in demand for labour.** It is clear that a socialist community, if it desires to make the best use of the resources at its disposal, must pay special attention to the economic allocation of labour to jobs. If it adopts the principle of free choice of occupation at a wage, it must, above all, avoid the temptation to retain more men in a particular job than are really needed, either by subsidizing particular trades and occupations at the expense of the whole community, or by employing more men than are needed at a wage lower than the normal rate. The latter case is specially liable to occur in the case of agriculture. In practically all capitalist countries, agricultural labour is worse paid than industrial labour. This is due, in part, to the relatively large toll taken by parasites of various kinds—landlords, moneylenders,

---

[1] For a discussion of inter-regional variations in real wages and in standards of leisure see Chapter VIII of L. Robbins's *Economic Planning and International Order*.

middlemen, &c.—but in part also to inadequate mechanical equipment and the continued use of primitive, labour-wasting methods of production. Judged by the test of marginal productivity, agriculture in all capitalist countries is not under- but over-manned. Instead of aiming at the most efficient use of human labour power and the highest output per worker (which would probably mean a diminution of the number employed), public policy usually aims at making work for the largest possible number of men on the land (especially in countries that have a large peasant population). This excessive number is maintained in agriculture at the cost of a low marginal productivity per worker occupied. If there is no subsidy to agriculture in the way of tariffs and quotas (and even if there is such a subsidy in many cases), the uneconomic surplus of men is maintained in the industry at a low level of real wages. Thus, in effect, the uneconomic employment is subsidized out of the earnings of the workers themselves. In a capitalist state this is sometimes justified by the plea that the men are better working on the land at low wages than totally unemployed. In a planned socialist community this excuse would have no validity: the men would be needed to produce other goods and services, which would be in demand after the community's needs in the way of food and agricultural products had been satisfied.

In some cases subsidies to an industry may be justified— temporary ones in the case of sudden large changes in demand and in technical methods, permanent ones in the case of a permanent discrepancy between market demand and real social utility—but subsidies whose effect is simply to keep at work in an industry an unnecessarily large number of people at a low rate of productivity per head must be ruthlessly opposed.

The most serious problems in connexion with labour arise when, owing to changes in consumers' demand or to the introduction of improved machinery and organization, the demand for a given kind of labour falls off. The immediate effect of such a happening is, partly, a fall in the economic value of labour and so of wages, and, partly, actual unemployment or short time. The number of workers originally employed could be offered work at a sufficiently reduced wage; but this is objectionable on both social and economic grounds. On social grounds, because a lowering in wages (even when wages is not the workers' sole source of income) causes discontent; on economic grounds, because it perpetuates an uneconomic allocation of labour to different occupations. The true solution is an outflow of workers from the affected trade, until the economic return of labour of the particular quality under consideration is once more equal in all occupations. This transfer will, in part, be effected automatically, through the voluntary response of workers to the change in the remuneration offered, but to a large extent the transfer must be organized systematically. The S.E.C. must decide what other occupations need labour and what openings are suitable for the particular quality of labour displaced. It must plan the transport and rehousing of the transferred workers, and, most important, it must arrange for their retraining. Every reduction in the demand for labour in one direction should be accompanied by a definite offer of work of equivalent skill and amenity in another direction. This policy implies that, as invention and improved organization makes less labour necessary to satisfy human wants, society should set itself to discover new wants to satisfy. Of course, at some time a point will be reached at which the utility of increased leisure is greater than that of increased consumption. When this point is reached, the hours of labour should be reduced, and the days of holiday increased. But this should be done uniformly throughout all industry. It is in accordance neither with economic equilibrium nor with social justice to reduce hours in one industry, simply because the demand for labour in that particular industry has fallen off, while other industries work as long hours as before.

4. Wages and Equality

It will be objected to the method of basing individual income on the value of work done that it is incompatible with the principle of equality. To this it may be answered: firstly, that a rigid and arithmetical equality is no part of the socialist programme; secondly, that even if personal income was based solely on earnings, inequality would be less than in capitalist society; thirdly, that this method of distribution might be modified by a system of taxes and allowances based on one or other of the alternative principles.

(a) The essence of socialism is the abolition of class rather than the achievement of perfect equality of income. The *origin* rather than the *amount* of income is here the decisive moment. A society in which the means of production were socially appropriated and income from ownership had disappeared would be a socialist society, even though it tolerated considerable personal inequality. It would not involve exploitation, and the inequality that it tolerated would be personal inequality and not class inequality. Nevertheless we must admit that large personal inequalities would tend to destroy the character of a socialist society by laying the foundations of a new class stratification.

In an originally class-less society, economic classes can arise out of inequalities in work-incomes, given either of two conditions: (i) purchase of the means of production; (ii) preference in the recruitment of personnel for high-paid work given to persons already doing such work (or to persons associated with them in a narrow group, such as blood-relations, former school-fellows, &c.). The first condition is excluded *ex hypothesi* in a socialist economy. (A socialist community that tolerated small-scale capital-less private enterprise, as considered in Chapter VI, would have to be specially vigilant lest capitalism re-emerge from such a matrix.) The second condition might be fulfilled in a socialist economy. Only free political institutions and vigilance on the part of the lower-paid workers will prevent new class stratifications from emerging in this way. (We may add that so long as educational opportunities are effectively open to all irrespective of their means, this danger is small. This seems a sufficient answer to those critics of the U.S.S.R. who assert that a 'new bourgeoisie' is arising in that country.) It appears, therefore, that it is desirable to achieve a large measure of personal equality of actual income, as well as of equality of opportunity. We shall see how a large measure of personal equality can be attained in practice.

(b) If obstacles to the mobility of labour were removed and if education and vocational training were really free and available to all who cared to take advantage of them, the supply of kinds of labour that are to-day scarce (skilled and professional labour) would probably increase and its economic value fall, so reducing the inequality in personal earnings. Under such a system variations in personal income would be very different to those that actually exist in a world in which inequality of parents' means, and not inherent scarcity of natural abilities, is the chief source of disparities in wages and salaries. In a socialist community it is possible that the dirty and unpleasant occupations would come to be the best paid, instead of, as at present, the worst; that a cabinet minister or a bank director might elect to serve for a few months as a dustman or a lavatory attendant in order to get enough money for a holiday trip.

Nevertheless, so long as the worker is remunerated according to the economic value of the work done, some incomes will be markedly greater than the general average.

These incomes will be composed chiefly of rent of ability.[1] However, they will be much fewer than in capitalist society. Most large earned incomes in the present system are dependent on the existence of large unearned incomes or on the competitive activities of large capitalistic concerns: e.g. the earned incomes of society portrait-painters, of fashionable physicians and surgeons, of corporation lawyers, and of advertising experts. But even in an equal-opportunity society, of the kind here outlined, where personal income was for the most part roughly equal, some individuals with a genius for appealing directly to large numbers of people— e.g. a popular writer, singer, comedian, lecturer, or artist— would earn big incomes. Since these incomes would be of the nature of a rent—that is, the return to a factor whose supply is independent of its remuneration—they could bear a heavy weight of taxation without drying up the supply of the services which they remunerated. Such people as Edgar Wallace, Gracie Fields, or Harold Lloyd would probably maintain the output of their services even if they were quite heavily taxed, provided they retained some portion of their more-than-average earning power.

(c) Even though value of service is the main principle involved in the distribution of individual income, the principles of equal division or of distribution according to need may also find a place. Thus the existence of a large number of free social services (medical, cultural, and recreational) would diminish inequalities in real income due to inequalities in money earnings. In addition to providing social services free of charge, the community may decide to distribute a portion of its income to individuals in the form of freely disposable purchasing power. Thus a certain minimum income per head (the 'vagabond wage') might be a first charge

[1] For a discussion of Rent of Ability see the present author's *Institutional Revenue*, ch. v, § 29.

upon industry. Certain payments according to need, such as children's allowances, mothers' allowances, old-age pensions, pensions to the blind and crippled, would come under this head. This element in income would not belong, strictly speaking, to the division of communal consumption, because the purchasing power would be spent individually, but the cost of it would be borne by a general levy on the income of society, like the rest of the communal division. It would come out of the Social Fund: if that was insufficient, out of a proportionate deduction from earnings. Thus each individual in a socialist community might receive part of the national income as a fixed money allowance—a real national dividend—paid to him regularly throughout his life irrespective of his efforts and deserts. Varying in amount according to the time of the recipient's life, it would be in succession a child's allowance, a subsistence grant for scholars and students, a 'vagabond wage' for adult workers (which would make any special unemployment insurance payments superfluous), and an old-age pension. It could be supplemented by special allowances in the event of invalidity, blindness, and other disabilities.

Complementary to this system of allowances would be a system of progressive taxation on large incomes. Inequality could be reduced by a steeply graduated surtax levied on all earnings over a certain amount. (This tax would go into the Social Fund.)

5. General Scheme of Distribution of Income

It is clear that, in a socialist society, the return to natural resources, interest on capital and the surcharge on uncertainty are mere accounting terms. They would be calculated as described above (Chapter III, section 3 (1)–(3)), but, instead of accruing directly to individuals as personal income, they would be paid into a general fund to be at the disposal of the community as a whole. This is what has been called the Social Fund (Chapter III, section 3 (4)): into it would also go all net surpluses of selling price above cost realized by the productive and marketing organs, the proceeds of taxation on socially undesirable lines of consumption, and the proceeds of taxation on abnormally high personal earnings.[1]

The balance of the social product, after deduction of the Social Fund, is the product of labour. It does not, however, follow that this balance is the net sum available for distribution as personal income. It is conceivable that either more or less than this sum would be so available. For the whole product of industry cannot be distributed as personal income. There are two prior charges on the aggregate social income. One is capital accumulation; the other is the cost of communal consumption. The obvious source for these is the Social Fund. If this fund is not sufficient, then a levy must be made on the product of labour. If, on the other hand, the fund is more than sufficient to supply all the needs of the community for social services and capital formation, then the balance may be distributed among the citizens as individual income.

If the Social Fund happened to be exactly equal to the sum of the amounts required for capital accumulation, communal consumption, and personal allowances, then each worker could be paid in wages (as distinct from personal allowances) the exact economic value of his labour. If this coincidence was not achieved then two cases arise: either the Social Fund falls short of the sum of the claims made upon

---

[1] If the principle of basing price on marginal cost, instead of average cost, were adopted for diminishing-cost goods (Chapter III, section 4 (2)), the (debit) balance of the Marginal Cost Equalization Fund would be a further charge upon the Social Fund.

it, or it exceeds that sum. In the first case the Social Fund must be augmented out of the product of labour. A levy must be made on earnings. This might be either proportionate to actual wages or salary or graduated progressively (it would be in addition to the special surtax on abnormally high earnings). In the second case part of the Social Fund would have to be distributed, either by increasing capital investment, by expanding the social services, or by making a cash dividend. The latter could take the form either of a proportionate bonus on wages, a graduated (progressive or regressive) bonus on wages, or a flat-rate allowance per head (a true Social Dividend).[1]

The general picture of distribution is, then, of a society in which the imputed product of land, capital and uncertainty-bearing, and a portion of that of exceptional personal gifts would be paid into the Social Fund. Subject possibly to a levy for new capital and for social services, the imputed product of labour (wages) would be paid over to the worker, under contracts of employment with the organs of collective economy, forming part of his individual income. A large measure of equality in wage-income could be attained, partly by maintaining the fullest equality of opportunity, partly by the development of social services, and partly by special taxation on high incomes.

Thus the total economic advantages enjoyed by an individual would be composed of two parts: one the use of the free goods and services (communal consumption); the other the goods and services purchased on the market (individual consumption). The money income to purchase the latter purchase might also consist of two parts: one would be earnings (less taxes and levies) for work done for the community; the other would be a payment irrespective of work done, in the form of allowances based on need or of a Social Dividend.

[1] See note on National Income, p. 238.

6. Women's Work and Wages

It is worth noting that the system of distribution of income here described (the payment of earned income or wages, involving a moderate degree of inequality, supplemented by free social services and personal allowances payable from birth) is the only one which renders possible the achievement of the feminists' ideal of equal pay for work of equal value, irrespective of sex.[1] The variability of earnings according to the value of labour will make possible the free choice of occupation: the free services and the payment of personal allowances will equalize the economic advantages of workers of either sex who have different numbers of dependants. In the absence of such services and allowances (or even in their presence, if the inequality of earned incomes is great enough) the male wage-earner with dependent children will be driven to demand higher earnings than his female colleague and to exclude women from the better-paid posts. But, under the system described above, it will be possible to open up all occupations to both sexes on equal terms and to permit the selection of workers on the basis of their personal merits without penalizing large families or unduly favouring the bachelor or the spinster. Only so will it be possible for women to make a really free choice, based on personal preferences and abilities, between the alternatives: (a) motherhood, (b) industrial or professional career, (c) the combination of both activities.

These matters of the right to work, equal pay for equal work, and the payment of adequate family allowances are those most relevant to the scope of the present book. Other matters—hours and conditions of labour, maternity leave, the administration of the social services—are not less important to the welfare of women and children, but they cannot

[1] See E. Rathbone, *The Disinherited Family*.

be discussed in detail here. The example of the U.S.S.R. shows how much in this direction can be done by a socialist community even when it is still, by occidental standards, relatively poor. It would appear that only under socialism can the feminist realize the aspiration that women should become fully human beings and enjoy full citizen rights in a community of human beings.

7. POPULATION

We have so far considered the problem of the supply of labour as one of allocating a given supply among different occupations; that is to say, the problem of the supply of labour in particular. There now remains the problem of the total quantity of labour forthcoming; that is to say, of the supply of labour in general.

Within certain limits, the effective supply of labour as a whole can vary without a change in the total population. Thus, changes in the number of hours that people are willing to work, in the holidays that they demand, in the ages at which people normally enter and retire from industry, in the relative number of women offering themselves for gainful employment, are some of the ways in which the supply of labour as a whole can be stimulated or checked. But these means are effective only within narrow limits: to effect greater variations in the aggregate supply of labour the size of the whole population will have to be varied. And the means that will have to be used to influence the numbers of the total population are quite different from those which influence the supply of labour in other ways.

Some people will object that, since every consumer is also a producer, the absolute magnitude of the population is of no importance and the only things that matter are the proportion between workers and non-workers and the allocation of workers to different occupations. According to this view there is no difference except one of scale between a socialist community of a million persons and one of a hundred million persons; the latter would be just the former multiplied one hundred times.

This point of view, however, ignores two things. One is a static and the other a dynamic consideration. (i) The static consideration is the twofold relation of population (*a*) to land and natural resources, (*b*) to produced means of production. (*a*) An increase in the number of people living in the same limited area of ground will entail a more intensive use of natural resources and a fall in their yield per unit of human effort expended on them. If this were not so, then the entire human race could be supported on the proceeds of cultivating a single acre of ground. (*b*) On the other hand, given a certain equipment of fixed plant, an increase in the number of people directly or indirectly making use of it will make it necessary to spread the costs of maintaining this equipment over a larger number of persons, and so will decrease the unit cost of maintaining a given level of output per head. This proposition is true of all the capital equipment of industry, but it is especially applicable to such social capital as roads, railways, telegraphs, and telephones, supplies of water, gas, and electricity, all of which may be termed the overhead costs of civilized existence. Between these two tendencies—which are our old friends Diminishing Returns and Increasing Returns—there must be at some point or other a balance. That is to say, for a country of given size and natural resources, for a given accumulation of instrumental goods, and for a given level of scientific and technological knowledge, there must be a population of a determinate magnitude such that the output per head obtainable with the most suitable use of labour and other means of production is greater than for a population of any other magnitude. For a larger population the law of diminishing returns to land and natural resources would indicate a lessened product per head: for a smaller population the greater burden of social overhead would diminish product per head. The population for which output per head is a maximum may be termed the optimum population. With changes in the quantity of accumulated resources and in scientific knowledge and industrial technique, the maximum *per capita* product and with it the optimum population will change. As accumulation increases and knowledge advances, the maximum product will increase. But it is not certain in what direction the optimum population will move. It may be that, to take full advantage of technical improvement and the increase of material equipment, population should decline a little, or it may be that population should advance a little. Generally, however, we may expect the optimum population to rise with economic progress.

(ii) The dynamic consideration is the fact that, the more rapid the rate of population growth, the greater is the annual provision that must be made out of current resources for the annual increment of new citizens. Means of production must be created for their useful employment, houses and schools must be built, means of transport and other public services must be developed, *within a given period of time*. Thus, a population of such a size as, considered in its static relation to natural resources and other means of production, would be compatible with quite a high standard of life might not be so compatible if it were growing rapidly.

A society organized economically on rational lines should aim at control of the quantity of the population so as to achieve the maximum product per head, that is to say, to aim at the optimum population. The size of the population depends ultimately on two factors: natality and mortality.[1]

---

[1] Measured not by the *crude* birth-rate and death-rate respectively, but by the *corrected* birth-rate and death-rate (corrected for variations in the sex and age composition of the population).

Since it may be assumed that the lowest possible mortality would be aimed at by a society that attempted to guarantee the highest possible standard of life to its members, it follows that natality is the only factor that can be varied in order to regulate the size of the population. In other words, control of population is, in the last analysis, control of the birth-rate.

In the matter of population a socialist commonwealth cannot, in principle, follow a policy of *laisser-faire*. If society guarantees every individual born into its fold not only subsistence but a substantially equal share in the social product, then society cannot be indifferent to the number and quality of the individuals that come to claim its bounty. Thus we are faced with a twofold problem, quantitative and qualitative.

(*a*) To take the quantitative problem first, there are two opposite dangers to which a socialist society might be liable. One is a high birth-rate, leading to over-population (in relation to the optimum); the other is a low birth-rate leading to under-population and, finally, to extinction. Since the days of Malthus, one of the stock objections to schemes of communistic reorganization of society has been that, once a livelihood is guaranteed to every member of the community from birth, irrespective of his or her parents' abilities and resources, the only incentive to a prudent restraint in the matter of procreation is removed, and the community will increase in numbers by reckless breeding. The relation of workers to natural resources will become progressively less favourable to production, so that the standard of life of the community, however high it may originally have been, will fall steadily until it reaches the point of bare subsistence, where a rising death-rate will arrest the increase in numbers. No improvements in the technical arts of production, although they may delay the onset of the evil hour, will avail in the long run to avert the consequences of over-population.

The means of checking an undesirably high rate of multiplication are twofold, partly in awakening in the people tastes
for comforts and amenities which will compete with the
pleasures of philoprogenitiveness, partly in enforcing strict
individual responsibility of parents for the upkeep of their
children. Under the first heading it may be noted that the
development of extra-domestic pursuits and entertainments
and, in particular, the participation by women on equal
terms with men in intellectual, political, and sporting interests,
all tend to weaken the desire for numerous offspring, since
even if the community assumes the whole material burden
of their support, the burden of responsibility and of being
tied to the nursery still remains on the parents, especially on
the mother. If, in spite of counter-attractions, the flood of
babies still tends to submerge the community's accepted
standard of comfort, more drastic methods must be adopted.
H. G. Wells, writing at a time when men did not yet think
that the Malthusian devil had been safely chained up, suggested that a community which accepted responsibility for
the education and for part of the maintenance of every child
born into the world would have to impose upon the pros-
pective parents definite conditions of health, good conduct,
intelligence, and economic efficiency. The latter condition
may be interpreted as ability to earn an income of a prescribed amount above the minimum. Individuals who, not
fulfilling these conditions, nevertheless became parents would
be subject by law to some form of deterrent treatment and
forced to contribute out of their income as much as they
could of the cost of maintaining their offspring.[1]
The bulk of the world's population still lives under conditions that conform to Malthus's thesis. Before these
peoples can be incorporated into a socialist society their way
of life must be changed. In some cases, education and the

[1] H. G. Wells, *Anticipations; A Modern Utopia*, p. 182.

opportunity of a higher standard of life would effect this. In other cases, however, powerful social forces, especially religion, are opposed to a rational control of population. The religious beliefs of Hindus and Chinese and, perhaps to a less extent, of Roman Catholics and Jews, are incompatible with the existence of a socialist society such as is here described.

But recent social trends suggest that the danger besetting a socialist community would be not over-population but under-population. Modern communities of the occidental type are all rapidly approaching or have already reached a level of fertility which is insufficient, even with the lowest possible death-rate, to prevent the population from actually declining. The net reproduction rate, defined as the number of female children born to a thousand females in the course of their child-bearing lives, is falling or has fallen below 1,000.[1] This is a fact: as to its explanation, opinions differ. It may be the insecurity and pessimism engendered by capitalism in its decline—the unwillingness of people to bring children into a world threatened by unemployment, fascism, and war. It may be the competitive struggle for wealth and social position and the continuous emulation by every social group of the standards of living of the group just above it in the income-scale, in which the possession of children is a handicap. Or it may be that the rise in the material standard of living has led to the development of ways of life in which children have no place, of interests, occupations, and amusements that are incompatible with the care and attention that young children continually need—in particular the entry of women into spheres previously monopolized by men or the determination of married women not to lose the social contacts of the unmarried, and the extension to the middle and working classes of leisure and leisure-time interests without

[1] See R. R. Kuczynski, *The Balance of Births and Deaths*, and Enid Charles, *The Twilight of Parenthood*

the menial service that enabled the aristocracy to combine these with child-rearing. In the first two cases we may say that the decline in the population is due to capitalism—in fact, it may be that the most fundamental objection to capitalism is not economic but biological, that it is a system under which society can no longer reproduce itself.[1] But if the last explanation is the true one it augurs ill for a socialist community since no sooner would it have achieved the prosperity, freedom, and equality (social and sexual) that socialists desire than it would tend to die out. Between these rival views it is difficult to decide. The rapid population growth of the Soviet Union might suggest that capitalism is the culprit, and that the security and optimism of a socialist society would stimulate healthy biological growth. But it must be remembered that the Soviet Union is still a country with a low standard of living (although rapidly rising) and that peasant ways of life still survive in the majority of families. And even in the Soviet Union the birth-rate is beginning to decline.

In any case what measures could a socialist community take to revive a flagging birth-rate? The most obvious measure is to create institutions which will make leisure and amusement, freedom, and equality for women, compatible with child-rearing. The provision of crèches and nursery schools, reduction of domestic drudgery by machinery and by communal effort, the organization of means whereby young children could be looked after while their parents went together to the theatre or to the evening-class—all these would help. Above all, suitable housing must be made available for families with children—houses at ground level with

[1] This is true only of capitalism in its late period of degeneration and decline. In its middle period of rapid technological expansion (exemplified in Great Britain between 1750 and 1870) it was responsible for a historically unprecedented growth of population.

no dangerous balconies and stairs, with plenty of floor-space and separate sleeping-rooms, with playrooms and play-grounds, situated in the country with access to fields and woods. If, in spite of these measures, people still refuse to reproduce, more positive measures must be taken. Economic advantages (as by money allowances, subsidized housing, subsidized holiday facilities, supplies of certain goods free or at reduced prices) must be given to parents in proportion to the number of their children; and the unmarried and the childless must be economically penalized (as by extra taxa-tion, discriminating rents, or exclusion from the most desi-rable housing sites and holiday resorts). (The one type of economic discrimination that should *not* be used is the giving of preference in employment to parents; this should be avoided as interfering with the choice of the most suitable personnel and thus tending to lower the efficiency of pro-duction.) The general principle involved might be described as that of greater eligibility—to make the social and economic position of the parent more eligible than that of the non-parent and to make the position of the parent of several chil-dren more eligible than that of the parent of few children. It should be remarked that, in a community enjoying a high standard of life, the application of this principle would probably involve a far greater measure of redistribution of income in favour of parents than any scheme of family allow-ances hitherto contemplated.

Above all, a socialist society must endeavour to make motherhood a career which an intelligent and educated woman might gladly choose. Motherhood must be made compatible with the social equality of the sexes and the eco-nomic emancipation of women. To achieve this at least two things are necessary. One is that the social and economic status of the woman who chooses motherhood must be at least as good as that of the woman who chooses paid work outside the home. The other is that the economic position of the home-keeping mother should be secured to her independently of her husband's economic success or failure and that she should cease to be personally dependent on him for her and her children's livelihood. Both of these things will be far easier to realize in a society which does not tolerate great inequalities of personal income and which has entirely abolished functionless income derived from property. All this means that motherhood must be made a professional career and that a woman who raises efficiently a family of children must be paid for her services by the community.

(b) The qualitative aspect of the population problem is much more knotty. In the present stage of social biology our knowledge of the innate qualities of different human stocks is so scanty and uncertain that there is little scope for any measures of discrimination between potential parents. A few definite defects are known to be hereditary, and persons who are genetic carriers of these defects should be encouraged to refrain from parenthood. If necessary they must be segregated or sterilized. If their unsuitability for parenthood is biological, not social (e.g. if they are persons whose children are liable to inherit some physical disability, but if they are good citizens and able to make a good home for children), they should be allowed to adopt children, if they so desire. But beyond such measures of negative eugenics there is little that can be done in the present state of our scientific knowledge. Until one or two generations have grown up in good physical and social surroundings, with equal opportunities of good food, shelter, and education for all, it is impossible to distinguish between the effects of environment and those of heredity.[1]

1 See L. Hogben, *Genetic Principles in Medical and Social Science*, chaps. iv, vi, and viii; *Nature and Nurture*, ch. v; also J. B. S. Haldane, *Heredity and Politics*, ch. i.

On the other hand, there are some people about whose biological fitness we can make no certain statement, but who are socially unfit for parenthood. Such are those who, by reason of criminality, mental defect, or physical incapacity, cannot create an environment in which children can live a healthy and happy life. The children of such people would have to be maintained as wards of society, apart from their parents,[1] but receiving the same advantages of environment and education as, say, orphaned children of normal parents. The question arises, should such people be permitted to produce as many children as they like and leave them to be brought up by the community free of charge to themselves? Most people, particularly the socially fit parents, would probably answer, No. It must be noticed that the point at issue is not the multiplication of the unfit, in the eugenic sense, but simply the responsibility for the support of children.

It appears that, if parenthood is to be subsidized, the subsidy should be selective. It should be restricted to those who in the course of their life as citizens make some contribution towards the cost of the social services which they and their offspring enjoy. The economic encouragement accorded to parents should be confined to those who rise above a certain minimum standard of physical health, mental capacity, economic efficiency, and absence of judicially proved criminality. It might be necessary to restrict by law the right of parenthood to such persons as satisfied these minimum conditions, and to deter the illegal production of children in some way that would penalize the parent but not the children. Children brought into the world in contravention of these regulations would have to be maintained as wards of society, while the parents would be liable to some form of forced labour as a

[1] This does not necessarily mean that their parents should never see them. It does mean that they should not permanently reside in their parents' home.

partial contribution towards the cost of maintaining their offspring.

The question of migration is closely linked to that of population. In principle, every citizen of a socialist commonwealth should be guaranteed free choice of domicile just as he should be guaranteed free choice of occupation. This principle has been admitted implicitly, in the section dealing with regional variations in the efficiency of labour. One real obstacle exists, however, in the way of the full application of this principle. If the level of efficiency in a given region is low, due to over-population, and if the inhabitants of that region have procreative habits that tend to create and to intensify over-population, then freedom of migration will simply enable them to export their habits and their poverty into regions inhabited by other cultural groups. Two methods of dealing with this problem offer themselves. One is to draw a sort of *cordon sanitaire* round the region in question and, suspending for the nonce the right of migration, to leave the inhabitants to pullulate in their own squalor until they learn sense. The other is to initiate a vigorous educational campaign (even at the cost of restricting the liberty of obscurantist ecclesiastics) against the social forces that lead to increase of population beyond the point of maximum productivity per head.

CHAPTER V

PRICE POLICY OF PUBLIC UTILITIES

1. Public Utilities in General

A PARTICULAR case of importance in the theory of pricing is afforded by undertakings of the kind usually known as public utilities, exemplified by railways, electricity-works, gas-works, postal services, telephones, &c., which are characterized by three peculiarities. (*a*) One is a very high proportion of fixed costs to prime costs (many of them can scarcely be said to have any prime costs at all). (*b*) The second is that maximum economy of operation is obtained only with a very large output. (*c*) The third is that the products of these industries are services rendered directly to the consumer and incapable therefore of being transferred by re-sale to another consumer.

The first peculiarity means that the price of particular services is almost entirely independent of cost and that, consequently, a wide discretion in the matter of charges is possible to the operating authority. Thus, competition, instead of establishing stable prices, results in a high degree of instability. The second peculiarity means that undertakings of this type tend towards monopoly. The third means that the operator of these enterprises, if he obtains monopoly power, can charge discriminating prices.[1] Thus, these enterprises are, even under capitalism, usually subject to some form of public control, especially with regard to their charges and profits. If they remain competitive, their charges are regulated by public authority, in order to secure some kind of stability. If they become monopolistic, their charges are regulated by public authority, in order to protect consumers

---

[1] See Pigou, *Economics of Welfare*, part ii, ch. xvii.

from extortion. Thus, in either case, they tend towards public control of price policy. (This often takes the form of public ownership, which of course includes control of price policy.) The system of prices resulting from public control may be, and generally is, discriminating. Thus, different prices are charged for the same service (transport of a ton of cotton and of a ton of coffee over the same distance, use of 1 kw.-hour of electricity for lighting and of 1 kw.-hour for heating); and the same price for different services (penny post irrespective of distance).

It may be added that even public control does not prevent competition, in the indirect form of competition between alternative services (railway and road transport, gas and electricity). If there are discriminating charges in one or both of the competing services, competition is particularly anarchic and unstable.

The problem before a socialist administration is, then, on what basis it is to fix its charges. This involves the further questions whether price discrimination is to be retained or not, and how competition between alternative services is to be dealt with.

The alternative price policies are (1) charges based on cost of service, (2) charges based on value of service. In case (1) the charge will be uniform for services of a similar kind; in case (2) it will tend to be discriminating.

The cost-of-service principle raises the further issue of average versus marginal cost, already discussed in Chapter III, section 4 (2). It also raises the problem of averaging in a different form. No two ton-miles of transport are provided, no two kw.-hours of electricity generated under precisely similar conditions; hence their cost of production is never exactly the same. But in practice it is impossible to make a separate charge for each individual unit of output; services must be classified into categories, and a uniform charge made for each category. Therefore a rate system based on cost, whether average or marginal, will have to average cost over a whole category of services evolved under similar, but not identical, conditions. We shall call these mean costs to distinguish them from average, as opposed to marginal, costs.

Professor Pigou[1] concludes that the output proper to simple competition (which he assumes to involve prices based on average cost) is likely to be nearer the ideal output (from the social point of view) than that proper to discriminating monopoly. He admits, however, of some possible exceptions, which he considers unlikely to occur in reality, where discrimination would produce *some* output and simple competition none at all. Mrs. Robinson[2] desires to extend the scope of Professor Pigou's exceptional categories. She also suggests that, if the monopolist is limited to a fixed rate of return on his capital, discrimination may enable the weaker consumer to be subsidized out of the surplus exacted from the stronger consumer, so increasing output above that proper to single competition.

This argument is plausible, and if a socialist community desired to develop public utilities by means of discriminating charges, this is the principle on which it should do so. But, in the writer's opinion, the argument is fallacious and the practice based on it should be rejected. Although at first sight this increased output seems to be a gain that no one loses, yet an uneconomic diversion of resources may occur. If the service is developed in this way, a need for increased capital equipment will come about earlier than it otherwise would. Thus resources will be diverted from industries in which it is impossible to make discriminating charges.

Another way in which the imposition of discriminating charges might be justified is the following. Assume the

---

[1] *Economics of Welfare*, part ii, ch. xvii.
[2] *Economics of Imperfect Competition*, ch. xvi.

undertaking to be yielding the maximum service under a system of prices based on average cost (output proper to simple competition). Suppose then that some increase of output can be effected by charging some consumers a price less than average cost, and that the net additional return at this price just covers the net additional cost of the extra service. Then, it may be argued, the favoured consumers obtain an advantage that causes nobody any loss. There is no subsidy, since non-favoured consumers pay no more than they would have done had the discrimination not been made. The additional service is provided, not at any one's expense, but out of the more intensive utilization of plant. It is thus a net social gain. This argument, however, really justifies, not discrimination, but a system of non-discriminating charges based on marginal cost.

It should be remembered that a sound system of social costing should render possible a threefold equilibrium: (1) within the enterprise, a balance of receipts and costs in each line of production where separate costs are ascertainable; (2) between different ways of rendering similar services (say gas and electricity, rail and road transport) a balance between the economic use of each kind of service; (3) in the economic system as a whole a balance between the relative worthwhileness of different ways of utilizing the community's resources. In the case of transport, for example, this last point means that a balance must be struck between the advantages of increased transport facilities and a more widespread distribution of factories. Neither transport nor the generation of electric power are ends in themselves, and it may well be that a policy that increases the use of transport facilities or the consumption of electrical energy is simply multiplying unnecessary journeys and hindering the most economic location of producing plants. A system of transport, electricity, gas, and water charges based on mean cost of service would afford a reliable indication to the planners of socialist industry of the most economic size and location for the manufacturing unit in different industries.

Wherever competition is possible between alternative services, as in the cases of gas and electricity, rail transport and road transport, where each alternative has a definite range of undoubted superiority, but where there is a wide overlap of competitive uses, equilibrium can only be maintained by a rigorous method of cost-accounting. Each service should be charged with its own proper costs, all its own proper costs, and nothing but its own proper costs. The concealed taxes and subsidies that so often exist under capitalism must be abolished. Then the choice between the alternatives can be made on their merits.

It would thus appear that the proper basis of charging for a public utility in a socialistic economy is cost; and where, as generally happens with public utilities, the cost of a particular unit of service cannot be separately ascertained, the proper basis is the mean cost of a category of services that are similar from the point of view of supply. That is to say, in power production one kw.-hour of energy is similar to any other kw.-hour of energy if generated at the same time and by the same plant: differentiation of charge on the basis of use (e.g. for lighting or for heating, for private houses or for shops) is not justifiable; but differentiation on the basis of load factor is. In transport one ton-mile is the same as another ton-mile carried over the same line or road in the same type of vehicle: differentiation of charge is not justifiable on the basis of the kind of good carried (between iron ore and copper ore, between wheat and oats, between kitchen tables and grand pianos); but differentiation is justifiable on the basis of ease of loading, or between full wagon-loads and half-filled wagons, or between ton-miles carried on a line of dense traffic and on one of sparse traffic.

Thus we conclude that in the case of electrical energy the two-part tariff is to be recommended. This consists of an annual (quarterly or monthly) charge based on maximum demand plus a charge per unit of energy consumed, the two rates of charges being adjusted in such a relation to each other that, as far as possible, the sum of the receipts under the first head will cover the capital costs of the power installation, and that under the second head will cover the operating costs. Differential charges are also to be recommended if they are likely to lead to an improvement in the load-factor, i.e. to a more uniform distribution of demand throughout time: on this account some charges that apparently discriminate between different uses of current may be justified—e.g. domestic users of current may be charged less for cooking and heating than for light because their demand for the former comes at a time when their demand for the latter is low, and so evens out the total demand. As between localities, charges will tend to vary according to the size and efficiency of the local generating plant; but, with the full development of a national electric grid, it should be possible to establish a uniform rate (at least, a uniform unit-charge) throughout the entire country.

The subject of transport rates will be dealt with in more detail later, but one or two points emerge directly from the preceding discussion. One is that the rate system that should be adopted is much more like the present system of road rates, systematized and uniformized, than like the present system of railway rates. There is no economic justification for the present complication of class rates and exceptional rates on the railway. The principle of 'charging what the traffic will bear' or even of 'not charging what the traffic will not bear' is fundamentally wrong. If the traffic will not bear the charge, it should not exist. If it must exist, it must bear the charge. Uniform ton-mile rates over a given route should be established, except where differences in rates are justified by differences in cost.

Uniform rates over different routes and in different parts of the transport system are a different matter: on the cost principle every part of a transport system should be a separate accounting unit and should have its charges based on its own costs. Uniformity over an extended system, where traffic conditions vary greatly in different parts, means that one part of the system subsidizes another part. This would be a serious consideration in an area like the U.S.S.R., the North American continent, or the Australian continent; in an area like Britain, where traffic conditions are relatively uniform, this would matter less. Within the area of a single West European country a uniform system of mileage rates might be established, ignoring the differences between one line and another, for the sake of simplicity.

Apart from local variations in rates, the cases where differentiation is justifiable are as follows: (a) between different technical forms of transport, as between rail, road, and canal, each of which has its own schedule of costs; (b) between goods involving different degrees of care or auxiliary services such as covering with tarpaulins or the use of special wagons (e.g. bananas, fish, milk); (c) between full train-loads or wagon-loads and less-than-car-load consignments.

Attention should also be drawn to the possibility of applying to transport the principle of the two-part tariff. An enterprise that makes use of the socialized transport service might be charged an annual charge based on its maximum loadings in any one week plus a ton-mile rate for each consignment. The charges would be designed so as to make the standing charges cover the capital costs of the transport system (road, rail, and water transport would have to be accounted for separately) and the unit rate cover the operating costs. This would be a much more logical and economic system than the 'agreed charges', recently introduced on the British railways, which, by making transport charges vary only with the tonnage (or value) of traffic and not at all with distance, tend to make impossible any rational localization of industry. The two-part system would be difficult to work under capitalism, but it could be introduced into a socialist economy. It is more appropriate for goods than for passenger transport.[1]

A strong case can be made out on social grounds for a greater measure of 'tapering' in transport charges than would be justified on private-economic grounds. Wherever large aggregates of population come into existence they exert a powerful attractive force upon industry, since, other things being equal, it is most convenient to locate an enterprise near the market for its products. (The growth in the importance and variety of consumption goods as compared with capital goods, and the increase in the relative importance of home production over foreign trade may be expected to reinforce this tendency.) But the establishment of new enterprises in a particular region involves a local increase of population, both direct (workers in the new enterprise) and indirect (people satisfying their needs). These people now constitute a market for goods and attract new enterprises into a region. Thus a cumulative process is set up which, in a region that is relatively independent of external sources of supply, may lead to an overwhelming concentration of the population into one or a few areas where (possibly for fortuitous or transient reasons) a tendency to concentration had first shown itself. Now this tendency is undesirable both for social and for purely economic reasons. Economically, urban concentration involves costs in the form of traffic congestion, new road-building, housing, providing local services, &c., which are

---

[1] See M. Farrer, *How to Make the British Railways Pay*, for an exposition of a scheme on these lines for both passenger and goods transport, proposed for immediate adoption under capitalism.

not ordinarily taken into account in fixing transport charges nor in the original calculations of cost that led to the setting up of the enterprise (a case of divergence between net private and net social marginal product). Socially, costs that are hard to estimate in definite figures but are none the less real are incurred in the form of loss of amenity.

One remedy for this state of affairs is, of course, control exercised over the establishment of new enterprises in urbanized areas. But a strict all-or-nothing rule is uneconomic. *Some* enterprises should be established in a congested area, even though fewer than would be established on the basis of a purely business calculation of costs. To deal with every proposal 'on its merits' would soon result in hopeless inconsistency and confusion. To avoid both the clumsy rigidity of an all-or-nothing rule and the random results of deciding every question on its merits, some general method of calculating the advantages and disadvantages of industrial locations must be devised that will automatically exercise a deconcentrating influence. One method would be a system of local taxes on industrial sites that rose steeply with the density of industrial enterprises in the locality. Another method would be a system of strongly tapering transport rates, enabling enterprises at a distance from their markets to compete successfully with those nearer to their markets if they had even a slight advantage on grounds other than transport costs. This principle might be extended, in the form of a general subsidy given out of social revenue to transport as a whole, but at a higher rate to longer hauls (negatively tapered subsidy).

2. SOCIALIST TRANSPORT

We may conclude this chapter with a sketch of the working of the transport system in a socialist community, as an example of the principles discussed above.

We must first distinguish between land transport, air transport, and sea transport. (Coastal traffic competitive with land transport and sea transport over short lengths of sea, as between England and Ireland or between the North and South Islands of New Zealand, are reckoned as land transport.)

(1) All land transport would be in the hands of a single operating organization, the Land Transport Corporation, which would sell *transport*, not rail transport or road transport or transport by coastal vessel. In it would be vested all railways, canals, road vehicles, and coastal vessels. It could be divided into separate sections for different types of transport and into geographical areas and divisions, but as an enterprise it would be a single unit. We may think of it as a unified railway enterprise (like the German Reichsbahn) operating road, canal, and coastal services as an integral part of its undertaking (as the British railways are beginning to do). We will discuss first goods and then passenger transport.

A. In the case of goods transport the Land Transport Corporation would be in a position to offer a completely co-ordinated, door-to-door service. It would be a common carrier for private individuals. It would probably take over all transport outside the factory-gates for the organs of collective economy. It would contract with the consignor (whether a private individual or an organ of collective economy) to transport for a stipulated charge, fixed and known in advance, a given load between two given places (within certain definite limits of time) and then please itself whether it used rail, road, canal, or coastal-vessel transport. In this way the operating Corporation itself would have to settle internally all questions of competition between alternative forms of transport. If the consignor wished to send freight by a special form of transport (e.g. if he wished specially to designate road transport) he should be free to do so (in some cases on payment of a special surcharge).

The rates charged would be based on two principles: (1) cost, (2) simplicity. Since in general the specific costs of a particular consignment cannot be ascertained, charging according to cost implies charging according to mean cost. For goods this means a uniform ton-mile rate for all commodities and for passengers a uniform mileage rate. But, wherever possible, special costs should be ascertained and allowed for. Thus in the case of goods, terminal costs can be partly separated from forwarding costs and should be separately charged for. Long hauls promote fuller utilization of rolling-stock than short ones, thus justifying a fall in the ton-mile rate as the distance increases (tapering rates). Again, small consignments mean more handling, and use of rolling-stock below capacity. This justifies different rates of charge according to the size of the consignment: say a less-than-truckload rate, a less-than-trainload rate, and a full-trainload rate. Finally, some commodities require special care in transport and involve special risks that others do not. A higher rate per ton-mile is justified in this case. Thus commodities such as fruit, fish, furniture, milk, delicate machinery, or explosives, with special requirements in the way of speed, covering, care, or special type of vehicle, would be subject to higher rates, while commodities such as coal, iron ore, wheat (in grain-producing countries), which can be transported in bulk with little in the way of special care and covering, would receive special low rates. By dividing a railway into divisions and keeping cost accounts for each, as if it were an independent undertaking, the mean cost in each division (even in each branch-line) can be ascertained: the same principle can be followed with road transport and canal transport. Here, however, the principle of simplicity enters. Although it would be possible to vary the basic rates of charge for every division and branch of railway or canal, and for every road-transport area, it would probably be inadvisable to do so, although it would be desirable nevertheless to keep accurate cost accounts.

Thus our system of charges for the carriage of goods resolves itself into one based on a uniform rate per ton consisting of a terminal charge and a mileage charge (tapering), with three main classes, according to size of consignment, together with a few special classes for particular commodities. These special rates would be applicable all over the system and would, like the general rates, consist of a terminal charge and a tapering mileage charge. The classification would be based not on the *value* of the commodity carried but on the *cost* of transport. A rate system on these lines, unlike the present one of charging 'what the traffic will bear', would reflect the real social costs of transport, and could thus serve as a reliable index to the relative advantages of different locations for industry. The transport undertaking would become an arbiter, but not a dictator, of economic development.

The container system could be considerably developed under a common administration for rail, road, canal, and coastal-shipping transport. Its working would be simplified by the adoption of a uniform tariff for all commodities sent in containers, irrespective of the normal classification.

B. Passenger transport is a simpler proposition than goods transport. A co-ordinated system of rail and road passenger transport should be set up. The same fares should apply to both rail and road transport; and, where both forms of transport serve the same route, all tickets should be available indifferently for either form. The present process of closing down less important railway lines and stations, concentrating traffic (especially local traffic) on the roads, might probably continue; but proper co-ordination should avoid the loss to the public of such facilities as proper waiting-room and lavatory accommodation at wayside stations, transfer from main-line to local transport under cover and without a long distance to walk, and complete time-table information regarding local as well as main-line services.

With regard to the tariff of passenger fares, the best principle for charging is a uniform rate per mile, based on mean costs. There is a less strong case for tapering rates in the case of passenger traffic than in that of goods traffic, but a moderate taper in the mileage charge would be justified. The whole of the present jumble of excursion, week-end, and other special rates would disappear; but season tickets at reduced rates would be continued, since the season-ticket passenger gives a guaranteed steady volume of traffic and ensures a good load-factor. There seems no adequate reason for a division of passenger accommodation into classes, since special accommodation involves extra weight hauled per passenger and more work in marshalling and assembling trains. Already, in Great Britain, only 6·2 per cent. of passenger journeys are made in the first and second classes (only 1·7 per cent., excluding season-ticket holders). The continental system (now being introduced into Britain) of charging higher fares for fast trains is justifiable on the basis of cost, but is complicated and vexatious. Both British and American experience suggest, by comparison with continental practice, that discrimination of this type not only irritates passengers but delays progress by making transport administrations tolerant of low speeds by ordinary trains. Fares should be fixed on a uniform basis, as low as possible, and all passengers admitted to the fastest means of conveyance.

The roads would be built and maintained either by the same Transport Corporation or by a special Road Board. In view of the facts (a) that roads are used by other vehicles than those of the Transport Corporation, and (b) that complex problems of local use and local finance emerge, the latter method may be preferable. In any case it will be necessary for accurate costing, in order that the Transport Corporation may keep an exact balance between road and other forms of transport, to calculate the cost of road construction and maintenance and to allot it to different types of vehicle on the basis of their number, average speed, and gross laden weight. Vehicles in private ownership or owned by public bodies other than the Transport Corporation would be subject to taxation on the same level as the costs allotted to vehicles used by the latter body. This taxation might be on any of three bases: (1) an annual licence duty per vehicle, graduated according to its weight and normal working speed; (2) a tax on fuel consumption; (3) a mileage tax, graduated according to the vehicle's weight and normal speed. This last kind of tax would give rise to administrative difficulties in a capitalist order of society, but would be applicable to all publicly owned vehicles in a socialist community. For privately owned vehicles, two possibilities exist. One is a mileage tax, based on an officially sealed mileage-counter; the other is an extra licence duty, or an extra tax on fuel sold to private persons, in lieu of the mileage tax.

Canals give rise to no problem that has not been treated, in principle, under the heading of rail-and-road transport. Contrary to popular prejudices on the subject, canals have few advantages that would justify an extensive development of this form of transport. Although the cost per ton-mile of pure transport is lower by water than by either road or rail, this is in most cases offset by other factors. One of these is the slowness of canal transport, even on the level: where locks or lifts are necessary, this defect is even more marked. Another is the fact that the canal network is not and cannot be as ubiquitous as the rail or the road network: many places cannot, for geographical reasons, be served by canal except at great capital cost, and in many cases the route between two places that are served by canal is exceedingly circuitous. Hence canal transport will often involve transhipment, with all its attendant costs. In special cases, as the transport of coal in special containers on the Aire and Calder Navigation, canals have their secure place in the transport system. For the carriage in bulk of goods, where speed is not essential, over a fixed route or a few fixed routes (e.g. between a number of collieries and a coaling port) this form of transport will continue in use.

Much the same can be said about coastal shipping as about canals. Here, too, is a limited but definite field of usefulness, restricted mostly to the carriage of goods in mass over definite routes.

The socialist administration of docks and harbours should not occasion any special difficulties.

(2) Air transport, because of its much higher range of costs, should for the present be organized as a separate service under a separate operating body, the Air Transport Corporation. The sphere of air transport to-day is mainly threefold: (a) provision of transport for isolated communities where the capital cost of road or rail communication would not be justified by the returns (e.g. in Northern Canada, Central Australia, New Guinea, and the Asiatic part of the U.S.S.R.); (b) emergencies; (c) luxury travel. In all these cases, air transport is not seriously competitive with land transport; nor will it be in the future, unless its cost is very considerably reduced. If it does become competitive with land transport, it will have to be operated by the same organization as operates land transport.

(3) Sea transport, in the special sense of the word used here, includes ocean transport and transport in smaller seas between distinct land masses, but excludes coastal and local river traffic, and such transport as that between Great Britain, the Isle of Man, and Ireland, and that between the North and South Islands of New Zealand, which is simply a link between two closely co-ordinated systems of land transport. Border-

line cases of course will arise, such as the case of cross-channel communication between Britain and the European continent, which is here provisionally reckoned as sea transport. Difficult problems also arise when what is undoubtedly sea transport partakes also of the character of coastal trade, such as traffic between the Atlantic and Pacific seaboards of North America, via the Panama Canal, or such as traffic between Australia and the rest of the world, which usually touches at a number of Australian ports.

The problems of sea transport, in the special sense, are sufficiently different from those of land transport to warrant a distinct organization. Here discrimination between different kinds of goods is less important than the variation in the general level of rates in accordance with the fluctuations of supply and demand in the market. The administration of the mercantile marine of a socialist country that entered into trade relations with the capitalist world would have to be prepared to face competitive rate-cutting on the part of capitalist steam-ship companies. It would probably be best to concentrate in the hands of one administration *all* overseas transport, whether it was shipped in socialist or capitalist bottoms. This administration would maintain a fairly stable schedule of rates, based on mean costs, applicable to all consignors, whether private or public, within the socialist country, and then ship the forthcoming traffic either in its own vessels or in capitalist vessels chartered at current market prices, whichever seemed best to it.[1]

[1] For a discussion of socialist transport see chapter ii of *Britain Without Capitalists*.

CHAPTER VI

PRIVATE ENTERPRISE WITHIN THE SOCIALIST COMMUNITY

1. The Private Sector in General

WE have hitherto assumed that all production is in the hands of economic organs of the community and that all income is either earned by working for these organs or distributed as a Social Dividend. We must now see whether it would be possible to relax this collectivistic rigidity so far as to allow of private persons' engaging in production or rendering services to other private persons; or, to use the Soviet phraseology, whether it would be possible to tolerate a private sector of industry side by side with the socialized sector, with which we have been solely concerned up to this point.[1]

Here two apparently conflicting considerations present themselves. On the one hand, from the point of view of production, there are a number of branches of personal service and petty production that do not lend themselves well to collectivistic provision. Also, there are activities of a highly individualized nature, such as the production of works of art and the printing of political and religious literature. In many cases they might be organized on the principle of producers' co-operation (cf. the Russian 'artel'), but in others they would be best suited by the one-man business or by the small firm with a few employees. If what is chiefly desired is economic efficiency, such businesses should be allowed to extend where they can produce a better or cheaper product than the socialized sector can, and, in order to achieve eco-

[1] Note the distinction between the *divisions* of communal and individual consumption and the *sectors* of socialized and private production.

nomic equilibrium, they should be placed, as far as possible, on the same basis as socialized industry in the matter of costs. This would only be possible if prices in the socialized sector were based on average costs. On the other hand, from the point of view of distribution it is desirable to prevent the private appropriation of rent, interest, and profit. Any extensive toleration of private enterprise, especially with the use of large-scale capital, would tend towards the enhancement of economic inequality and the re-establishment of a class society. Less objection would attach to enterprises analogous to personal service, involving little capital, such as restaurants, tea-shops, garages, and petrol filling-stations; the making of pickles, jam, and cakes for sale; bespoke shoe-making, tailoring, and dressmaking, &c. Let us, therefore, consider the conditions on which a socialist community could tolerate a private sector of industry, at least in such small-scale branches of production as are mentioned above, without endangering the fundamentally socialist basis of society.

Since all land and natural resources would belong to the community, it would be possible to charge the private employer a full economic rent for his premises. His capital would be obtained partly from the Central Bank and partly from private sources. The Bank would charge on loans the normal rate of interest in the socialized sector, and the private trader would be required to pay on the rest of his capital a tax equivalent to the normal rate of interest. The result of this would be the social appropriation of income derived from land and capital, leaving the owner of a private business with only the surplus that might fairly be considered to be derived from his own exertions and organizing ability. Furthermore, he would pay on this residue of his income whatever tax was payable on abnormally high individual earnings.

If the worker in the socialized sector was paid in the form of wages the full economic value of his labour, no more and no less, there would be no objection to private employers' competing with the public for the services of workers. All trade-union regulations and all laws designed for the workers' protection would, of course, apply with equal force to the private and to the public sector. Their enforcement would probably need greater vigilance in the private sector.

A difficulty would arise in the case where, owing to a general levy on wages, the worker in the socialized sector received less in wages than the economic value of his labour. To put the employee in the private sector upon the same footing as the worker in socialized employment, a tax would have to be levied on private employment (its ultimate incidence would be the same whether it was laid upon the employer or the employee). The private employee would participate, like every citizen, in free social services and in social dividend. (It would not be desirable to allow him to contract out of these in return for exemption from the private-employment tax.) The same treatment would apply to free-lance professional workers, artists, writers, doctors, &c., not employed by organs of the community.

With regard to contracts of personal service, that is to say, employment by private persons not for gain, the only things necessary would be the employment tax, designed to equalize the position of the private and the public employee, and the enactment of a strict code of labour laws for the protection of the private employee.

2. AGRICULTURE

The most important branch of the private sector will probably be agriculture. Although the technical arguments for conducting some branches of agriculture by means of large, publicly owned estates, worked by employed labour, are very strong, there are other branches where the small family unit is economically preferable. Moreover, there are social and psychological considerations which may result in the retention for some time of the small, privately worked farm over a great part of the range of agricultural production. This is especially likely to be the case where, as in Scandinavia, Australia, New Zealand, and parts of North America, small, one-family farms worked with little or no hired labour have achieved a considerable degree of technical efficiency (thanks usually to the help of co-operative or state activities) and account for a very large proportion of agricultural output.

It will be particularly difficult to fit private agriculture into a planned collectivistic economic system, especially where it is a question of co-ordinating the national production of agricultural commodities with a general plan of exports or imports. Large-scale, directly collectivist agriculture could of course expand or contract its output and its labour-force in accordance with the social plan, just as collectivist industry could. But a multitude of petty commodity producers is not so amenable to direct regulation. Moreover, a complication is introduced by the fact that the small farmer's income consists of the proceeds of the sale of his product. He, like the industrial worker, should be sheltered from the major fluctuations of a market valuation of his services; this protection should, however, be afforded at a minimum loss of economic efficiency. Four ways of controlling the output of the private sector of agriculture may be mentioned.

(1) **Price-control.** The planning authority for agriculture might regulate the supply of different products by varying the prices which it offered for them. Each year it would decide how much wheat, say, was required from the private sector, and then fix a price for wheat that, in its estimation, would elicit the desired supply. If more was forthcoming, the price could be lowered, or purchases could be stopped. The question is more complicated if it is desired at the same time to guarantee the farmer's livelihood. In this case the

purchasing board would have to make a guaranteed price—that is to say, announce a price that would be fixed for a definite period of time and undertake to buy the whole of the individual farmers' output (subject of course to its satisfying a certain minimum standard of quality) during that period. If its calculation was wrong and, say, more wheat was offered than it expected, it would have either to cut its losses and learn to make better estimates next time, or store the excess and offer a lower price next year. In the case of a perishable commodity, such as strawberries, the purchasing board would have to sell at a loss.

(2) **Rent-control.** The planning authority might control the supply of commodities by adjusting the rents charged by the community for the use of agricultural land. The rent of different kinds of land would be calculated so as to make it profitable for producers in the private sector to grow just the desired quantity of the different products. By itself this is probably a less flexible method than price-control, but it might be convenient in the case of crops of minor economic importance. Its principal sphere of use is probably in conjunction with price-control. Prices and rents are naturally complementary in an exchange economy, and the simultaneous manipulation of prices and rents would give the planning authorities greater freedom, e.g. in adjusting home production to the import and export trade.

(3) **Licences.** The planning authority, having decided how much of a particular crop it requires during a given year, might issue licences to produce the desired quantity, and sell them to the producers by public auction or by public tender. This would ensure the most productive use of land and would tend to concentrate production in the hands of the most efficient farmers. It would not be so effective as some of the other methods in guaranteeing the producers' livelihood. It could be combined with guaranteed prices and rent-control.

(4) **Quotas.** If the minimum disturbance to established expectations is sought, the method of quotas is the most obvious. Existing producers could be registered and given a quota based on their past output, the sum of the quotas constituting a standard output. Changes in output required would be effected by expressing the desired output as a percentage of the standard output and then authorizing all producers to produce this percentage of their quota. This method is particularly suitable where the probability is that planning policy will reduce the quantity of home production and it is desired to let existing producers down lightly. This may happen either because the demand is declining (as in the case of flax), or because the imported product is cheaper (as in the case of wheat in France), or because the product in question is produced mainly for export and the foreign markets are becoming less remunerative (as in the case of butter in New Zealand).

This method (the simple quota) is subject to serious economic defects. The chief one is that it tends to stereotype the use of land as it was at the moment of introducing the quota system. But as time goes on, new methods of cultivation are discovered, new land is opened up by improved means of transport, new crops are introduced, and the relative suitability of land for different purposes becomes quite other than what it was originally. Thus the simple quota perpetuates an increasingly uneconomic use of land.

This objection can be avoided by the device of making the quotas transferable. They will then acquire an economic value. Thus in the case of a butter-fat quota, a farmer cultivating land that is intrinsically more suited to dairying than some other land and having himself no quota or a small one, will find it worth his while to buy quotas from men on worse land who have larger quotas than they want to use. In this way the production of butter-fat will be concentrated upon the land more suitable for the purpose, while less suitable land will be driven into other uses. Also it will be worth while for the personally more efficient man to extend his production, at the expense of the less efficient, through the purchase of quotas. Meanwhile old producers who are displaced will obtain some compensation through the sale of their quotas.

The simple quota system will tend to break down if the permitted output increases above standard. It may be physically impossible, or at least economically very costly, for farmers to produce more than 100 per cent. of their existing output. This situation can be dealt with, either by authorizing the sale of quotas, thus transferring the extra production to the next most suitable sites, or by combining the quota with the licence method, and issuing new quotas to be sold at competitive prices to whoever will buy.

CHAPTER VII

FOREIGN TRADE

So far we have described price-formation and economic regulation in an isolated socialist community. Such a community, far from being parasitic on capitalist states outside, in the sense of basing its price-system on theirs, would find it possible, at any rate in theory, to determine all necessary prices and costs in an isolated economy. We have now to consider how this community would be economically related, through imports and exports, to other communities.[1]

(1) TRADE IN GOODS

Comparative costs. The principle of comparative costs applies to a socialist economy as to a capitalist one. If a good *A* can be obtained from abroad in return for the export of other goods whose cost is less than the cost of producing *A* at home, then a net gain of economic welfare results from importing the good *A* instead of producing it at home. This is subject to distinctions and qualifications. For example, it is only true of costs reckoned in the long run, and not of short-period prices, which may diverge considerably from cost. The S.E.C. must discriminate between supplies of cheap foreign goods that are permanently cheap owing to low real costs of production and those that are only temporarily cheap. It ought to take advantage of temporarily cheap goods whenever it can do so without dislocating its own plans of production or incurring more than countervailing costs of

---

[1] These other communities are assumed to be non-socialist. It is improbable that a number of independent socialist commonwealths would isolate themselves, each in its own distinct economic system, when self-interest and socialist principle alike would impel them to adopt an integrated system of economic planning and costing.

transference. But it is not worth while importing goods that are temporarily cheap owing to a foreign seller's price-cutting policy, if their introduction necessitates changes in the allocation of capital and labour at home that will soon have to be reversed. If, however, the foreign goods are permanently cheap, the S.E.C. ought to substitute them for those of native manufacture, transferring labour and other resources to alternative branches of production, until the cost of the home-produced goods is equal to that of the imported. (This may involve, in some branches of industry, abandoning home production and relying entirely on importation.) Even if the imports are permanently cheap, the cost of the necessary adjustments in home production may be greater than the savings effected by importation. Now a socialist community can make allowance in its estimates of *all* the relevant costs (e.g. retraining of skilled labour), and can spread the charge over that period of time during which equipment and labour would naturally be renewed. The problems of transference involved in the case of foreign trade are precisely similar to those which arise in a self-contained economy owing to technical improvement or to changes in demand. (See pp. 86–7; and Chapter IV, section 3 (3).)

In order to give effect to the principle of comparative costs the S.E.C. will have to make a survey of domestic manufactures with a view to their disposability in foreign trade. It will then have to compute price indexes for export goods and for import goods, and work out, on the basis of the bargains that its foreign trade organs actually make with external trading bodies, the real rate of international interchange between its imports and its exports (the barter terms of trade). On the basis of these figures it can compare the costs of any particular branch of domestic production and compare its costs with those of importation. An increase in imports will make it necessary to dispose of more exports abroad; this will in general be progressively more difficult and involve a worsening in the real rate of interchange, thus raising the cost-coefficient of all imported goods.

An important qualification of the comparative-cost principle is that it is static, it considers only actual economic relations as they exist at a given time. A planning authority ought to be able to look ahead and forecast future trends (a) in costs of export goods, (b) in costs of goods that compete with or might compete with imports, and (c) in the barter terms of trade. It ought in its decisions to take into account these trends as well as the actual conditions of the moment. The most usually quoted example of the importance of future trends is the case of the industry that is not at the moment capable of surviving in the face of foreign competition, but could do so after a sufficient period of development. This is the 'infant industry' argument in favour of fiscal protection. A socialist community could foster infant industries without the fear that they would become infant Gargantuas devouring the substance of whole provinces in their greed. No private vested interests would be created by such a policy of development, nor would protected industries develop that penumbra of sub-marginal undertakings which makes it almost impossible to remove protection from an industry under capitalism even though the more efficient establishments no longer need it.

Another qualification of the comparative-cost principle is that there may exist political reasons for not being dependent on foreign countries for particular products or on certain foreign countries for any product. Again, there may exist social reasons for developing certain branches of domestic production, beyond the point indicated by the principle of comparative costs, such as the necessity of developing factory industry in agricultural districts and of establishing proletarian settlements there, or of developing agriculture in regions considered to be unduly urbanized. In all these cases definite subsidies should be made out of the social income to the industries concerned and the ordinary calculation of costs then applied. In this way it will be possible to see clearly the real social cost of such a policy of protection, and, moreover, to apply quantitative methods to the case where, while it is undesirable for political or social reasons to admit a large quantity of some imported product, it may not be desirable to exclude it entirely.

But these exceptions apart, the policy of a socialist community with regard to foreign trade should be, not free trade, which is inconsistent with the principles of collectivism, but *non-discrimination* between foreign and domestic sources of supply. We may note in this connexion that the orthodox argument in favour of free trade involves two propositions:
  (1) that specialization of industries within nations according to their comparative costs of production will yield the maximum aggregate real income to every nation;
  (2) that free competition is the best way of achieving this specialization.

Now in controverting the free-trade position the ordinary protectionist attacks proposition (1)—usually with scant success. The socialist can accept (1) with a good conscience, but rejects (2). He may consider desirable the distribution of resources that would result from an ideal free-trade policy, while doubting the capacity of capitalist society to achieve it. The only way to achieve this ideal distribution, according to him, is deliberately to plan it. There is need of a term to describe this policy of deliberate planning of production on a basis of comparative costs. It cannot be called 'free trade' because this phrase implies a policy of *laisser-faire*. The term 'non-discrimination' is here suggested. It is non-discrimination rather than freedom that is proved to be economically advantageous by the orthodox argument in favour of 'free trade'. A socialist community could practise non-discrimination while protecting the home market from dumping and short-period fluctuations; it could encourage infant industries; and, since production would not be in the hands of completely independent bodies of entrepreneurs with interests opposed to the social interest, there would be no danger of such protection and encouragement being used as a screen for monopolistic depredations. It is true that prejudice and mental inertia on the part of groups of producers might perhaps create a demand for restrictions not socially justified; but within the 'glass walls' of socialist economy it would be difficult to maintain unreasonable discriminations for long.

A difficulty arises inasmuch as the orthodox theory of international trade assumes that, at least on one side, trading units are small and that goods are offered and taken in small lots (small compared with the magnitude of aggregate trade between any two countries or in any one commodity). Where a socialist community was trading with another socialist community (if such existed) or with a capitalist community that had adopted the now popular policy of totalitarian state regulation of foreign trade, a situation would arise, similar to that called 'bilateral monopoly' by theoretical economists, in which it is probable that there is no determinate stable position of equilibrium, but in which either party has an incentive to get the better of the other by the use of fraud or force. The investigation of this problem leads us too far afield, but one may remark that, in these days of marketing boards, quotas, and clearing agreements, it is not a problem that faces a socialist commonwealth exclusively.

In order to safeguard the policy of the S.E.C. with regard to importation and exportation, the community should maintain a monopoly of foreign trade. Although there would not be any harm in individuals' ordering small quantities of goods from abroad for their own personal use,[1] the private sector should be excluded from direct participation in foreign trade. The private trader, if tolerated, should be obliged to make all his purchases from and sales to traders in foreign countries through socialized export and import organizations.[2]

2. FOREIGN EXCHANGES

Purchasing-power parity. The question of foreign exchanges should present no difficulty. If the outside world adhered to the gold standard, the socialist community would have to conduct its foreign-trade transactions in terms of gold. The S.E.C. would have to see to it that imports were paid for by exports. But there is no necessity for the internal currency to be linked to the external. The conversion of one into the other would only be necessary for the use of travellers and for remittances between private individuals. The central bank would have a monopoly of foreign exchange and could fix what rates it liked. The greatest economic and administrative convenience would, however, result from its fixing the rate of exchange at a figure corresponding nearly to the true purchasing-power parity between the internal currency and gold. This figure could be changed from time to time, as the internal value of gold varied.

It may be objected to this that purchasing-power parity is a concept of dubious validity in theory and difficult to determine in practice. In particular, the purchasing-power parity between a socialist and a capitalist country would be difficult to establish because of (a) the different price-structures, and (b) the different proportions in which things were consumed in the two countries. In so far as the socialist community

---

[1] The right of individuals to order books and newspapers from abroad would be an essential guarantee of political freedom.

[2] For foreign trade under socialism see G. D. H. Cole, *Principles of Economic Planning*, chaps. vii, x, xiii; R. L. Hall, *Economic System of a Socialist State*, ch. xii.

conducted its external trade on the lines laid down here, its price-structure would approximate to that of the countries with which it traded and objection (*a*) would cease to have effect. Objection (*b*) would remain true, but the more closely the two price-structures come to resemble each other the less importance will attach to differences in weighting due to different schemes of consumption. In any case no great accuracy is needed. If the control of external trade is rigid enough, any rate of exchange can be maintained. The more nearly this arbitrary rate approximates to the ratio of the purchasing powers of the two moneys the less temptation there is to smuggling of currency, 'black bourses', and other forms of illicit trade. Also less inconvenience is caused to tourists, and to persons in the socialist country who desire to make odd purchases (say books) or remit money to friends abroad. A quite rough approximation to purchasing-power parity in the rate of exchange will avoid these inconveniences.

If the outside world abandoned the gold standard, the socialist community would have a choice of alternative policies. (1) It could either conduct its external trade in terms of some capitalist country's stable managed currency (if such existed). (2) It could persuade capitalist countries to trade in terms of its own domestic money. If this was maintained stable in terms of general prices (see Chapter VIII, section 3) it might easily commend itself to the use of a capitalist world in the throes of dissolution. (3) It could contract and liquidate obligations in terms of some commodity chosen as a measure of value. This commodity might be gold (used as a commodity of trade and not as money), copper, steel, coal, wheat, cotton, coffee, butter, wool, or any other standardizable staple product. (4) It could conduct its trade on barter lines by means of clearing-house agreements. This last expedient, although it is one to which capitalist nations are forced in the extremity of the present crisis, is the last that should be adopted, since it is lacking in elasticity. It is ill-adapted to three- and more-sided exchange, and it therefore makes difficult rational economic choice between different commodities and between different sources of supply.

Under these circumstances the socialist community would still have to fix rates of exchange between its currency and other currencies. The principle of purchasing-power parity would still hold good. In the absence of gold pars, special steps might have to be taken in order to check speculation.

3. Capital Movements

More difficult problems of foreign trade are involved in the case of the import and export of capital. We must distinguish between short-period and long-period movements of capital.

(1) **Short-term capital.** Some form of short-term borrowing and lending must exist if a socialist community is to have any foreign trade at all. Even if all imports are paid for by exports the account does not balance accurately day by day: the temporary fluctuations between one month and another and those due to seasonal commodity movements (harvests, &c.) must be evened out by short-term capital movements. In the past these were provided by means of bills of exchange, which, being of short currency and called into existence by the commodities which they helped to pay for, automatically adjusted themselves to the needs of trade and, what was still more important, could not pile up a large unbalanced volume of debt on one side of the account. Nowadays a process of increasing differentiation and specialization has tended to separate the movement of goods from the movement of credit. The bill of exchange is being supplanted by the simple bank credit and the telegraphic transfer. Bills, if still in use, are to an ever-increasing extent finance bills, not based directly on transactions in goods. This development,

although it makes for greater flexibility, is liable to lead to greater instability in foreign trade; since transactions in goods do not automatically cancel each other out, and an unbalanced short-term debt can come into existence almost unperceived by the financial houses which handle foreign trade, leading on occasion to 'frozen credits' and to financial crises.

A socialist community which decided to trade with its non-socialist neighbours but did not wish either to make long-period loans (investments) to them or to accept such from them, would nevertheless have to make use of some machinery of short-period finance. It could either use that of its capitalist neighbours (as the U.S.S.R. has used that of London, New York, or Berlin), or set up its own. In the latter case, proper methods of inspection and control would enable it to know exactly where it stood: in the former case the danger would exist that the socialist community would find itself more deeply involved than it cared to be in the financial complexities of non-socialist countries. This could perhaps be guarded against by the devising of some new form of automatic and self-liquidating document against goods.

(2) **Long-term capital.** We must now consider long-term capital movements, or international investment. Under certain circumstances a definite economic advantage can be obtained by both the borrower and the lender from the movement of capital between countries. From the point of view of the socialist community, if the rate of interest on long-period loans outside the community is lower than the rate prevailing within, the community's real income can be increased by borrowing from abroad until the increased supply of capital lowers the domestic interest rate to the world level. Similarly, if the outside rate of interest is higher than that of the socialist community, the latter can increase income per head by using its resources to finance foreign undertakings instead of domestic ones and consuming additional

imported goods with the proceeds. Note that in making these calculations the planning organ of a socialist community would need to take into consideration the *net* effect on the national dividend of foreign borrowing and lending. That is to say, it would have to compute not only the return on capital at home and abroad but also the effect of the import or export of capital on the return to labour. This suggests that a socialist community, acting on purely economic calculations, would be more ready to import capital and less ready to export capital than a capitalist economy under similar conditions. In the former case it would set an increase in economic wages against the extra burden of interest payments: in the latter case it would set against the receipt of interest payments the increased return to labour that would have resulted from keeping the capital at home instead of exporting it.

Both borrowing and lending are theoretically possible. Subject to the qualification in the preceding paragraph, both borrowing and lending would be economically beneficial from the point of view of immediate gain, both to the socialist community and to the outside countries with which it entered into relations on capital account. But there are grave objections against both borrowing from and lending to outside communities (especially if they are non-socialist) on the part of a socialist commonwealth. Borrowing from abroad makes the socialist community dependent on foreign and possibly hostile countries; hence it should be avoided as much as possible on political grounds. Lending abroad, if carried out on a large scale and over a long period of time, would turn the community into a corporate exploiter of workers living in other communities; it would undermine its morale and create in the debtor country a sense of resentment that would embitter international relations and might lead to conflict. On social and political grounds, therefore, there is a case against it. Nevertheless, both the borrowing and the lending of capital resources are such sources of potential welfare that it seems difficult to renounce them altogether. A possible policy to recommend would be to borrow or lend subject to two conditions: (a) the total sum of foreign loans not to exceed a certain low proportion of the aggregate national capital; (b) all loans to be accompanied by sinking-fund provisions which would extinguish indebtedness within the lifetime of the physical assets acquired thereby or within half a generation (say fifteen years) at the most. The first provision would obviate excessive dependence of the national economy on external conditions. The second would prevent the development of usurer-nations, with accompanying resentment on the part of the debtors.

An exception to this self-denying ordinance may be admitted in the case of capital transactions between two socialist communities (if indeed they remain independent). A situation might arise, particularly if one country was technically backward and the other advanced, in which one might have a greater need of capital than the other and in which the transfer of part of the second country's surplus to the first might be effected in terms agreed on by the planning authorities of the two countries on terms mutually advantageous. (The actual transfer of resources would, of course, take the form of an export of goods or services—e.g. employment of experts—for which no immediate return would be made.) Even this, however, would have in it an element of possible exploitation. Against this danger the best safeguard would probably be the rapid extinction of debt by a sinking-fund. An ultimate safeguard is, of course, the possibility of repudiation by the community that came to feel itself exploited.

The further problem arises of what a country should do if it goes socialist when it is, like Britain or the United States, a large creditor on international account under capitalism. For example, Britain receives annually something like £200 millions of tribute from the workers of other countries as dividends on foreign investments, interest on foreign loans, and the net balance of repayment (the balance of principal of old loans and investments and loans repaid over new investments and loans made). It has been suggested that a socialist Britain should nationalize this stream of wealth along with the rest of the income of the property-owning classes. But there is a difference in principle between exogenous and endogenous income from property. The expropriation of capital invested at home simply restores to the workers of Britain what they have been robbed of. But the expropriation of capital invested abroad places the British people as a whole in the position of the capitalist, extracting surplus value from workers in other countries.

The exercise of elaborate moral casuistry by the British workers will, however, probably be obviated by the action of governments of debtor countries who, however deeply they honour in their own lands the sanctity of contract and the institution of private property, will almost certainly take advantage of the establishment of socialism in Britain to repudiate their obligations in that direction.

4. WILL SOCIALISM LEAD TO WAR?

This is perhaps the place to deal with the objection made against socialism that, if adopted by single countries, it would embitter international relations and lead to war. Under individualism the terms in which, say, wheat in one country is exchanged for machinery in another, concern a multitude of individual trades: if the terms alter, some traders gain and some lose in both countries; the populations as a whole do not feel concerned. But, it is claimed, if countries trade with each other as single units, every change in the conditions of trade, every time that one country establishes an industry to produce something that it previously imported, every time that one country decides to alter the channels of trade and buy from or sell to a third country in preference to the country with which it formerly dealt, any change of this kind will become a matter in which the entire population of two or more countries will acquire a material interest, and the occasions of conflict and quarrel between nations will be multiplied.

This, however, is precisely what is actually happening, on an ever-increasing scale, under capitalism. It occurs because, under capitalism, there is a separation of interests between the capitalist class (or certain sections of it) and the population as a whole. This separation of interests makes it possible for capitalist interests within a country to pursue a foreign policy in which the economic welfare of the people is sacrificed to the real or imagined economic interests of a small minority. Economic nationalism and economic imperialism impoverish not only the world as a whole but the great bulk of the people in the countries that practise them; nevertheless, they do enhance the profits of certain sections of the capitalist class. As long as free competition is maintained under capitalism, this separation of interest, although productive of *domestic* disharmonies, does not strongly influence *foreign* policy, since no one capitalist is strong enough to influence the state machine. Thus competitive capitalism does not display a marked tendency to economic nationalism. The more capitalism assumes a monopolistic form, however, the stronger is the tendency to economic nationalism. Moreover, a cleavage of interests occurs even within the ranks of capital; heavy industry allied with finance sacrifices other and weaker capitalist interests to gratify its own urge to export capital. It is often stated that the policy of modern states, as in the era of mercantilism, places power above welfare. This is not strictly true. The fascist state—even the liberal-'democratic' empire—sacrifices welfare, it is true, and may even sacrifice profits, temporarily; but the power at which it aims is sought for the sake of ultimate profit—a 'place in the sun' for heavy industry and the export of capital, the exclusive control of minerals or of territory suitable for plantation economy, access to reservoirs of cheap and docile labour.

But it is precisely because this separation of interests would no longer exist under socialism that we have little reason to expect that a socialist country would pursue a policy of economic nationalism. If the gains of economic imperialism were balanced against its real cost it would be found in nearly every case to be unjustified on purely material grounds. The liberal economists are perfectly right in asserting that it does not pay from the point of view of the national economy as a whole.[1] What they sometimes fail to see is that it pays from the point of view of a class or a section of a class. Where one party takes the risk and bears the costs of an enterprise and another gets the profits, it is likely that investment in that form of activity will be pushed far beyond the point of economic equilibrium. (In fact, economic nationalism and economic imperialism are outstanding examples of divergence between marginal private net product and marginal social net product.) But once let the profits and the costs be spread over the same body of persons (to wit, the entire population of a socialist community) and the folly and futility of imperialism will become obvious. No socialist country would treat imports as curses and exports as blessings, seeking to restrict the former and maximize the latter: nor would it imagine that it could make itself richer by giving away its substance (as in the case of subsidized export schemes). The U.S.S.R. almost alone among national economies at the present day treats exports as the necessary price to pay for desired imports, and deliberately diminishes its exports of certain goods (timber and foodstuffs) as its own productive powers increase. Trade between socialist countries will

[1] See N. Angell, *The Great Illusion; This Have and Have-Not Business.*

exemplify the principles of nineteenth-century economic liberalism: it will be a mutual benefit and a force making for peace.

Strictly speaking, however, this harmony of interests applies without any serious qualification only to the exchange of goods. In the movement of capital and of human beings, cases of disharmony can arise. The import and export of capital, although immediately beneficial to both parties, may give rise to conflicts of interest between debtor and creditor communities. Such transactions should therefore be entered into with peculiar circumspection. The migration of peoples, especially where they are of widely different social conditions, may also be grounds of economic disharmony (see Chapter IV, section 7). Capital transactions are not, however, likely to lead to serious conflicts of interest, since the net addition that any country could hope to make to its national income by international usury is a trifle in comparison with the cost of collecting interest from an unwilling debtor.[1]

There remains, as the only possible source of international conflict, the problem of migration. War for possession of territory is conceivable between a community with a sparse population, abundant natural resources, and a high standard of life, and a community with a dense population, few natural resources, and a low standard of life. Even this danger, though it must be admitted as a theoretical possibility, is improbable in practice. The spread of birth-control throughout the world is leading to a state of affairs in which

---

[1] Britain's income from overseas investments was £212 millions in 1929 (Sir Robert Kindersley, *Economic Journal*, December 1937). This amount of capital invested at home would have brought in *some* return, so the *net* addition to British income was much less than this. Assume that the return at home would have been one-half that of foreign investment (it would probably have been more), and we get a net addition to British income of not more than £106 millions, which amounts to less than £2 10s. per head per annum, or about 3 per cent. of the national income.

population dearth and not population pressure is the most
likely danger to civilization. Moreover, the peoples whose
rulers talk most aggressively of requiring territory for overseas
expansion, of being hemmed in by other countries, of being
'people without room', are suffering more from the mili-
taristic policy of these same rulers than from population
pressure. (In many cases the same dictators who demand
colonies for a surplus population are frantically trying to
reverse the trend of a falling birth-rate.) Reduce military
expenditure, abolish black-shirt militias and the corruption
of functionaries who may not be criticized or brought to
account, return to the people the profits, rent, and interest
that their rulers extract from them under the protection of
this same army and militia: and there would be few symp-
toms of population pressure.

The same considerations apply to the case of raw materials.
A policy of exclusive territorial possession and monopolistic
exploitation of raw-material supplies brings profits to small
sections of the capitalist class, sections which tend, in the
age of monopoly capitalism, to become politically dominant.
But the people of any country will nearly always stand to
benefit by a policy of the open door and of exchange on non-
discriminating terms.[1] The profits of an exclusive policy
will always be small and uncertain, outweighed, moreover, by
the costs of aggressive armaments. In a world containing
both socialist and capitalist-imperialist countries, however,
it might be necessary for the former to arm themselves, not
in order to secure exclusive control of raw materials for
themselves, but to prevent the latter from doing so.

---

[1] A possible exception is in the case of a small nation that controls
the *sole* supply of an indispensable commodity. Such a nation could
raise its collective standard of living to a certain extent by a monopolistic
policy. But no source of supply nowadays remains for long the sole
source. Chile's monopoly of nitrates was soon broken by the Haber
process of fixing atmospheric nitrogen.

CHAPTER VIII
MONEY AND PRICES
1. MONEY

THE adoption of a pricing system by our socialist commonwealth involves the use of money. In the economic arrangements that we have sketched out there will be three kinds of money payments: payments between one organ of collective economy and another, payments between an organ of collective economy and a private individual, and payments between private individuals. The first kind of payment corresponds to inter-firm transactions in capitalist economy. To effect it no material current money of any kind (notes or coins) is necessary. As goods are transferred from one Corporation or Trust to another or from a producing organization to a co-operative society or other sales agency, the one will be credited and the other debited with their value in the books of the Central Bank. Payments of the second and third kind will create the need for some form of individually disposable purchasing power (i.e. money). This will be required for effecting the sale of goods at a price to the consumer (Chapter II, section 4) and the distribution of individual income through the payment of wages and other allowances (Chapter IV, section 5). The same form of money would presumably be used for payments between individuals (the third kind of payment mentioned above). These payments would be multiplied by the development of a sector of private enterprise, but even in the absence of a private sector there would presumably be some transactions between individuals—gifts, odd loans of small sums, sale of second-hand goods and of the product of spare-time activity, subscriptions to clubs and other voluntary associations.[1]

Such freely disposable tokens of purchasing power may take either of two forms: (i) current money (notes or coins); (ii) book-entry money (bank deposits transferable by cheque or by a giro system).

It has been suggested that current money could be dispensed with in favour of transfers in individual ledger accounts in some central institution. Every citizen would be credited in the books of this institution with his income, calculated in some definite unit of value, and he would make payments, by a sort of cheque or giro system, to the retail trading organs of the community for all goods and services that he purchased. Convenience would probably dictate the development of some such system, just as the well-to-do citizen to-day deposits most of his income in the bank and pays his tradesmen by cheque. In a socialist community probably every citizen would have his wages and other allowances paid into his savings-bank account and would make a monthly settlement with the co-operative society where most of his purchases would be made. But even so, the book entries under such a scheme still remain money, in the sense of freely disposable purchasing power.

However, it would appear difficult to generalize the book-entry system for all transactions. In particular, there remain the problems of the traveller and of the casual disbursement of small sums. One cannot pay by cheque for tram-rides, postage-stamps, telephone calls, and newspapers. One wishes to buy cigarettes or sweets or flowers when one's own co-operative store is not handy, and to have occasional meals

---

[1] Cf. H. G. Wells in *New Worlds for Old* (p. 143). '. . . Money is indispensable to human freedom. The featurelessness of money, its universal convertibility, gives human beings a latitude of choice and self-expression in its spending that is inconceivable without its use.'

and drinks when away from home. Of course, things like trams, letter-post, and newspapers might, in time, come to be provided free, and an extension of the co-operative retail trading system might make it possible for an individual to walk into any shop, anywhere, and buy as much as he wanted simply on presentation of his savings-book or his co-operative pass book. Under these circumstances the use of coins and notes might dwindle to vanishing point. Even so, it would scarcely be possible to eliminate *all* occasions for petty-cash disbursements. Moreover, the cheque system is uneconomical for small transactions, since the administrative cost of cheque clearings depends on the *number* and not on the *magnitude* of the transactions.

One reason why many socialist writers object to the use of current money in their ideal commonwealth, but permit the use of book-entry money, is their fear of the anonymity of the former. If all transactions went through the medium of a single banking institution, it would be easier to trace and control transactions between individuals of an anti-social nature. Bribery, gambling, and private trading for a profit would certainly have a much greater chance of flourishing where notes and coin were in general use, transferable without formality and without record, than where all payments went through the books of an omnipresent, omniscient organ of the collective economy. (Even in the latter case, however, if private individuals really wanted to evade social control of such activities, they would probably evolve their own unofficial token currency, to be used for gambling or private trade, and either exchanged for official bank money in devious ways or redeemed in terms of commodities that were both produced and consumed outside the ambit of socialist economy.)

However, it will be assumed that current money is in use for small payments in the socialist community. That it ought to be purely token money should be clear for two reasons. One is that the use of full-value coins represents an entirely useless waste of natural resources: there are better uses for the precious metals than to serve as a medium of exchange.[1] The other is that the community's current money ought to be purely domestic money. The influx and efflux of money from outside communities would be an element too disturbing of the planned economy. If citizens wish to buy goods from outside they must obtain foreign exchange from the Central Bank, in whose hands all foreign trade transactions will be centralized (see Chapter VII, section 2).

2. CIRCULATION

The circulation of money against goods must be carefully controlled in the economic plan. Every part of the plan must be worked out in two distinct ways; in terms of real goods and services produced and consumed, and in terms of money payments. Thus a kind of double-account book-keeping will check every stage and department of production.[2]

In particular, care must be taken in the issue of individual purchasing power (currency or credit) in the division of individual consumption. The issue of money must be carefully co-ordinated with the whole economic plan for this division.

[1] It may be that, since metal disks are more hygienic and convenient than paper notes, part of the large stock of gold now held as monetary reserve will be made use of in the form of a gold coinage. But these coins will be essentially gold tokens bearing the same relation to full-value gold pieces as our present silver coins bear to the florins, thalers, and five-franc pieces of the mid-nineteenth century. In this case, gold will return to monetary use, but this time as the servant of society and not as its master. Even so, it is probable that gold would be of more use in fountain-pen nibs, electrical contacts, crucibles and containers for acids, than in coinage.

[2] Cf. the practice of the planning organs of the U.S.S.R., which draw up both a money-balance and a goods-balance for every large enterprise and for every considerable region of the country.

The correct circulation of money against goods will only be achieved if the sum total of purchasing power flowing into the market during a given period in the form of wages, social dividend, and other money allowances is equal to the sum of the prices of all consumption goods offered for sale during the same period. That this can be achieved is seen by considering the facts (*a*) that the total value of consumption goods is equal to the total value of all goods produced, less the deductions for new capital formation and for communal consumption, (*b*) that the sums distributed in personal income equal the earnings of all factors of productions, less deductions for the same two purposes. Since the sum of all prices of goods equals the earnings of all factors of production, the distribution of purchasing power given above will, in principle, ensure equilibrium.[1] However, various unpremeditated occurrences may upset this equilibrium. The first two of these are due to the irruption of unexpected elements from unplanned portions of the social economy, the third is due to deviations from the plan itself.

(1) Consumers may vary the rate of expenditure of purchasing power in their hands. Even though private investment is forbidden, saving in the sense of hoarding may exist. Thus consumers may hoard money instead of spending it, or may dishoard from previous accumulations.[2] This factor depends on the personal decisions of millions of individual consumers. Normally, the statistical average of their decisions may be taken by the planning authority as constant over fairly long periods, but in some circumstances it may undergo a biassed change in one direction that would affect the price-level in an unforeseen manner.

[1] See Note on National Income, p. 238.
[2] This is equivalent to a change in what Marshall and Pigou would call the proportion of resources that consumers elect to hold in the form of money, what Hawtrey would call their unspent margin, and what Fisher would call the velocity of circulation of money.

(2) If a private sector (Chapter VI) exists, its activities may disturb the calculations of those who manage the socialized sector. Since the products of private enterprise enter into the social income, changes in their prices, over which the S.E.C. has no direct control, will affect the general price-level. Moreover, variations in the real turnover of the private sector, equally withdrawn from the direct control of the general planning authority, will cause variations in the total demand for currency. A further disturbing factor is that the velocity of circulation of money will in general be different in the two sectors. Thus, any ebb and flow of money between the two sectors will upset the monetary circulation and the price-level of socialized production.

(3) In the system of combined planning and free price-formation here outlined, only general directives are given and in most branches of production prices and quantities are not rigidly decreed. Schedules of demand and supply prices are drawn up and, within the framework so made, actual prices and quantities are allowed to adjust themselves. Variations in the circulation of money and in the level of prices may occur through unforeseen changes either on the demand side or on the supply side. (a) Owing to variations in consumer's demand goods may command a higher or lower price in the market than that accounted for in the plan. Some things may be all the rage, and the price will have to be raised in order to prevent their being sold out before new stocks can be got ready: other things may have to be sold at a big reduction, in order to clear warehouse and shop space for other more urgently desired commodities. Price changes of this sort may be expected to cancel each other out, but there may be, at a given time, an appreciable balance one way or the other. Alternatively, if prices are not altered, variations in demand may produce unexpected variations in stocks. Those of suddenly popular commodities may decline more than the

plan took into account, and others may pile up. Here, again, there will be a certain amount of off-setting, but it may not be complete. One particularly unobtrusive way in which this may happen is in the case of services, and the use of fixed equipment which is not consumed in use. In this case the commodity sold is produced as it is required and not in anticipation of consumption; a great variation is possible in the amount of it produced without any change in the use of labour and other means of production. Thus a hot summer may increase the use of communally owned swimming-pools. If a charge is made for their use, the receipts from them will go up, diverting consumers' purchasing power from the purchase of other goods, lowering the price of these without raising the price of a swim. (b) In the calculations of the planning authority on the supply side, certain assumptions, which may not be realized in practice, will be made as to the efficiency of productive factors. If production tended, on the average, to fall below the level of efficiency postulated by the S.E.C. in its calculations, prices would tend to creep steadily upwards. If workers and managers in productive enterprises showed conspicuous energy and enthusiasm in reducing costs, prices would tend in the same way to fall. Corresponding to these upward or downward tendencies in prices would be tendencies in the same direction of the amount of purchasing power distributed in the form of wages.

Notice that while changes in the unspent margin and in relative importance of the private and the socialized sectors will create a disequilibrium in monetary circulation, in the sense that there will be a failure of prices and purchasing power to equate in the market, changes of the kind discussed in this heading will not create a disequilibrium, since changes in prices of goods will be exactly balanced by changes in the earnings of factors of production. The level of prices will alter and with it the absolute volume of the circulation, but aggregate prices will equal aggregate purchasing power.

How then can the influence of all these disturbing factors be corrected? There must be some elastic element in the monetary circulation, capable of being varied so as to offset unplanned changes. We will return to this problem in the next section under the heading of the control of the price-level.

3. THE PRICE-LEVEL

The system as described so far implies the existence of a stable price-level as a basis for economic calculations. A stable price-level will not necessarily be maintained of itself unless special steps are taken to control it. It is true that in a rigidly controlled collectivist economy, where the planning authority fixed prices and quantities of output absolutely, the price-level would be unable to change except by design, although even so there might appear a slow cumulative rise or fall of general prices. But in the partially free economy described above there would always be the possibility of appreciable fluctuations in general prices. There are three loopholes for the introduction of unplanned fluctuations. They have been previously considered under the heading of circulation (changes in the unspent margin; vagaries of the private sector; the degree of free play permitted to the pricing process through the autonomy of the various organs of public economy).

The control of general prices is, therefore, a matter that calls for attention. What then must be done? Three things are necessary. First of all, a method must be devised whereby a price-level can be measured. Secondly, a decision must be taken as to what price-level is to be stabilized. Thirdly, a method must be found for correcting undesired changes in it.

(1) **Measurement of the price-level.** Measurement of

the price-level can be effected by means of an appropriate index number, calculated by the statistical organization of the S.E.C. Probably several price index numbers would be constructed, for different classes of goods. There would be indexes for consumption goods, for capital goods, for wages, and for special categories of goods, such as foodstuffs, textiles, metals, &c. Indexes of aggregate and *per capita* production (real volume and money value) would also be required, for total production, production of consumption goods, of capital goods, and of special categories of goods. But the two indexes that would chiefly serve as guides to the price policy of the S.E.C. would be the price index of consumption goods and the index of money value of consumption goods produced *per capita*.

(2) **Monetary policy.** As to *what* price-level should be established, at least two possibilities present themselves. Either the goods-value or the labour-value of the monetary unit of account could be kept constant. In the first case the purchasing power of the unit would be maintained constant in terms of a standard collection of consumption goods. Increase of production *per capita* would result in the distribution of a proportionately greater average money-income to each individual. In the second case, the unit would be adjusted as always to correspond to a fixed fraction of the total production *per capita* of the community. The average money-income of every individual would remain constant, but increase of production *per capita* would raise the purchasing power of each monetary unit. Which of these alternative policies is to be preferred? Either would be workable, but the balance of preference, in the writer's view, inclines towards the first, for three reasons.

(*a*) First of all, with a constant purchasing power of money, a rising level of physical productivity would be reflected in rising money incomes. The incomes of classes of workers whose productivity was increasing slower than the average would rise more slowly, but only in the cases of an *absolute* fall in productivity would there be the necessity for any diminution of money-income. With a constant labour-value of money, on the other hand, since the average money-income would remain constant, any worker whose productivity was increasing more slowly than the average would suffer a reduction in money wages. Moreover, under both policies, the flow of labour to different occupations could be effectively controlled; only, while the second policy would drive labour out of less productive occupations by the pressure of lower money wages, the first policy would attract them into more productive occupations by the lure of higher wages. Thus the psychological effect of the first policy would be much more satisfactory than that of the second.

(*b*) Secondly, the first policy would be more convenient for adding totals of different goods to obtain a figure illustrative of aggregate production. If the monetary unit represents a constant purchasing power in terms of goods a figure expressed in monetary units always represents a constant volume of real production. Thus statistics of output convey a clear idea to the ordinary citizen. If the labour-value of money was kept constant, a new unit of account, a goods-unit, based on an index-number of general prices, would have to be introduced for the purpose of statistical comparisons.[1]

(*c*) Thirdly, the method of the constant goods-value of money would make it easier to maintain fixed prices for certain classes of goods and services, such as transport, postage, and telegraph rates (see p. 62), since they would

---

[1] This might have to be done in any case for particular classes of goods. For instance, if the prices of capital goods diverged appreciably from those of consumption goods, special index-numbers for capital goods might have to be used in making estimates of the physical volume of capital goods.

retain for a long time a fairly fixed relation to the prices of other goods.

(3) **Methods of control.** How is the level of prices to be controlled, according to whichever policy is chosen?

The causes of variation in the general price-level can be divided into two groups: changes in the prices of factors of production, which will affect all prices throughout the system; and changes in the velocity of circulation of money, due either to changes in the consumers' unspent margin or to fluctuations in the private sector. It should be noted that changes of the first kind produce changes of equal magnitude in the volume of consumers' money demand, thus affecting the price-level without disturbing the equilibrium of monetary circulation, while changes of the second kind produce changes in the volume of demand that are not balanced by changes in the aggregate sum of costs, thus disequilibrating the monetary circulation.

It would, therefore, seem desirable that the S.E.C. should have at its disposal two kinds of methods of regulating the general level of prices: those which act directly on factor prices, and those which act on consumers' effective demand. Of course it would be possible, taking a leaf out of the book of capitalism, to use methods of the second kind only. Changes in the volume of consumers' demand will percolate through the whole system of price determination and will ultimately produce an effect on factor prices; but it would seem more rational in a planned economy to operate directly on factor prices if indeed they are responsible for the disturbance in the price-level.

(*a*) *Control of Factor-prices.* It is true that factor-prices could be acted on directly. Whenever the price-index showed a tendency to go up or down too far, the S.E.C. could either order an all-round reduction or enhancement, as the case might be, of the prices of factors of production. But this method is somewhat crude and happy-go-lucky. What is wanted is a way of influencing prices generally and uniformly that is capable of quantitative adjustment and that does not involve arbitrary interference with the pricing system described above. One possible method would be to regulate wages by means of percentages on or off basic rates, the percentages to depend on some objective index of productivity, absolute or relative, calculated for the whole community or for the particular industry. The prices imputed to land and natural materials could be similarly adjusted. Smaller adjustments of the price-level could be effected by varying the rate of interest on short-term capital or by varying charges for uncertainty-bearing. In the first case, if the Central Bank provided all or a part of working capital by short-term advances, the rate of interest on these could be set at a small amount above or below the rate fixed for permanent investments, according as it was desired to make the price-level rise or fall.

(Note that under socialism the short-term interest rate would have an influence diametrically opposite to that which it actually has under individualism. This is because in the first case it would affect costs alone, while in the second case it affects the volume of money, through the creation of credit, much more than it affects costs.)

(b) *Control of consumers' money demand.* If it is required to keep the level of prices stable, or to cause it to move in any predetermined way (such as inversely with physical productivity), it seems necessary to have at hand some means of neutralizing changes in the velocity of circulation of money, either arising spontaneously among consumers as a result of changes in the quantity of reserves which they keep (their unspent margin) or arising as a result of alterations in the relative importance of the private and the socialized sector.

Many reformers of capitalism have advocated deliberate

control of the volume of investment (generally by means of public works) as a method of regulating consumers' outlay, and hence the monetary circulation and the price-level. This method would not be suitable to a planned socialist economy, where the volume of investment would be governed by other and more fundamental considerations. Three methods of regulating consumers' outlay would be available to the monetary authority of a socialist community: (i) through the Social Fund; (ii) through a system analogous to the 'dividend' of co-operative societies; (iii) through control of individual savings.

(i) The Social Fund (Chapter III, section 3 (4); Chapter IV, section 5) might be used as an adjustable reservoir of purchasing power. By accelerating or retarding the flow of money out of this reservoir into the pockets of the public, the price-level of consumption goods could be raised or lowered. This acceleration or retardation could be effected in various ways, as by changes in the flat-rate Social Dividend, changes in the rate of payment under particular social services, or special bonuses to persons who fulfilled certain conditions (comparable to bonuses paid nowadays by insurance companies to policy holders).

(ii) Alternatively, if the present system of dividend on purchases, as at present in vogue in co-operative stores, were taken over and generalized in retail trade, the flow of purchasing power could be adjusted by changes in the rate of 'divi.' paid to consumers.

(iii) A third method might be by control of savings. In order to prevent effectively sudden changes in the volume of the circulating medium and to be in a position to detect hoarding and dishoarding, the S.E.C. might find it convenient to establish a Savings Bank, which would receive savings deposits, repayable only after a certain definite, though short, notice. In order to attract deposits it might be necessary to offer a small rate of interest. Then a rise in the rate of interest offered as deposits would contract the volume of purchasing power appearing on the market, reduce the velocity of circulation of money, and lower the price-level, or counteract a tendency for it to rise. A fall in the deposit rate would tend to raise the price-level, or counteract a falling tendency. It is important to note that this Savings Bank would be primarily concerned with the circulation of money: the deposits in it would not be necessary to the community for the purpose of capital accumulation (although they would be available for that purpose), since capital accumulation would be provided for, independently of any voluntary saving, out of the Social Fund.

Let us now describe both these forms of price-control operating under various types of monetary policy. (1) Suppose first that it be decided to stabilize the goods value of money (that is to say, keep the general commodity price-level constant). Then any increase in the material production of society must be accompanied by a proportionate increase in the volume of money in circulation. This increase in production might come about in two ways, either through an increase in population or through an increase in productivity per head. In either case new money would normally flow into circulation in the form of enhanced money earnings of factors of production, either because there were more factors or because each factor was earning more in terms of money. This would be reflected in a rise in the money value of wage payments and in an increase in the amounts credited to the Social Fund by way of rent, interest, and profit. The former could be effected (in the case of rise in *per capita* productivity) by percentage additions to basic rates of wages, the latter by means of a planned increase in the outgoings from the Social Fund. (Note that wages in all occupations need not rise in exactly the same proportion.) (2) Suppose, as a second case, that the labour-value of money be stabilized (that is to say, that the average money income per head be kept constant). Then any increase in productivity per head must be accompanied by a fall in general prices. This will normally occur automatically, provided average factor prices be prevented from rising. (If some factor prices rise, others must fall.) But to achieve this end considerable amount of adjustment of factor prices by the S.E.C. will probably be necessary, accompanied probably by a check to the out-flow from the Social Fund. If, under the same policy, popu-lation increases, then additional money must be issued. This would naturally take the form of increased issues from the Social Fund first as children's allowances, later as adults' Social Dividend, together with an increasing flow of wages as the number of wage-earners rose.

CHAPTER IX

EQUILIBRIUM, PRICING, AND PLANNING

1. The Pricing Process and Economic Equilibrium

WE have endeavoured to outline the principles that the economic organs of a socialist community should follow in using the resources at its disposal, according to a rationally co-ordinated plan for satisfying the needs of the citizens of that commonwealth. We have discussed (1) the allocation of finished goods to ultimate consumers; (2) the allocation of resources to the different branches of production and the calculation of the social cost of production; and (3) the distribution to the individual workers of a claim to a specific and definite share in their collective product. In our discussion we have seen that such a community would have to take over and develop, at least for the wide section of economic life that we have designated the division of individual consumption, the methods of pricing goods, of costing, and of determining wages that have been developed under the capitalist system. We have worked out sufficient of the details of such a collectivist economy to show that it is, in principle at least, workable. Given free choice of consumption goods at a price, we have seen how the process of price-formation can be carried back through the series of production goods and made an integral part of the process of costing. The imputation of values to the ultimate factors of production, moreover, results in the emergence of rates of wages and of a rate of interest. The former enable individual preference to be expressed by the citizen *qua* producer as well as by the citizen *qua* consumer, and the latter, applied systematically throughout the entire socialist economy, completes the process of rational balancing of economic means and economic ends.

Thus there is, in theory, no ground for the assertion that a socialist community, lacking a free market for intermediate goods, would be unable to regulate production in accordance with the principles of scarcity and utility. In fact, we may go so far as to say that only in a socialist community, where production can be carried on in the full light of statistical measurement and publicity, is it possible to realize the true principles of economic valuation. Capitalist society, with its deviations from equilibrium due to gross inequalities of individual income, to competition (overlapping, price-cutting), to monopoly (restriction of output, deliberate holding back of technical improvements), to the mutual ignorance of entrepreneurs concerning other entrepreneurs' activities, to the alternation of waves of cumulative and contagious optimism and pessimism, is a very imperfect approximation to the economic ideal. The beautiful systems of economic equilibrium described by Böhm-Bawerk, Wieser, Marshall, and Cassel are not descriptions of society as it is, but prophetic visions of a socialist economy of the future.[1]

2. ARBITRARY ELEMENTS

In the system of libertarian socialism that we have outlined there are a certain number of arbitrary elements—arbitrary in the sense that they do not depend on the freely expressed preferences of individual economic agents. The most important arbitrary elements are four:

(1) the allocation of resources between communal and individual consumption,

(2) the allocation of resources between present and future consumption,

(3) the choice between work and leisure,

(4) geographical planning and the pricing of land.

(1) **Communal and individual consumption.** The

---

[1] F. von Wieser, *Natural Value*, bk. ii, ch. vi.

setting aside of a certain proportion of the total social income for communal consumption represents a restriction of the free choice of the consumer, since the more spending power is reserved in this way the less remains at the individual's free disposal. The decision as to what proportion is to be so set aside is necessarily an arbitrary one. Theoretically the principle to follow is that the marginal utility of resources expended on communal consumption should be equal to that of resources expended on individual consumption (see Chapter II, section 3 (2)). But this criterion is largely inapplicable in practice for two reasons. (*a*) The first reason is because in neither division is the marginal utility of resources precisely the same for every consumer. This, which is an insuperable obstacle to rational allocation of resources under capitalism, is a less serious difficulty in a more equalitarian society. Under socialism it should be theoretically possible to achieve a right equality of marginal utility in the two divisions for a 'representative consumer'. (*b*) The second reason is because there exists in the case of communalized goods and services no method of measuring marginal utility comparable in precision with the method of pricing in the case of goods individually consumed.

Under capitalism the allocation of resources to the communal division is effected by the fiscal decisions of governments, central and local. The theoretical study of this problem falls under the caption of 'Public Finance'. For the reasons given above, it is an arbitrary action incapable of being brought under the categories of exchange economy. Under classical capitalism, however, it affected only a very small proportion of the total social income. (Those were the days when the Chancellor of the Exchequer believed in 'letting the money fructify in the pockets of the people'.) In recent times, however, the growth of social services has expanded the communal division, with the consequent introduction of a large alien element into capitalist economy. Under socialism this division would probably expand even more, although the prevalence of a greater measure of equality would eliminate some of the more violent disputes over social policy. Nevertheless the demarcation between the two divisions of consumption would involve an arbitrary decision.

(2) **Present and future consumption.** Another arbitrary element in our socialist economy is the allocation of resources between the satisfaction of present and future needs—in plain language, the decision as between spending and saving, or the proportion of the social income to be devoted to the production of new capital goods. The use of a rate of interest in a socialist economy as described in Chapter III, section 3 (2), would make possible a rational and consistent conduct of economic activity in so far as a uniform rate of time-preference could be established for all branches of economy, but the original decision as to the magnitude of this rate would not depend on the time-preferences of individual savers. It would represent the time-preference of the 'community' as a collective saver; but the 'community' in this sense is a purely metaphysical fiction—what would take its place in actuality would be some board or commission, taking a decision on the behalf of the individuals composing the community. And this decision would be arbitrary.

To this the socialist may retort that the rate of interest, and consequently the allocation of resources between present and future use, is arbitrary under the existing system. The capital market is dominated by the large corporate savers (banks, insurance companies, industrial joint-stock companies, co-operative societies, and municipalities, all with reserves to invest) whose decisions as to saving and spending are made with as little reference to the preferences of their constituent individuals as those of the most arbitrary Gosplan

or S.E.C. Further, in the short-term section of the capital
market, the formation of a rate of interest is disturbed by
such factors as currency policy, banking technique, and the
balance of international payments. The existence of 'forced
saving', due to the creation or destruction of credit, seriously
interferes with the decisions of the marginal saver. In fact,
the liberal individualistic view of the determination of the
rate of interest by the interactions in a free competitive
market of millions of distinct persons' individual 'time-preferences' is completely unreal. The economist's 'marginal
saver' is largely a mythical creature. Moreover, even if
the rate of interest were determined by the interaction of
individual time-preferences, it would have little claim to
represent *the* time-preference of the community, since the
distorting influence of inequality of income works more
powerfully in the region of interest-rates than in any other
part of the process of price-formation. Still, the fact remains
that, under socialism, the allocation of resources between
present and future use would be at least as arbitrary as
it is under capitalism.

(3) **The delimitation of work and leisure.** An individual who is working for the satisfaction of his own needs
divides his time between productive activities (making goods
to satisfy his needs) and leisure-time activities (consuming
the goods he has produced, or just enjoying nature and the
company of his fellow men). He can choose that division of
his time which affords him the maximum of satisfaction. If
he enjoys an increase in productive efficiency, as by the discovery of more fertile land or the invention of superior tools,
he may choose to work the same hours and produce more
goods than he did before, or to produce the same output of
goods as before with the expenditure of less time. In other
words, he has the choice between more material goods and
more leisure. What is true of an isolated economic agent is

true also of a petty commodity producer, making goods for the market, but using his own means of production and master of his own time. But as soon as production comes to involve an elaborate social organization and division of labour (i.e. either under capitalism or under any form of techno-logically advanced socialism), this no longer holds good. A few people—free-lance professional workers such as journal-ists and examination coaches, piece-workers in a few indus-tries, casual workers such as dockers—can please themselves as to what portion of their time they will devote to recrea-tion; but the great majority of workers must adapt themselves to the discipline of the social labour process. They must clock in and clock out of factory, mine, school, or office. The same division of time between work and leisure holds good for every member of the social labour force doing the same job. The difference between capitalism and socialism is that under the former, the division of time is not decided by the preferences of the workers at all, whereas under the latter, there is the possibility that the division of time may be de-cided by the workers themselves. Even if a separate, indi-vidual decision in each case is not possible, at least a collec-tive, average decision may be made. Under capitalism, the length of the working day is determined, in the first instance, by the employer, for whom profit and not the maximum satisfaction of the worker is the ruling consideration. To be true, of recent years, organized labour has used both indus-trial and political power to secure a national minimum of leisure, against the opposition of the employing class. (It is notable how, spontaneously and almost unconsciously, the workers have endeavoured to obtain their share in increased social productivity, in the form not merely of higher real wages but also of shorter hours, of more leisure as well as of more goods.) Nevertheless it remains true that in the last resort the division of time between work and leisure is made over the workers' heads by decisions of people who are not workers. Under socialism this decision could be made by the workers themselves, through appropriate democratic institutions, either regional or occupational. It must be noted, however, that the decision would have to be, in the majority of cases, not an individual and particular decision, but a collective and general one. It would thus be, from the point of view of individualistic market economy, arbitrary.

(4) **Geographical planning and the pricing of land.** In the pricing of land and natural resources for costing purposes (see Chapter III, section 3 (1)), there is a very considerable element of indeterminacy, and consequently of arbitrary choice on the part of the planning authority. Where their value is derived entirely from their technical efficiency in the manufacture of definite physical products—that is, where the fertility of land (in the narrow sense) and the physical productivity of mines and quarries is involved—the arbitrary element does not necessarily emerge. But where the value of a site is derived from its geographical relations, it often depends, to a very large extent, on other decisions of the planning authority.

Consider, for example, an extensive plain of uniformly fertile wheat-land with an excellent natural harbour at one edge of it. The value of the land depends on its proximity to the harbour: hence it falls steadily in a series of concentric zones, centred in the harbour. Now let a railway be built from the harbour inland. Any number of possible routes might have been adopted: the actual one chosen may be determined by relatively trivial considerations, or possibly by the need for communication with some point in a more distant region of the hinterland. As soon as the railway is in existence, the regions consisting in land of equal desirability at once became rearranged in a new pattern: instead of circular zones, we shall find longitudinal bands, paralleling the line of the railway. Now let a second line be constructed, parallel to the coast. It, too, might have followed a number of possible routes: the one actually taken may be determined by comparatively unimportant circumstances. Once, however, the second line is built, the regions of equal desirability will assume a roughly cruciform configuration. Moreover, a junction has come into existence. Traffic will be exchanged between the two lines, trains made up and dispatched; hence it will perforce be better served than other places in the matter of transport. A site in the neighbourhood of this junction, which, before the railways were constructed, was indistinguishable from thousands of similar sites in the plain, will now become a definitely more suitable location for a factory than any other site along the two lines. In other words, the decision to construct certain lines out of the many possible ones carries with it a long trail of consequences as to the most economic utilization of land and natural resources.

The same thing applies to the building of roads and harbours (in cases where there is no pre-eminently good natural harbour, but a number of moderately good ones, all in need of considerable improvement), the bridging of rivers, the location of aerodromes, the construction of dams and reservoirs, the location of power plants, and so forth. In some cases, the natural features of the country dictate the decision —a mountain pass constrains road and railway to one definite route, a river can be bridged at only one point—but in many cases there is a large element of indeterminacy in the problem, and a decision will frequently be taken on more or less arbitrary grounds. But once made, it becomes the basis of future decisions, it crystallizes the scheme of land utilization into a definite pattern which subsequent development has to follow.

What is true of things such as the location of railways and harbours, in which natural topographical considerations play a large part, is still more true of the location of different human activities within a given settled area, in other words, the problem of town-planning. The decision to demarcate a given region that is becoming or has become urban into residential areas, shopping centres, factory areas, areas for commercial and administrative establishments, areas for universities, museums and libraries, areas for theatres and amusements, and areas of open country (green belts), is a decision to allocate land to different uses on grounds other than the operation of consumers' demands on the market. Once the decision has been taken, then consumers' choice will determine what rent will accrue to a given housing site or shop-site or factory-site, but the decision that certain sites are housing sites and others shop-sites or factory-sites has already been made on other grounds. Before the decision was taken there may have been a very large number of possible arrangements, none of which could be definitely preferred to another on purely economic grounds, and all of which would have resulted in much the same *general* allocation of uses—that is to say, the same aggregate area devoted to different uses—but not the same *specific* allocation of definite pieces of land.

From this discussion it appears that town and regional planning involves in an eminent degree just that supersession of the indices of the market economy that characterizes economic planning in general. This fact justifies the application of the word 'planning' in the sense of town and regional planning. It also helps to explain much of the instinctive hostility shown towards even this small instalment of economic planning by the property-owning interests.

Reviewing as a whole this question of arbitrary decisions, it appears that the decisions in question are of the same kind as those already taken arbitrarily under capitalist individualism. Taking one thing with another, it does not appear that the arbitrary elements in a socialist society need be any greater than those which exist already, and are inevitably growing greater, in capitalist society. Moreover, they refer to fields of choice where individual decisions can never be more than very rough-and-ready, and where little loss of welfare can be expected to result from drawing the line a little above or a little below the ideal point. Against this small loss of welfare can be set the much greater gain of welfare resulting from greater equality and from a greater degree of collective control over his own destiny vested in the ordinary man.

3. The Entrepreneur in a Planned Socialist Economy

In the picture of a socialist economy that we have built up so far we have introduced various elements drawn from capitalist individualism. In order to make possible a proper equilibrium of cost and satisfaction we have admitted money and the price system, and we have assumed that economic activities are decentralized and carried on by a large number of separate organs of collective economy. These organs, although they will have incomparably more exact knowledge of one another's actions and of their own part in the whole economic system, will be financially independent of one another, having their own nominal capital and their own profit and loss account, and will be managed very much as separate enterprises are under capitalism. This raises the problem of the powers and remuneration of the individuals who are to manage them. If the establishment of a decentralized economic organization, co-ordinated by a price and cost system, is to realize its economic advantages to the full, a very large degree of independence must be given to the managers of the various economic organs of the community. They must be free to experiment with new products, with alternative methods of production, and with the substitution of one kind of material, machine, or labour for another. But independence involves responsibility. The manager must be made to realize his responsibility for the decisions that he makes. Now responsibility means in practice financial responsibility. The manager's personal remuneration must in some way reflect his success or failure as a manager. Unless he bears responsibility for losses as well as for profits he will be tempted to embark on all sorts of risky experiments on the bare chance that one of them will turn out successful. It will be 'heads I win, tails you lose' between himself and the community. Or else the attempt to check irresponsibility will tie up the managers of socialist enterprises with so much red-tape and bureaucratic regulation that they will lose all initiative and independence. In this case the chief advantages of the price system will be lost. In other words, the socialist manager must be invested with many of the attributes of the entrepreneur under capitalism.

This brings us to a highly contentious issue. Next in importance to the argument that socialist economy would be vitiated by the impossibility of pricing intermediate goods is the argument that planned economy is incompatible with the true entrepreneur function. It is asserted that the managers of factories, trusts, combines, selling syndicates and what not would be simply bureaucratic officials taking their orders from the supreme planning authority. They might criticize, perhaps, and suggest modifications in the plan through the medium of innumerable closely reasoned reports and minutes; but they would never be in a position to make independent economic judgements, to exercise choice between different markets or sources of supply, and, what is worse, they would have no financial responsibility for success or failure. A successful manager may receive the Order of Lenin and an official motor-car, an unsuccessful one may be shot for sabotage, but there can be none of that steady, ubiquitous, quantitatively adjustable and automatically self-regulating correspondence of judgement with reward that makes enterprise under capitalism the exact science it is. In any case the success or failure of a manager under planned economy would be a matter of technical or administrative competence, not of economic judgement. He would be an engineer and a civil servant, but not an entrepreneur. (One obvious reply to this is that entrepreneurs have made such a mess of society that it is about time that the engineers and the civil servants got their chance. They could scarcely do worse, and they might do better, than the business man.)

In his *Socialism*, Mises declares that socialists have no comprehension of the entrepreneur's function.[1] Even when they do not consider him merely as the 'capitalist'—a parasite, alien from the process of production, passively appropriating the 'surplus value' created by the workers—they think of him as a manager, with purely technical or clerical functions, in other words, an official and not an entrepreneur at all. Thus they think that his functions would remain unchanged in a socialistic reorganization of society. He would simply be a manager, appointed by the state to administer its economic affairs. Mises enlarges upon the distinction between the entrepreneur and the official. The official is, at the best, a functionary, a person trained to execute formal, prescribed, professional duties; at the worst, he is indolent and irresponsible. In business he is static, unoriginal, bound by precedents, and unwilling to take responsibility. Unless the manager of an enterprise has a free hand to dispose of resources at his own discretion, subject only to the control of objective market forces, and unless he is liable for any miscalculation with the whole (or with a substantial part) of his personal wealth, he is no true entrepreneur. Thus, by Mises, the attempt to solve the problem of pricing under

[1] L. von Mises, *Socialism*, pp. 208–10, 212–17, 233, 256–8, 487–8.

socialism by decentralizing the socialist economy into separate undertakings under 'business management' instead of
'bureaucratic control' is declared inadmissible, on the
grounds that the managers of such enterprises would be, in
fact, not entrepreneurs, but officials. Either, as good officials,
they would play for safety and be unprogressive routineers;
or, freed from the control of an official hierarchy and lacking
personal financial responsibility, they would embark on wild
and grandiose schemes that would squander the community's resources without satisfying the people's needs.

But this antithesis of the entrepreneur and the official is
an artificial one. Granted that at the two extremes the types
are vastly different, it does not follow that there is no range
of intermediate types.

According to this analysis two correlated characteristics
define the entrepreneur: (1) freedom in the disposal of resources within his enterprise; (2) full financial responsibility for his decisions, whereby, if successful, he makes a
profit and, if not successful, he makes a loss—extending if
needs be to the loss of all his property. But these characteristics do not necessarily follow an all-or-nothing law.
Possibly they are capable of being quantitatively graded.
What we need to do is to investigate (1) how much freedom
in the disposal of resources, and (2) what degree of personal
financial responsibility are necessary to constitute the manager of an undertaking an effective entrepreneur.

(1) Actually, in the real economic world of to-day, Mises's
ideal entrepreneur scarcely exists. Most entrepreneurial
functions are exercised nowadays by salaried managers of
joint-stock companies, whose financial responsibility is very
limited and whose freedom of substitution is often circum-
scribed by the fact that the directors of the company have
interests in other companies. (Mises would admit that managers of this type are mere officials. For him 'the type of man

to whom joint-stock companies owe their success is not the type of general manager who resembles the public official in his ways of thought. . . . It is the manager who is interested himself through his shares, it is the promoter and the founder —these are responsible for prosperity.')[1] But even where the individual entrepreneur still survives or where a joint-stock company is managed by a man of the type of those who 'manage business in their own interests, whether this co-incides with the shareholders' interests or not', who 'receive a large part of the profits of the enterprise' and are 'primarily affected by the misfortunes of the enterprise', even these men do not really conform to the ideal type. Trade associations and trade unions (condemned by Mises as hostile to all true economy) restrict their freedom of disposal of resources, to say nothing of such less tangible influences as trade customs, goodwill, family connexions, and the unorganized public opinion of a trade or a locality. Moreover, the law of bankruptcy can be used so as to relieve even the individual entrepreneur of personal liability for uneconomic decisions.

The views quoted involve, in the writer's opinion, the 'all or nothing' fallacy. Because the manager of socialist industry will be governed in some choices by the directions laid down by the planning authority, it does not follow that he will have no choice at all. His choice of alternative markets, alternative methods of production, alternative sources of supply, although limited in some ways (as it is even in capitalist society by tariffs, factory legislation, building regulations, town-planning, trade union rules, &c.) may be free over a fairly wide range. Moreover, his choice will be made on the basis of much more complete and accurate information than his capitalist confrère has at his disposal. (Any choice, once made by one industrial or commercial manager, will at once become part of the data accessible to the planning authority

[1] Mises, l.c., p. 209.

F f

and to all other managers.) This will reduce the penumbra of uncertainty which gives an exaggerated importance to the functions of the business man under capitalism.

(2) The same 'all or nothing' fallacy vitiates the argument drawn from the absence of financial responsibility. It is not necessary for the due performance of enterprise that the entrepreneur should himself bear the full brunt of the consequence of his decisions. (The capitalist entrepreneur who does so belongs to the last century or, if he survives at all, to the back streets. In these days of limited liability, highly-geared loan capital, and subsidiary companies, the entrepreneur has more sense.) Financial responsibility may exist in varying degrees. Provided that the entrepreneur's personal earnings reflect to some extent the consequences of his decisions, he bears some financial responsibility for them. How much responsibility he should assume is a problem of administrative technique rather than of economic theory; but it may be observed that, in a community founded upon a basis of economic equality, quite a small pecuniary interest in the concern he administered would give the socialist manager an incentive to responsibility and thus constitute him a genuine entrepreneur.

A few principles governing the remuneration of the socialist manager may be laid down. At its base should be a system of fixed salaries, graduated according to the magnitude of the enterprise. Promotion from one post to another should be as far as possible, not by seniority or any other automatic system, but by selection from a number of competing applicants drawn from as wide a range of other enterprises and services as possible. Supplementing the fixed salary there should be a number of bonuses, based upon various indices of efficiency, such as output, the cost of production, the margin between costs and receipts, &c. In every industry a special commission would have to be charged with the task of classifying enterprises according to their importance, or rather of devising objective indices of economic importance that would be suitable for each industry (output, turnover, labour force, quantity of fixed capital, &c.), and of devising suitable bases for payment of bonus. Generally speaking, the manager's bonus should not depend on profit in the ordinary capitalist sense of the word, because the emergence of profit is not necessarily a sign of efficiency, but may denote a failure to expand output. Only in a branch of production where there are many effective substitutes for the product, or where the optimum scale of production is small enough to permit numerous independent enterprises to coexist, so that a high degree of competition exists, is profit a criterion of efficiency. In other branches of production the efficiency of the individual manager is to be judged rather on such things as increase of output and reduction of cost. On the other hand, although the making of profits is not necessarily a sign of success, the making of losses is a sign of failure, although even here losses may be due to circumstances independent of the individual manager's control— such as changes in fashion or of technical methods. Comparative cost accounting as between different enterprises of similar kind should help to reveal the efficiency or inefficiency of management. If the bonuses were calculated so that the average manager earned a bonus of about half his salary, while the maximum bonus amounted to the whole of the salary or a little more and the minimum bonus was zero, the manager would have an incentive to experiment and improve the service and yet would be made to feel the consequences of imprudent and extravagant ventures.

4. PLANNING

So far, the reader will say, there has been little talk of planned economy. The S.E.C. has been described as a mere statistical board, collecting and publishing data of output, cost, price, capital and income, calculating demand and supply schedules, but not exerting any real directive functions. All that has been done is to set up within the socialist community a sort of simulacrum of a capitalist economy, purged from the latter's grosser errors, but, like it, actuated by the blind choice of millions of unco-ordinated consumers and producers. This is now the place to make clear the proper relation of economic planning to the price-process. The two are not opposed, but complementary, principles of economic regulation.

It should not be supposed that deliberate economic planning necessarily means the elimination of all economic indices and the deciding of every economic alternative 'on its merits'. The board of a capitalist firm when it draws up its policy does not ignore the data of internal costs, market prices, &c., put before it by its officials: it makes use of these data to check the soundness of its policy. So a socialist community, in its economic planning, should keep within the general limits imposed by the system of prices and costs described above.

There are four ways in which economic planning is required to supplement a system of quasi-individualistic pricing and costing. The first is to give general directives to socialist economy. The second is to make decisions where market indications are lacking. The third is to eliminate cyclical fluctuations in economic activity. The fourth is to deal with special emergencies.

(1) **General directives.** It is especially in the early days of a socialist commonwealth, during the period of transition from capitalism to socialism, that the positive directive functions of a planning organ would come to the fore. At the best the new government would take over a semi-derelict community, which capitalist sabotage had left cluttered up

with idle men and idle plant—the familiar paradox of poverty
in the midst of potential plenty. At the worst the new
government would have to rebuild the economic life of
society out of the ruins left by revolution and civil war. The
first thing to do would be to ensure a supply of bare necessities to the people without any consideration for the rights of
property and without much consideration for the niceties of
an elaborate system of pricing and costing. First things first—
and the first thing to do would be to feed, clothe, and house
the people *somehow*: one could leave till later the exact adjustment of silk stockings against light motor-cars. The
S.E.C. would have to make a survey of immediately available
resources (including stocks of possible exportable goods) and
a survey of the people's needs. These needs would then be
satisfied as far as possible with the available resources. The
basic needs of the people would probably be satisfied directly, without bothering about the measurement of effective demand. Probably some system of rationing would be
in use. A feature of this stage would be a considerable
development of free services—medical, educational, recreational, &c. If there were resources available for the satisfaction of needs above the minimum, the money-and-price
system could be left operating in this sphere.

The second stage in the building up of the socialist economic system would be the expansion of the means of production. The planning organs would have to make further
surveys of needs and resources, and draw up a general plan
of industrial development—rationalization and reorganization of industries whose existing equipment was up to date
and adequate, modernization and new capital equipment
for other industries. In the light of this plan the S.E.C.
should make a preliminary examination of a number of
highly important undertakings from each of which a widen-
ing stream of economic consequences would flow. It should

be the task of the subordinate planning organs to co-ordinate these consequences and determine to what extent the available resources would permit the carrying out of these undertakings. If the first examination should prove unfavourable, the S.E.C. would have to decide how far the original schemes should be modified. Once a few key undertakings had been decided upon,[1] their needs in labour and materials would involve planned economic development in a number of other industries in ever-widening circles. Thus the rest of the economic programme for the current period (whether one-year, five-year, or twenty-year) could be built up round them.

Up to this point, planning would have been very largely in terms of physical and technical quantities and objectives. But meanwhile the mechanism for the quasi-automatic determination of prices and costs by economic considerations would be in course of evolution. Gradually, as provision for primary needs became more abundant and as more complex needs came into consideration, the economic element in planning would supersede the more arbitrary methods. Finally, a stage would be reached in which the economic machine would practically run itself. The planning authority would need only to lay down a few very general leading principles, and to make definite decisions regarding the allotment of resources to new capital construction and to communal consumption. In one or two matters, perhaps, considerations of social policy would override purely economic considerations and certain undertakings would be planned 'on their merits'. (But even here the tendency would be to make specific grants to particular undertakings or to lay specific

---

[1] In many cases a decisive factor in the choice of key undertakings would be the necessity of developing backward areas. Large-scale irrigation, power, transport, or mining schemes might be instituted in potentially productive regions in order to realize their potentialities quicker than would be possible in the course of ordinary economic equilibrium.

burdens upon particular branches of productions, and then to leave them to the quasi-automatic working of market forces.) In all other matters, and in all questions of detail even within the special schemes, the normal indices of price and cost would be decisive. The great majority of lines of production would be carried on automatically within the given framework of costs and prices so as to supply goods to consumers according to their preferences as indicated in the market.

(2) **Lack of market indications.** The second function of economic planning depends on the existence, referred to in section 2 of this chapter, of certain decisions that cannot be taken on the basis of an automatic following of market indications. These decisions—the extent of communal consumption, the amount of provision to be made for new capital, the limits of leisure—are a legitimate sphere for the work of a general planning authority. Furthermore, an economic community that relies on the blind automatic working of market valuations will achieve *an* equilibrium, but not necessarily the only possible equilibrium in the allocation of resources; it will achieve *a* maximum of economic welfare but not necessarily the only possible maximum under the circumstances. The equations which express the working of a market economy may, and probably do, have multiple solutions.[1] The role of an economic planning authority is then to make a choice between different sets of conditions, each compatible with economic equilibrium; to give a general line to economic development, which will eventuate in one particular state of equilibrium rather than another.

Wherever, for instance, there is the possibility of discriminating charges, several different positions of equilibrium may be possible. Thus the problem of the co-ordination of different means of transport (railway, road, inland waterway,

[1] See Pigou, *Economics of Welfare*, part ii, ch. iii, sections 4–5.

coastal shipping, &c.) and that of the most economic use of
electricity and gas are probably not capable of unique solutions under individualist conditions, since in each case the
charges of one of the competitors embody the principle of
discrimination (classified railway rates, multiple-part electricity tariffs); and in such an event there may be open to
either competitor a number of alternative rate-policies, to
each of which the rival services may adapt themselves, producing *an* equilibrium but not necessarily *the* equilibrium
corresponding to the greatest attainable social income. Under
socialism, as we have seen (Chapter V, section 1), discriminating charges would be avoided as far as possible, but it
might not be possible to avoid them entirely. In any case
the prevalence of joint-cost in public utilities may introduce the possibility of indeterminacy, even where discrimination is absent.

A similar situation exists in the case of town and country
planning, in the sense of the division of land into specific
use-categories. As is shown in this Chapter, section 2 (4), there
is an element of arbitrary choice in this. Here, too, the automatic machinery of the market has proved inadequate under
capitalism. In such cases even capitalist society feels the
need for some authority that can impose from above, not
the actual solution of the problem, but the appropriate set of
conditions within which the solution is to be worked out.

We have thus seen that some indeterminacy is almost inevitable in many cases. Our socialist commonwealth needs
some organ for choosing between alternative states of equilibrium. This is precisely one of the functions of the planning
authority.

(3) **Elimination of cyclical fluctuations.** The third
function of economic planning is the elimination of cyclical
or quasi-cyclical fluctuations. It is possible that this can be
achieved by some form of monetary stabilization (see Chapter

VIII, section 3 (2)), but this is by no means certain. The tendency of a free-price economy to produce self-stimulating and self-perpetuating fluctuations of activity is enhanced by monetary instability, but it is by no means certain that this tendency is caused by such instability. A free economy with stable money might still show a tendency towards cyclical fluctuations in output. One of the functions of the economic planning authority in a socialist community would, therefore, be to watch for such a tendency and to correct it, if it appeared, by judicious use of the mechanism of monetary control (see Chapter VIII, section 3 (3)).

(4) **Emergencies.** The fourth function of the economic planning authority is to be prepared for unforeseen happenings and for economic changes that demand more than the small adjustments of a free price system. Extensive crop failures, inventions and discoveries that render obsolete the equipment or methods of whole industries, the rise of new and efficient competitive industries on a large scale in foreign countries—these are some of the emergencies that planned economy must be prepared for. Finally, a socialist community of the sort here described would be well prepared to meet the greatest emergency of all—war.

CHAPTER X
FREEDOM

IN a scheme of socialist economy such as has been outlined here, the author maintains, three objects could be simultaneously effected. Firstly, with the aid of a calculus of cost and value, a balance of efforts and satisfactions could be attained and carried through all the branches of economic life, at least as effectively as, and perhaps more effectively than, in an individualist economy. Secondly, an incomparably greater degree of economic equality could be established among men. Thirdly, economic freedom could be achieved in as great a measure as, or even in a greater measure than, under individualism. The principles and machinery necessary for the attainment of the first object, economic equilibrium, has been the main topic of this book. The second object, economic equality, has been discussed in Chapter IV, section 4. The third object, economic freedom, has been discussed by implication throughout this book, whenever economic equilibrium has been dealt with. It must now be considered explicitly.

1. PLANNING AND FREEDOM

The usual objection that is made to economic planning of any sort (and *a fortiori* to socialist planned economy) is that it necessarily destroys freedom. 'Goods will be provided according to need, but according to the planning authority's idea of what people need and not according to their own idea of what they need.' 'People will be regimented and ordered to their various jobs without being allowed any say in the matter.' The planner's motive, when it is not 'the sadistic desire to destroy the rich', is 'meddlesomeness', 'the desire to assert themselves at the expense of others', or a plain 'lust for power'. 'Scratch a would-be planner and you will find a would-be dictator.'

Now there is no doubt that a planned economy affords great opportunities to any dictator who manages to capture the planning machinery; but dictatorship is not an inherent characteristic of planned economy. So much of the liberal indictment of planning must be admitted as refers to the *possibility* of the destruction of freedom under planned economy. In the hands of an irresponsible controller (or group of controllers) it *could* be made the greatest tyranny that the world has ever seen. But must we admit the *necessity* of such a destruction of freedom? Planning involves a conscious choice of ends. But may not freedom be the end chosen? Is it not possible to plan for freedom, for the abolition of the inequality which makes freedom a sham under capitalism, and yet retain enough of the price-system to ensure the satisfaction of a plurality of ends as expressed by individual consumers? Planning is a means, not an end, and it is as possible to plan for freedom as to plan for anything else. The end to which planning is directed depends on the wishes of that section of the community which can, in the ultimate analysis, control the actions of the planning body. The price of liberty is eternal vigilance, under planning as under any other system, and if people wish to be free they must deliberately choose freedom and pursue it.

It is claimed, however, that freedom is essentially incompatible with planning; that even if a socialist planner wished to realize freedom he could not do so and remain a planner. The argument is that, since planning involves the deliberate choice of an end to be followed, it necessarily involves the rejection of all alternative ends and the abandonment of all possibilities of change. Now I believe this argument to involve a false antithesis. It is like the argument which

asserts that import duties cannot be at the same time protective and remunerative. 'Either the duty keeps out the foreign
products or the foreign products enter in spite of the duty.
In the first case the duty brings in no revenue; in the second
case the domestic industry enjoys no protection.' Of course,
in actuality, *some* foreign wares may enter in spite of the duty,
but less than would be imported if there were no duty. There
may therefore be *some* measure of protection to home producers and *some* revenue for the treasury. So it is with the
presumed antithesis of planning and flexibility. A plan can
always be changed. When under the existing system a business man plans the construction of a factory or a government
commission plans the reform of an agricultural market, the
decisions taken are not immutable, nor are they put beyond
the pale of public discussion. What is true of the partial
plans that can exist in the interstices of capitalism may be
true of the more comprehensive plans of a socialist community.

But, it is agreed, decisions once taken cannot be modified
without loss. As soon as the possibility of change is admitted
the element of risk creeps into the economic problem. This
must be admitted. Elasticity of organization and technique
does introduce a penumbra of uncertainty into all economic
calculations. If the community desires an economic machine
that is responsive to changes in individual taste or productive
technique it must pay for the advantages of flexibility by a
certain margin of unavoidable loss. This is the cost of risk-
bearing. It exists in planned as in unplanned economy. But
is the only means of achieving flexibility the abandonment of
the whole direction of resources to the company promoter
and the advertising expert? It is argued that the social cost
of risk-bearing must be greater in a planned economy because
wherever a wrong choice is made its effects are more widely
spread, while individualism retains the saving grace of

averages and random samples. But could the errors of a socialistic order well exceed those of capitalism as exemplified in the British stock exchange boom of 1928[1] or the orgy of foreign lending by America in 1927-8?[2]

It might be argued that, nevertheless, a planned society would generate a psychological atmosphere in which it would be difficult to admit mistakes or to change fundamentals of a plan. In particular, an unwillingness to sacrifice sunken capital would lead to the suppression of the desire to experiment and innovate. But this argument is refuted by those who object against planning that it tends to push technical improvements further than economic calculus would indicate. Surely the truth is that both tendencies will exist: the purely administrative type of mind will favour routine and a static order, while the technical mind will delight in novelty for novelty's sake. An effective system of social cost-accounting should be capable of holding the balance between these two opposing tendencies. We must have recourse to the devices of Measurement and Publicity.

But suppose that, in spite of our devices for securing a flexible equilibrium within planned economy, society does rush to one or another of these extremes—either a slowing down of material progress or a misplaced zeal for technical improvements unrelated to economic welfare—what then? Even the sternest critic of planning admits that the standard of living need not necessarily *fall*: economic progress will be slower than it might have been under an alternative system. But may it not be possible to balance economic progress against other social ends—e.g. equality of opportunity and liberty for the common man? After all, the principle of marginal equilibrium applies to marginal equilibrium itself.

---

[1] See 'The Results of the 1928 New Issue Boom', *Economic Journal*, December 1931. Also *Macmillan Report* (Cd. 3897/1931), section 386.
[2] See League of Nations *World Economic Survey*, 1931–2, pp. 39, 42.

There is not an all-or-nothing choice between a planned economy, rigidly unchangeable and unchanging, on the one hand, and a perfectly flexible market economy, based on marginal equilibrium, on the other. It is a question of adjusting the proportions of conscious planning and of formal, market-economic, freedom in order to maximize real social freedom. Some inequality, some rigidity, some irrationality, some lack of ideal symmetry and order, must perhaps be tolerated; but the resultant balance might conceivably produce a more satisfactory blend of order and freedom than that which we enjoy to-day.

It is not difficult to detect the origin of the idea that planning is inimical to economic freedom. The partial and imperfect planning that occurs under capitalism is generally an attempt to circumscribe consumers' choice, either by restriction of output or by opposition to some change that is economically desirable. Examples of the first are the international rubber and tin restriction schemes, the coffee valorization in Brazil, the measures of the A.A.A. under the New Deal in America for ploughing in cotton and for 'not raising hogs', and the Coal Mines Act of 1930 in Britain. Examples of the second kind are the restriction of road transport in nearly every country in order to maintain the profit-earning power of railway capital, the protection by tariffs and subsidies of uneconomic branches of agriculture in some countries (e.g. the sugar beet subsidy in Britain) and of uneconomic industrial plant in others (e.g. the Australian iron and steel industry), persistent attempts made to preserve established trades and industries when they become superfluous because of either changes in consumers' tastes, technical change, or the growth of more efficient industries in other geographical areas. But this is easily explicable. So long as the private ownership of land and capital and the private organization of business enterprise for profit continue, the purpose of 'planning' is bound to be not the satisfactions of human needs but the preservation of the existing vested interest of rent, interest, and profit receivers. Competitive capitalism of the nineteenth-century type was forced by the invisible hand of competition to pay some attention to consumers' wants (as reflected in the distorting mirror of unequal incomes) and to economy (as reflected in money costs). 'Planning' under capitalism is simply another name for the tendency towards monopoly, whereby capitalism seeks to escape from the stern laws of consumers' sovereignty and of minimum cost while retaining all the advantages (to the capitalist) of the profit system. Capitalist planning is bound to be a conspiracy against the consumer. But that is not because it is planning but because it is capitalist. (See Chapter I, section 3 (3).)

2. FREEDOM UNDER SOCIALISM

Let us consider just what economic freedom means within the limitations of a socialist commonwealth. It certainly does not mean economic freedom in the sense in which the nineteenth-century economist understands these words. It does not mean freedom to own and to draw income from the ownership of land and other material means of production, although it is not incompatible with the personal *use* of such means of production (as under leases), nor with the personal ownership of tools and small machines such as an independent craftsman may use. But under modern conditions of technique the great mass of means of production exists in the form of machinery and equipment that can only be worked by labour associated on a large scale. And under socialism no individual or group of individuals may own the means whereby other men work and live. Nor does it mean freedom to organize production on individual lines for the sake of private profit, with all the secrecy, deception, speculation with other people's livelihood, and possibility of monopoly that this entails; although it is not incompatible with non-profit-making ventures on a co-operative basis for genuine experiment or for the provision by individually organized activity of highly specialized satisfactions of an aesthetic, literary, religious, or political nature. But it does mean freedom for the consumer, in the sense of a free choice of satisfactions within the limits of a system of prices reflecting the relative scarcity of different goods; and it does mean freedom for the producer, in the sense of a free choice of occupations within the limits of a system of wage-rates reflecting the relative social importance of different kinds of work. In other words, free price-formation is restored at the two ends of the chain of production, at the end of consumer's goods and at the end of personal productive services. It may be fairly claimed that, in these two respects, freedom will be more adequate than under capitalism.

For the consumer, liberty of choice will be implemented by the reduction of advertisement to its proper social function of stimulating interest and imparting information; whereas to-day the consumer is only too often 'free' to choose between commodities whose real properties are obscured in a smoke cloud of misinformation and irrational appeal. Standardization of consumption goods is often decried as an infringement of the consumer's liberty of choice. In truth a considerable measure of standardization is a necessary condition of any rational liberty of choice. In most lines of consumption the consumer is faced, to-day, with a veritable *embarras de choix*. An enormous variety of brands of chocolate, tooth-paste, or petrol, a bewildering range of diverse kinds of clothes, furniture, and household gear, differing from each other by almost imperceptible shades of quality, far from offering the consumer increased opportunities of choice, really paralyse his powers of discrimination and decision. Only when the number of lines competing for his notice are reduced to a few varieties with well-marked characteristics does choice cease to be a mere gamble and become a rational decision. Moreover, the index of consumer demand will no longer be distorted by gross inequalities in consumers' incomes or by monopoly elements in the prices of goods.

For the producer, liberty of choice will be a reality when it is exercised with a full knowledge of the possibilities of the labour market and with full opportunities for training and equipment, unhindered by lack of means on the part of the candidate or the candidate's parents. Moreover, for those who dislike the prospect of salaried or wage-paid public employment, there will always be the emergency escape of the free-lance occupations and (possibly) of the private sector (see Chapter VI).

Economic freedom in this sense is, however, only the beginning of freedom. Is it worth while, the critic might say, to turn society upside-down for the sake of enacting Books III to VI of Marshall's *Principles*? Should men carry out a revolution, and perhaps fight a civil war, in order to abolish patent-medicine advertisements and blind-alley occupations? This kind of freedom is necessary, but it is not sufficient. What socialists claim is that not merely economic freedom for consumers and producers but also liberty in the wider sense—political freedom as understood by the nineteenth-century liberals—is impossible under capitalism. Men cannot be free in a class-society: men cannot be free when the means whereby they live are owned by a few. The control over public opinion that is given by ownership of newspaper capital, like Beaverbrook's or Hearst's, the power of intimidation over votes that is possessed by a large local employer of labour, the power of wealth to impose its prestige upon wavering and indifferent voters—all these make a mockery of democracy under capitalism. Security of livelihood,

a large measure of economic equality, the conscious control
of social production by society—these are the guarantees
of true liberty. Only by such restrictions as those mentioned at the beginning of this section can insecurity, inequality, and the arbitrary control of the private owner over
men's destinies be kept at bay: only by these curtailments of
liberty in small things can liberty in great things be purchased.

Liberals profess to fear the possibility of tyranny under
socialism. As the sole employer and the sole purveyor of
goods, the socialist commonwealth is expected to exercise its
powers in the spirit of a monopolist under capitalism. But
this expectation is no more reasonable than the expectation
that a democratic state would reproduce all the vices of an
absolutist or oligarchical state. Not the formal relations of
economic or political organization, but the underlying social
relations (and, above all, the relations of classes), are the
decisive factor in the issue of freedom or tyranny. What is the
source and origin of tyranny? Exploitation. Men tyrannize
over other men, in political or economic relations, in order
to obtain their services otherwise than by voluntary consent
and co-operation. Abolish exploitation and substitute a
society of freely co-operating agents, then the root cause of
tyranny is taken away. If the basic cause of tyranny in the
exploitation of one class by another is removed, there still
remains the possibility of isolated and individual abuses of
communally delegated power. This danger is a real one and
the liberal's fear is to this extent justified. But the remedy
is suggested by the historical parallel between the struggles
for political and for economic rights. The task of the liberal
in winning political liberty and equality was a twofold one.
First, the control of the state-machine had to be wrested
from the class that had previously monopolized it. The
Sovereign People had to be placed on the throne of a Louis

XIV. Secondly, the nature of the state-machine had to be transformed from an instrument of power into an instrument of service. The arbitrary elements in its action had to be abolished and it had to be made the means of serving the interests of all citizens on equal terms. In Dicey's words, the Rule of Law was set up. The same twofold task awaits the socialist, in establishing economic liberty and equality. First, the control of the economic machine must be wrested from the class that now monopolizes it. The community as a whole must step into the shoes of a J. P. Morgan or a Harry McGowan. Secondly, the nature of the economic machine must be transformed from an instrument of profit into an instrument of service. As part of this change a machinery of constitutional safeguards and guaranteed rights must be evolved. The Rule of Law must be extended from the political to the economic sphere. The part played in the bourgeois liberal order by property rights and enforcement of contract will be played in a socialist order by a Labour Code, which will enforce reasonable workshop customs and give remedies for victimization, and by a legally enforceable code of Consumers' Rights.

In a socialist society the distinction, always artificial, between economics and politics will break down; the economic and the political machinery of society will fuse into one. The problem of economic liberty will then become the same as the problem of political liberty. During the period of transition from a capitalist to a socialist society both forms of liberty may be abridged, just as during the early phases of the struggles which made possible the establishment of religious and political liberty those very liberties were temporarily eclipsed. Luther and Calvin persecuted, yet the ultimate influence of their teaching was tolerance; Cromwell and Robespierre ruled arbitrarily, yet the ultimate influence of their rule was to establish civil liberty. So Lenin and Stalin have shown scant respect for the preferences of the individual consumer, yet, if they shall have been the means of establishing a classless society, their ultimate influence will be for economic liberty. After a socialist order has been safely established, the *raison d'être* of restrictions on liberty will have ceased. There will no longer be a class with a privileged relation to the means of production. The planning authorities will become responsible to the whole body of the community.

This may be so, is the reply, but even a classless society may deny freedom of experience to minorities. Will those who manage the printing presses of the perfect socialist community be as ready to print Bibles or copies of *Science and Health* as to print Marx's *Capital*, in response to an equivalent effective demand of consumers? There is no reason why a socialist economy should not have room for voluntary associations formed for the publication of books, pamphlets, and periodicals. In this way, political, religious, and cultural minorities could express and propagate their views. But such associations would require, in addition, to obtain paper and the use of printing machinery from those organs of collective economy that owned and controlled them. Thus we arrive at the necessity of some machinery for vindicating consumers' rights, analogous to the legal machinery evolved by liberalism from 1776 onwards for vindicating the individual's political rights to life, liberty, and the pursuit of happiness.

Just as in the liberal political society of the nineteenth century the law was conceived of as a sort of automatic machine for defining and vindicating personal rights, that would operate indifferently whoever dropped the penny in the slot, whether he belonged to a majority or a minority; so a socialist community should conceive of the economic organization of society as a machine for satisfying individual needs, accessible on equal terms to all citizens. The socialist commonwealth ought to write into its constitution explicit guarantees of economic as well as of political liberty, and implement them by due process of law, especially in the matter of the printed and broadcast word.

We should not conceive of the administrative organs of a socialist economy as an extension of the powers of the *state*, but rather as the creation of a new form of activity of *society*. The state, as it exists under capitalism, is a product of class antagonism, and of national antagonism ultimately rooted in class antagonism (see Chapter VII, section 4). With the achievement of a classless society, the state will undergo a complete transformation. Its functions as the bearer of authority will diminish largely in importance; its functions of impersonal administration in matters of common interest will probably gain in efficiency by being freed from association with its coercive functions. If it is desired to compare the organs of a socialist economy with existing institutions, an enlarged and universalized consumers' co-operative society would afford a better parallel than the political state.

But even under the most perfect constitution a democracy may act tyrannously to minorities: the ultimate guarantee resides not in written constitutions, but in the social structure of the community, thus ultimately in the material relations of production. The guarantee of liberty in a socialist community would be the absence of the causes which nowadays make human beings desire to deny one another liberty; in other words, the true pledge of freedom is the abolition of economic classes.

NOTE ON NATIONAL INCOME

Put $P =$ aggregate value of all goods produced.

       $I =$ aggregate value of goods sold for individual consumption.

       $C =$ aggregate value of goods provided for communal consumption.

       $K =$ aggregate value of capital goods produced.[1]

Then $P = I+C+K$.

Put $E =$ aggregate value of all factors of production.

       $L =$ aggregate value of labour services.

       $S =$ aggregate value of factors other than labour (Social Fund).

Then $E = L+S$.

Assuming that goods are valued according to average cost, the aggregate value of all goods produced is equal to the aggregate value of all factors of production.

$$\therefore P = E$$

and
$$I+C+K = L+S.$$

If goods are valued according to marginal cost (see Chapter II, section 4 (2)), the aggregate value of all goods is equal to the sum of marginal costs, while the aggregate value of all factors of production is equal to the sum of average costs, the sum in each case being taken over the entire national product. In this case put

       $M =$ sum of average costs $-$ sum of marginal costs.

(Thus M is the debit balance of the Marginal Cost Equalization Fund.)

Then
$$M = E-P$$
or
$$P = E-M.$$

$$\therefore I+C+K = L+S-M.$$

Put $S' = S-M$, and use S' instead of S in the argument of the remainder of this Note. (It is possible that S' may be negative.)

Put $W =$ Total sum paid out in wages.

       $D =$ Total sum paid out as Social Dividend.

[1] Including additions to stocks of consumption goods.

Then a condition of equilibrium is that the aggregate value of goods sold for individual consumption must equal the disposable money income of consumers.[1]

That is
$$I = W+D,$$

$$\therefore W+D+C+K = L+S.$$

Then
$$W = L \quad \text{if} \quad S = D+C+K.$$

That is to say, the imputed value of labour can be paid as wages if the Social Fund is just exhausted by social dividend, communal consumption, and capital accumulation.

Otherwise, put $W = L(1+k)$ where k represents a uniform proportional addition to the imputed value of labour.

Then
$$W = L+S-D-C-K,$$

$$\therefore k = \frac{S-D-C-K}{L},$$

$\therefore k$ is positive or negative according as $S \gtrless D+C+K$.

If $S > C+K$, there arises a surplus of individually spendable income over the economic value of labour. This surplus can be distributed in three ways: (a) by issuing a social dividend $(D = S-C-K)$; (b) by paying wages for labour at a rate higher than its economic value $\left(k = \frac{S-C-K}{L}\right)$; (c) by a combination of both methods (any D being chosen, $k = \frac{S-D-C-K}{L}$; in this case, if $D > S-C-K$, k becomes negative).

If $S < C+K$, spendable income is less than the value of labour, and it is impossible to pay wages at their full economic value.

---

[1] This assumes that no individual saving takes place (see note 1 on p. 83). If saving of an amount H occurs, then, in equilibrium, $I = W+D+H$. An appropriate scheme of distribution involves either $D = S-C-K+H$ or $k = \dfrac{S-D-C-K+H}{L}$. In other words, individual saving can be compensated for by an increase in the social dividend or in the percentage addition to wages.

That is to say a levy must be made on the value of labour $\left(k = \dfrac{S-C-K}{L}\right.$, which is a negative quantity$\Big)$. Even in this case it is still possible to issue a social dividend, provided an increased levy on the economic value of labour is made $\left(k = \dfrac{S-D-C-K}{L}\right)$.

Alternative Method

An alternative method would be to pay wages strictly according to the imputed value of labour, but to make a uniform proportional addition k' to the price of all goods sold in the market.

Then the condition of equilibrium is

$$I(1+k') = L+D.$$

$$\therefore k' = \frac{L+D-I}{I} = \frac{D+C+K-S}{I}.$$

Thus k' is positive or negative according as $S \lessgtr D+C+K$.

BIBLIOGRAPHY

Abbreviations

A.E.R.	*American Economic Review*	*M.S.*	*Manchester School*
		P.Q.	*Political Quarterly*
Arch. d. Soz.	*Archiv der Sozialwissenschaft*	*Q.J.E.*	*Quarterly Journal of Economics*
Eca.	*Economica*	*R.E.S.*	*Review of Economic Studies*
E.J.	*Economic Journal*	*Schm.J.*	*Schmollers Jahrbuch*

1. ECONOMIC THEORY

1. GENERAL

HEARN, W. E. *Plutology*. 1864.

WAGNER, A. *Grundlegung der politischen Ökonomie*. 1876 (rev. ed. 1892). (Vol. i of *Lehr- und Handbuch der politischen Ökonomie*.)

SIDGWICK, H. *Principles of Political Economy*. 1883 (rev. ed. 1901).
—— *Elements of Politics*. 1891 (rev. ed. 1908).

HOBSON, J. A. *Industrial System*. 1909 (rev. ed. 1910).
—— *Work and Wealth*. 1914 (new ed. 1933).

OPPENHEIMER, F. *Theorie der reinen politischen Ökonomie*. 1910 (rev. ed. 1923). (Bd. III of *System der Soziologie*.)

BÖHM-BAWERK, E. v. *Macht oder ökonomisches Gesetz*. 1914. (In *Gesammelte Schriften*. 1924.)

CANNAN, E. *Wealth*. 1914 (rev. ed. 1928).

CASSEL, G. *Fundamental Thoughts in Economics*. 1925.

HAWTREY, R. G. *The Economic Problem*. 1926.

VAN DEN TEMPEL, J. *Macht en Economische Wet*. 1927.

ROBBINS, L. *Nature and Significance of Economic Science*. 1932 (rev. ed. 1935).

WELLS, H. G. *Work, Wealth and Happiness of Mankind*. 1932 (rev. ed. 1934).

MUMFORD, L. *Technics and Civilisation*. 1934.

GRANT, A. T. K. *Society and Enterprise*. 1934.

FISHER, A. G. B. *Clash of Progress and Security*. 1935.

HOGBEN, L. *Retreat from Reason*. 1936.
—— (ed.). *Political Arithmetic*. 1938.

WOOTTON, B. *Lament for Economics*. 1938.

242   BIBLIOGRAPHY

2. PRICE SYSTEM

JEVONS, W. S. *Theory of Political Economy.* 1871.
MENGER, C. *Grundsätze der Volkswirtschaftslehre.* 1871 (rev. ed. 1923).
WALRAS, L. *Éléments d'Économie Politique Pure.* 1874 (éd. déf. 1926).
WIESER, F. VON. *Über den Ursprung und die Hauptgesetze des wirtschaftlichen Wertes.* 1884.
—— *Der natürliche Wert.* 1889. (Trans. *Natural Value.* 1893.)
BÖHM-BAWERK, E. V. *Grundzüge der Theorie des wirtschaftlichen Güterwerts,* 1886 (reprint 1932).
—— *Positive Theorie des Kapitals.* 1889. (Trans. *Positive Theory of Capital.* 1891.)
—— *Wert, Kosten und Grenznutzen.* 1892. (In *Gesammelte Schriften.* 1924.)
MARSHALL, A. *Principles of Economics.* 1890 (rev. ed. 1920).
WICKSELL, K. *Über Wert, Kapital, und Rente.* 1893 (reprint 1933).
—— *Lectures on Political Economy.* 1934.
GREENE, D. I. 'Pain-Cost and Opportunity-Cost.' *Q.J.E.* viii. 218, Jan. 1894.
CANNAN, E. *History of Local Rates in England.* 1896 (rev. ed. 1927).
SCHUMPETER, J. *Das Wesen und der Hauptinhalt der theoretischen Nationalökonomie.* 1908.
DAVENPORT, H. J. *Value and Distribution.* 1908.
—— *Economics of Enterprise.* 1913.
WICKSTEED, P. *Commonsense of Political Economy.* 1910 (reprint 1933).
TAUSSIG, F. W. *Principles of Economics.* 1911 (rev. ed. 1921).
PIGOU, A. C. *Wealth and Welfare.* 1912.
—— *Economics of Welfare.* 1920 (n. eds. 1924, 1929).
CASSEL, G. *Theoretische Sozialökonomie.* 1918 (rev. ed. 1932). (Trans. *Theory of Social Economy.* 1932.)
—— *On Quantitative Thinking in Economics.* 1935.
KNIGHT, F. H. *Risk, Uncertainty and Profit.* 1921 (reprint 1935).
HENDERSON, H. D. *Supply and Demand.* 1922 (rev. ed. 1932).
CLARK, J. M. *Economics of Overhead Costs.* 1923.
CLARK, J. B. *Essentials of Economic Theory.* 1924.
CHAMBERLIN, E. H. *Theory of Monopolistic Competition.* 1933.
ROBINSON, J. *Economics of Imperfect Competition.* 1933.

PHELPS-BROWN, E. H. *Framework of the Pricing System.* 1936.
HICKS, J. R. *Value and Capital.* 1939.

3. DISTRIBUTION

CLARK, J. B. *Distribution of Wealth.* 1899.
EDGWORTH, F. Y. 'Theory of Distribution.' *Q.J.E.* xviii. 159,
    Feb. 1904 (reprinted in *Papers Relating to Political Economy*,
    vol. i, p. 13. 1925).
SCHUMPETER, J. 'Rentenprinzip in der Verteilungslehre.' *Schm. J.*
    xxxi. 31, 591, 1907.
——— 'Grundprinzip der Verteilungslehre.' *Arch. d. Soz.* xlii. 1,
    1917.
CANNAN, E. 'Division of Income.' *Q.J.E.* xix. 341, May 1905.
    (Ch. VII in *Economic Outlook.* 1912.)
ELY, R. T. *Property and Contract.* 1914.
DALTON, H. *Inequality of Incomes.* 1920 (rev. ed. 1925).
WEDGWOOD, J. *Economics of Inheritance.* 1929.
DICKINSON, H. D. *Institutional Revenue.* 1932.

4. LABOUR AND WAGES

THOMPSON, H. M. *Theory of Wages.* 1892.
TAUSSIG, F. W. *Wages and Capital.* 1896 (reprint 1932).
PIGOU, A. C. *Unemployment.* 1913.
——— *Theory of Unemployment.* 1933.
ROBBINS, L. *Wages.* 1926.
DOBB, M. H. *Wages.* 1928 (rev. ed. 1938).
CANNAN, E. 'Problem of Unemployment.' *E.J.* xl. 45, March 1930.
——— 'The Demand for Labour.' *E.J.* xlii. 357, Sept. 1932.
LEDERER, E. *Technischer Fortschritt und Arbeitslosigkeit.* 1931.
    (Trans. *Technical Progress and Unemployment.* 1938.)
HICKS, J. R. *Theory of Wages.* 1932.
DOUGLAS, P. *Theory of Wages.* 1934.
NASH, E. F. *Machines and Purchasing Power.* 1935.

5. CAPITAL AND INTEREST

BÖHM-BAWERK, E. v. *Positive Theory of Capital.* 1889 (1891).
WICKSELL, K. *Geldzins und Güterpreise.* 1898. (Trans. *Interest and
    Prices.* 1936.)
CASSEL, G. *Nature and Necessity of Interest.* 1903.
FISHER, I. *Nature of Capital and Interest.* 1906.
——— *Theory of Interest.* 1930.

BICKERDIKE, C. F. 'Individual and Social Interests in Relation to Saving.' *E.J.* xxxiv. 408, Sept. 1924.

RAMSEY, F. P. 'Mathematical Theory of Saving.' *E.J.* xxxviii. 543, Dec. 1928.

MARSCHAK, J. 'Note on the Period of Production.' *E.J.* xliv. 146, March 1934.

6. UNCERTAINTY-BEARING AND PROFITS

LAVINGTON, F. 'Uncertainty in its Relation to the Rate of Interest.' *E.J.* xxii. 398, Sept. 1912.

—— 'Social Interest in Stock-Exchange Speculation.' *E.J.* xxiii. 36, March 1913.

—— 'Approach to the Theory of Business Risk.' *E.J.* xxxv. 186, June 1925.

KNIGHT, F. H. *Risk, Uncertainty and Profit.* 1921 (reprint 1935).

DOBB, M. H. 'The Entrepreneur Myth.' *Eca.* iv. 66, Feb. 1924.

7. DIFFERENTIAL RATES

ACWORTH, W. M. *Elements of Railway Economics.* 1905 (rev. ed. 1924).

CLARK, J. M. *Standards of Reasonableness in Local Freight Discriminations.* 1910.

EDGWORTH, F. Y. 'Contributions to the Theory of Railway Rates.' I. *E.J.* xxi. 345, Sept. 1911; II. *E.J.* xxi. 551, Dec. 1911; III. *E.J.* xxii. 198, June 1912 (reprinted in *Papers Relating to Political Economy*, vol. i, p. 172); IV. *E.J.* xxiii. 206, June 1913.

PIGOU, A. C. *Wealth and Welfare*, 1912, pt. ii, ch. 13; *Economics of Welfare*, 1920, pt. ii, ch. 15; ibid., 1924, pt. ii, ch. 17; ibid., 1929, pt. ii, ch. 18.

TAUSSIG, F. W. 'Railway Rates and Joint Costs Once More.' *Q.J.E.* xxvii. 378, Feb. 1913.

PIGOU, A. C. 'Railway Rates and Joint Cost.' *Q.J.E.* xxvii. 535, May 1913.

—— 'Railway Rates and Joint Costs.' *Q.J.E.* xxvii. 687, Aug. 1913.

LORENZ, M. O. 'Cost and Value of Service in Railroad Rate-making.' *Q.J.E.* xxx. 205, Feb. 1916.

HANEY, L. H. 'Joint Cost with Especial Reference to Railways.' *Q.J.E.* xxx. 233, Feb. 1916.

WATKINS, G. P. 'Electrical Rates: Local Factor and Density Factor.' *Q.J.E.* xxx. 519, May 1916.

—— 'Theory of Differential Rates.' *Q.J.E.* 682, Aug. 1916.

GLAESER, M. G. *Outlines of Public Utility Economics.* 1927.

8. INTERNATIONAL ECONOMICS

BASTABLE, C. F. *Theory of International Trade.* 1887 (rev. ed. 1903).
TAUSSIG, F. W. *Tariff History of the United States.* 1888 (rev. ed. 1931).
—— *Theory of International Trade.* 1927.
WHALE, B. *International Trade.* 1932.
OHLIN, B. *Theory of International and Interregional Trade.* 1933.
HABERLER, G. *Internationaler Handel.* 1933. (Trans. *Theory of International Trade.* 1936.)
KINDERSLEY, R. 'New Study of British Foreign Investments.' *E.J.* xxxix. 8, March 1929 (and articles in *E.J.* nearly every year since).
CANNAN, E. 'Incompatibility of Socialism and Nationalism.' (Ch. X in *The Economic Outlook.*) 1912.
ROBBINS, L. *Economic Planning and International Order.* 1937.

II. CRITIQUE OF INDIVIDUALISM

VEBLEN, T. *Theory of the Leisure Class.* 1899.
—— *Theory of Business Enterprise.* 1904.
—— *Absentee Ownership.* 1923.
—— *Engineers and the Price System.* 1934.
TAWNEY, R. H. *Acquisitive Society.* 1921.
—— *Equality.* 1929 (rev. ed. 1931).
SODDY, F. *Cartesian Economics.* 1922.
—— *Inversion of Science.* 1924.
—— *Wealth, Virtual Wealth, and Debt.* 1926.
WEBB, B. and S. *Decay of Capitalist Civilisation.* 1923.
LEWIS, E. LL. *Children of the Unskilled.* 1924.
DOBB, M. H. *Capitalist Enterprise and Social Progress.* 1925.
—— *Introduction to Economics.* 1932.
—— *Political Economy and Capitalism.* 1938.
LINDSAY, K. *Social Progress and Educational Waste.* 1926.
CHASE, S., and SCHLICK, F. J. *Your Money's Worth.* 1927.
ANON. 'Results of the 1928 New Issue Boom.' *E.J.* xli. 577, Dec. 1931.
HARRIS, R. A. 'Re-analysis of the 1928 New Issue Boom. *E.J.* xliii. 453, Sept. 1933.
SCOTT, H. (*et al.*). *Introduction to Technocracy.* 1933.
MUMFORD, L. *Technics and Civilization.* 1934.
HALL, D. (ed.). *Frustration of Science.* 1935.

DICKINSON, H. D. 'Failure of Economic Individualism' (in *Studies in Capital and Investment*, ed. Cole, G. D. H. 1935).

DURBIN, E. F. M. 'Social Significance of the Theory of Value.' *E.J.* xlv. 700, Dec. 1935.

HOGBEN, L. *Retreat from Reason.* 1936.

—— (ed.). *Political Arithmetic.* 1938.

III. PLANNING

LANDAUER, C. *Planwirtschaft und Verkehrswirtschaft.* 1931.

LEDERER, E. *Planwirtschaft.* 1932.

SALTER, A. *Recovery.* 1932 (rev. ed. 1933).

—— *Framework of an Ordered Society.* 1933.

MACMILLAN, H. *Reconstruction.* 1933.

—— *The Middle Way.* 1938.

FENN, L. A. *Project of a Planned World.* 1933.

GREGORY, T. E. 'An Economist Looks at Planning.' *M.S.* iv. 1, 1933.

DICKINSON, H. D. 'Freedom and Planning: a Reply to Dr. Gregory.' *M.S.* iv. 82, 1933.

GREGORY, T. E. *The Planned State and the Equalitarian State.* 1934.

WOOTTON, B. *Plan or No Plan.* 1934.

COLE, G. D. H. *Principles of Economic Planning.* 1935.

HAYEK, F. A. (ed.). *Collectivist Economic Planning.* 1935.

BEVERIDGE, W. H. *Planning under Socialism.* 1936.

SMITH, H. 'Planning and Plotting: a Note on Terminology.' *R.E.S.* iii. 193, June 1936.

BURROWS, H. R. *Problems and Practice of Economic Planning.* 1937.

ROBBINS, L. *Economic Planning and International Order.* 1937.

IV. SOCIALISM

1. GENERAL

SHAW, G. B. (ed.). *Fabian Essays in Socialism.* 1889 (rev. eds. 1920, 1931).

—— *Intelligent Woman's Guide to Socialism and Capitalism.* 1928 (rev. ed. 1937).

—— *Essays in Fabian Socialism.* (Collected in 1932.)

BERNSTEIN, E. *Die Voraussetzungen des Sozialismus und die Aufgabe der Sozialdemokratie.* 1899. (Trans. *Evolutionary Socialism.* 1909.)

WELLS, H. G. *Anticipations.* 1902.

—— *A Modern Utopia.* 1905.

—— *New Worlds for Old.* 1908 (rev. ed. 1914).

WICKSELL, K. *Socialiststaten och Nutidssamhället.* 1903.

WEBB, B. and S. (*et al.*). *Socialism and Individualism.* 1909.

—— *Towards Social Democracy?* 1916.

—— *Constitution for Socialist Commonwealth of Great Britain.* 1920.

CANNAN, E. 'Economics and Socialism.' (Ch. I in *The Economic Outlook.*) 1912.

RUSSELL, B. *Roads to Freedom.* 1918 (rev. ed. 1919).

TAYLOR, F. M. 'Guidance of Production in a Socialist State.' *A.E.R.* xix. 1, March 1929.

DICKINSON, H. D. 'Economic Basis of Socialism.' *P.Q.* 1. 561, Sept.–Dec. 1930.

MORREAU, G. 'De Economische Structuur eener Socialistische Volkshuishouding.' *De Economist,* lxxx. 445, 566, 645, June, July–Aug., Sept. 1931.

LANDAUER, C. *Planwirtschaft und Verkehrswirtschaft.* 1931.

HEIMANN, E. *Kapitalismus und Sozialismus.* 1931.

—— *Sozialistische Wirtschafts- und Arbeitsordnung.* 1932.

LEDERER, E. *Planwirtschaft.* 1932.

JEVONS, H. S. *Economic Equality in the Co-operative Commonwealth.* 1933.

DICKINSON, H. D. 'Price Formation in a Socialist Community.' *E.J.* xliii. 237, June 1933.

DOBB, M. 'Problems of a Socialist Economy.' *E.J.* xliii. 588, Dec. 1933.

LERNER, A. P. 'Economic Theory and Socialist Economy.' *R.E.S.* ii. 51, Oct. 1934.

DOBB, M. 'Economic Theory and Socialist Economy—a Reply.' *R.E.S.* ii. 144, Feb. 1935.

LERNER, A. P. 'A Rejoinder to Mr. Dobb.' *R.E.S.* ii. 152, Feb. 1935.

LANGE, O. 'Economic Theory of Socialism.' I. *R.E.S.* iv. 53, Oct. 1936; II. *R.E.S.* iv. 123, Feb. 1937.

LERNER, A. P. 'A Note on Socialist Economics.' *R.E.S.* iv. 72, Oct. 1936.

LANGE, O. 'Mr. Lerner's Note on Socialist Economics.' *R.E.S.* iv. 143, Feb. 1937.

DURBIN, E. F. M. 'Economic Calculus in a Planned Economy.' *E.J.* xlvi. 676, Dec. 1936.

LERNER, A. P. 'Statics and Dynamics in Socialist Economics.' *E.J.* xlvii. 253, June 1937.

COLE, G. D. H. *Simple Case for Socialism.* 1935.

—— *Principles of Economic Planning.* 1935.

—— *Machinery of Socialist Planning.* 1938.

DALTON, H. *Practical Socialism for Britain.* 1935.

BEVERIDGE, W. H. *Planning under Socialism.* 1936.

JAY, D. *The Socialist Case.* 1937.

HALL, R. L. *Economic System in a Socialist State.* 1937.

PIGOU, A. C. *Socialism and Capitalism.* 1937.

LANGE, O., and TAYLOR, F. M. *On the Economic Theory of Socialism.* (Reprint with an Introduction by Lippincott, B. E., of Taylor's *Guidance of Production in a Socialist State,* 1929, and of Lange's *Economic Theory of Socialism,* 1936–7.) 1938.

HOFF, T. J. B. *Økonomisk Kalkulasjon i Socialistiske Samfund.* 1938.

2. MARXIAN

MARX, K. *Lohnarbeit und Kapital.* 1849 (new ed. 1891). (Trans. *Wage-Labour and Capital.* 1886 (new ed. 1932).)

—— *Zur Kritik der politischen Ökonomie.* 1859. (Trans. *Critique of Political Economy.* 1904.)

—— *Kapital,* vol. i, 1867; vol. ii, 1885; vol. iii, 1893. (Trans. *Capital.* Vol. i, trans. by Aveling, E., and Moore, S., 1886, reprint, 1938; another trans. by E. & C. Paul, 1928. Vol. ii, 1907. Vol. iii, 1909.)

—— *Value, Price and Profit.* 1898.

ENGELS, F. *Herrn Eugen Dührings Umwälzung der Wissenschaft.* 1878 (rev. eds. 1885, 1894). (Trans. *Anti-Dühring.* 1935.)

—— *Entwicklung des Sozialismus von der Utopie zur Wissenschaft.* 1883 (rev. eds. 1891, 1907). (Trans. *Socialism, Utopian and Scientific.* 1892.) (Extracts from the preceding, first published in a French translation, 1880.)

BEER, M. *Life and Teaching of Karl Marx.* 1921.

KAUTSKY, K. *Economic Doctrines of Karl Marx.* 1925.

LINDSAY, A. D. *Karl Marx's Capital.* 1925.

HOOK, S. *Towards the Understanding of Karl Marx.* 1933.

LENIN, V. I. *State and Revolution.* 1919.

LASKI, H. J. *Communism.* 1927.

HOOVER, C. *Economic Life of Soviet Russia.* 1931.

OBOLENSKY-OSSINSKY, V. (*et al.*). *Socialist Planned Economy in the U.S.S.R.* 1932.

WEBB, B. and S. *Soviet Communism: a New Civilisation.* 1935.

BRUTZKUS, B. *Economic Planning in Soviet Russia.* 1935.

HUBBARD, L. E. *Soviet Money and Finance.* 1936.

—— *Soviet Trade and Industry.* 1938.

ANON. *Britain without Capitalists.* 1936.

BUKHARIN, N. *Economic Theory of the Leisure Class.* 1927.

LANGE, O. 'Marxian Economics and Modern Economic Theory.' *R.E.S.* ii. 189, June 1935.

DICKINSON, H. D. 'Comparison of Marxian and Bourgeois Economics.' *Highway*, xxix. 82, Jan. 1937.

3. CRITICAL

SCHÄFFLE, A. C. F. *Quintessenz des Sozialismus.* 1875. (Trans. *Quintessence of Socialism.* 1889.)

MALLOCK, W. H. *Labour and the Popular Welfare.* 1893.

—— *Critical Examination of Socialism.* 1908.

BÖHM-BAWERK, E. v. *Zum Abschluss des Marxschen Systems.* 1896. (Trans. *Karl Marx and the Close of his System.* 1898.)

SIMKHOVITCH, V. G. *Marxism versus Socialism.* 1913.

JOSEPH, H. W. B. *Labour Theory of Value in Karl Marx.* 1923.

MISES, L. VON. *Gemeinwirtschaft.* 1922 (rev. ed. 1932). (Trans. *Socialism.* 1936.)

BRUTZKUS, B. *Die Lehren des Marxismus im Lichte der russischen Revolution.* 1928.

HALM, G. *Ist der Sozialismus wirtschaftlich möglich?* 1929.

HAYEK, F. A. (ed.). *Collectivist Economic Planning.* 1935.

ROBBINS, L. *Economic Basis of Class Conflict.* 1939.

V. FASCISM

VILLARI, L. *Fascist Experiment.* 1926.

—— 'Fascism.' (In *Encyclopaedia Britannica*, 14th ed., vol. ix, p. 101.) 1929.

—— 'Economics of Fascism.' (In *Bolshevism, Fascism, Capitalism.*) 1932.

SALVEMINI, G. *Fascist Dictatorship in Italy.* 1927.

—— *Under the Axe of Fascism.* 1936.

BARNES, S. J. *Universal Aspects of Fascism.* 1928.

—— *Fascism.* 1931.

AGRESTI, D. R. 'Economics of Fascism.' (In *Encyclopaedia Britannica*, 14th ed., vol. ix, p. 104.) 1929.

Goad, H. E. *Making of the Corporate State.* 1932.
—— and Currey, M. *Working of a Corporate State.* 1933.
Hoover, C. *Germany Enters the Third Reich.* 1933.
Pitigliani. *Italian Corporative State.* 1933.
Rosenstock-Franck, L. *L'Économie Corporative Fasciste en Doctrine et en Fait.* 1934.
Dutt, R. P. *Fascism and Social Revolution.* 1934.
Finer, H. *Mussolini's Italy.* 1935.
'Germanicus.' *Germany: the Last Four Years.* 1937.
Brady, R. H. *Spirit and Structure of German Fascism.* 1937.
Roberts, S. H. *House that Hitler Built.* 1938.

VI. IMPERIALISM

Hobson, J. A. *Imperialism.* 1902 (rev. eds. 1905, 1938).
Lenin, V. I. *Imperialism.* 1918.
Woolf, L. S. *Economic Imperialism.* 1920.
—— *Empire and Commerce in Africa.* 1920.
—— *Imperialism and Civilisation.* 1928 (new ed. 1933).
Moon, P. T. *Imperialism and World Politics.* 1926.
Bukharin, N. *Imperialism and World Economy.* 1929.
Hawtrey, R. G. *Economic Aspects of Sovereignty.* 1930.
Angell, N. *Great Illusion.* 1910 (rev. ed. 1933).
—— *This Have and Have-not Business.* 1936.
Stalin, J. *Marxism and the National and Colonial Question.*

VII. POPULATION

Carr-Saunders, A. M. *Population Problem.* 1922.
—— *World Population.* 1936.
Rathbone, E. *The Disinherited Family.* 1924.
Robbins, L. 'Optimum Theory of Population.' (In *London Essays in Economics,* ed. Gregory, T. E., and Dalton, H. 1927.)
Dalton, H. 'Theory of Population.' *Eca.* viii. 28, March 1928.
Kuczynski, R. R. *Balance of Births and Deaths.* 1931.
—— *Measurement of Population Growth.* 1935.
Charles, E. *Twilight of Parenthood.* 1934 (reprinted as *Menace of Under-population.* 1936).
—— *Effect of Present Trends . . . upon the Future Population of England and Wales,* &c. (London and Cambridge Economic Service). 1935.
Hogben, L. (ed.). *Political Arithmetic.* 1938.

INDEX OF PERSONS

INDEX OF SUBJECTS

for labour, machinery and, 131;
joint, 73, 99; methods of estimating, 43–51; regulation of, by
price-system, 28, 48–51, 189.
Demand schedules, 63–4; aggregation of, 82 *n.*, 83 *n.*, 99.
Differential charges, 151–3, 154–7,
160, 161.
Discriminating charges, 151–5,
223; monopoly, 150–3.
Distribution according to need, 10,
11, 118, 119–20, 135, 137; according to value of services, 118;
under planned capitalism, 21–2.
Distribution of income, 28–9, 49,
100–1, 118–49, 204; general
scheme, 135–7, 238–40; *see also*
Equality of income.
Docks and harbours, 164.

Economic calculation under socialism, 109–15.
Economic chivalry, orders of, 123.
Economic equilibrium, *see* Equilibrium.
Economic fluctuations, 220, 224–5.
Economic freedom, 235–7.
Economic imperialism, 4, 20; and
war, 185–6.
Economic organization, 30, 219.
Economic problem, 1–5; under
socialism, 24–9.
Economic relations essentially
social, 21.
Economics and politics, 23, 235; and
technology, 2–3.
Education, 32, 34, 47, 52, 109, 221.
Educational monopoly and inequality of income, 8, 133.
Efficiency, indices of, 219.
Emergencies, 220, 225.
Employment, full, of factors of
production, 99, 112; planned,
131.
Energy cost, 71–2.
England, *see* Great Britain.
Enjoyment, active and passive, 39–
40.
Enterprise, private, *see* Private
enterprise.
Entrepreneur function under

planned capitalism, 20; under
socialism, 13, 213–19.
Equality of income, 118–20, 226,
234; and socialism, 8, 9–11; and
social services, 134; and wages,
132–5.
Equality of opportunity, 133, 137,
229; and socialism, 10.
Equality of sexes, 138–9, 143, 144,
145–7.
Equilibrium, 73, 153–4, 174, 226,
229; multiple positions of, 210,
220, 223–4; in circulation of
money, 193, 238–40; and the
pricing process, 204–5.
Eugenics, 147, 148.
Europe, 29, 92, 127, 156, 165.
Exchanges, foreign, 178–80.
Experiment in patterns of social
life, 54.
Experts, 32, 44, 47–8.
Exploitation, 5–8; and tyranny,
234–5.

Factors of production, 65; in full
employment, 99, 112; pricing of,
73–5, 98–101, 204; return to, *see*
Marginal product; supply of,
100; ultimate, 28, 65.
Factor-prices, changes in, 199–200,
203; and monetary control, 199–
200.
Factory acts, 15, 217.
Family allowances, 138, 146, 203.
Fascism, 34, 185–6, 188 (*see also*
National Socialism); planned
capitalism tends to, 22, 23.
Fashions, women's, 97.
Feminism and socialism, 138–9.
Finance capital, 185.
Finance, public, 47, 59, 206.
Fluctuations, economic, 220, 224–5.
Foreign exchanges, 178–80; investment, 180–4; lending by U.S.A.
in 1927–8, 229; shipping, 165.
Foreign trade, in goods, 173–8;
bilateral monopoly in, 177; state
monopoly of, 177; private enterprise and, 177–8, 179; under
socialism, 29–30, 173–88.
France, 19, 171.